H. R. Fox (Henry Richard Fox) Bourne

The Romance of Trade

H. R. Fox (Henry Richard Fox) Bourne

The Romance of Trade

ISBN/EAN: 9783743394940

Manufactured in Europe, USA, Canada, Australia, Japa

Cover: Foto ©Suzi / pixelio.de

Manufactured and distributed by brebook publishing software (www.brebook.com)

H. R. Fox (Henry Richard Fox) Bourne

The Romance of Trade

THE

ROMANCE OF TRADE.

BY

H. R. FOX, BOURNE,

AUTHOR OF "ENGLISH MERCHANTS;" "MEMOIRS IN ILLUSTRATION OF THE
PROGRESS OF BRITISH COMMERCE;" "ENGLISH SEAMEN UNDER THE
TUDORS;" "A MEMOIR OF SIR PHILIP SIDNEY," ETC. ETC.

CASSELL PETTER & GALPIN:

LONDON, PARIS & NEW YORK.

PREFACE.

THIS volume aims to be a useful as well as an entertaining gossip-book about commerce. In the annals of trade are to be found incidents and episodes quite as striking and memorable as any in those fields of history which are commonly supposed to have a monopoly of romantic facts ; and these episodes and incidents, when traced back to their causes or followed out through their effects, furnish trains of circumstances that are full of romance. Some of them are here set forth in groups and series designed to illustrate certain notable phases of commercial progress. The whole history of commerce, if read aright, is as interesting as it is instructive. I have only selected pages from that history ; but I have endeavoured so to select and so to arrange as that the reader may obtain broad and comprehensive views of the great subjects handled. I trust that the work will not be less amusing than its title would lead the reader to expect, because it attempts to show that, if there is a romance, there is also a philosophy of trade.

CONTENTS.

CHAPTER VIII.

THE ROMANCE OF TRADE.

CHAPTER I.

THE WANDERING JEW.

The Connection of Jews with Commerce—The earliest Trading Nations—
Joseph as a Merchant-prince—Old World Commerce—The Trade of
the Phœnicians—The Commercial Alliance between Solomon and
Hiram—Jewish Trade before and after the Babylonian Captivity—
Nehemiah and the Money-lenders—The Wanderings of the Jews in
Christian Times—Their Employments in Alexandria and Venice—
Shylock and *Antonio*—The Jews in Northern Europe—Their Wealth
and Sufferings in Mediæval France—Their History in England—Their
Royal Patrons—Their Persecution in the Time of Richard I.—Their
Troubles under later Monarchs—Their Ways of Money-lending—
Popular Hatred of them—"Hugh of Lincoln"—Their Banishment by
Edward I.—Their Return in the Time of Oliver Cromwell—Their
Trading Exploits—Sampson Gideon—The Goldsmids—The Roths-
childs—The Extension of the Jews at the Present Time.

MORE than one famous work of fiction has been suggested
by the fable of the "Wandering Jew;" but the real story of
his adventures and experiences contains episodes as strange
as any that novelists have invented, and some of the strangest
and most memorable grow out of his connection with trade.
Though no single man has been released from the doom of
death, the race has been endowed with a remarkable vitality,
and an individuality no less remarkable, and its history
forms the completest link we have between past times and
the present, the Old World and the New.

The Jew was a wanderer long before he had a land of
his own, and from the first he had much to do with com-

merce. Abraham's purchase, for four hundred shekels of silver, "current money with the merchant," of the field and cave of Machpelah as a burial-place for Sarah, is almost the earliest instance on record of a money transaction; though it is probable that trade, as we now understand the term, was even then—nearly two thousand years before the time of Christ—an old institution. Mere barter of one commodity for another, which marks the transition of each nation or group of men from barbarism and theft to civilisation and commerce, had been superseded in those earliest communities that arose in the garden-land of the world. While Abraham's ancestors were leading a pastoral life in Ur of the Chaldees, their neighbours of the Aryan stock were building cities and developing commerce in Persia and India, and the patient settlers on the banks of the Nile were making Egypt a granary for all the nations. Abraham, "very rich in cattle, in silver, and in gold," going down to sojourn in Egypt, with his flocks and herds and tents, because there was a grievous famine in Canaan, only did what other fathers of nations often had to do in times when it was easier for men to travel hundreds of miles in search of food than to wait until the food was brought to them. It was so, two centuries later, when Jacob and his family went to settle in the land of Goshen; and the history of Jacob's son, Joseph—first a slave, then Potiphar's clerk, then Pharaoh's prime minister—is the earliest biography extant of a great merchant-prince. The industry and shrewdness, the skill in turning all things to his profit, and the fidelity to his own race which Joseph displayed, have been the inheritance of the Jews and the main source of their commercial success during the past five-and-thirty centuries.

The Jews, insignificant in numbers, hedged in by rival nations stronger than themselves, and generally forced to find their chief employment in other ways, were connected with, but played no important part in, the great commercial movements that occurred during their residence in Palestine. But the movements were great indeed. Egypt made itself powerful by fighting, but derived its main strength from its corn-producing wealth. Persia and India, and the many nations that existed on both sides of the Himalayas, paid most attention to the manufacture of clothing, the cultivation of spices and other luxuries, and the utilising of the precious stones and precious metals that abounded in their lands. Babylon and Nineveh, Bokhara and Oude, and half a hundred other great cities arose, to become the busy haunts of merchants and to extend their trading associations through every part of the then known world. Caravans travelled from the valley of the Euphrates to the walls of China, and down to the shores facing Ceylon; and wealth of every sort was exchanged, to the vast profit, not only of the traders, but also of the nations to which they belonged and to which they proved more useful servants than the warriors who had greater honour. The traditions of this Old World commerce, and often its exact methods, have been retained down to the present time, in spite of changes of empire, which have caused the ancient nations to crumble to pieces, and new ways of trade, that have helped to transfer the centres of civilisation from the East to the West.

The pioneers of these new ways were the hardy little race of Phœnicians, who had humble followers and comrades in their Jewish neighbours. The Phœnicians went eastward with the caravans that used Bokhara as their headquarters, and they brought to the shores of the Mediterranean abundant treasures, collected in the countries that they visited. But their enterprise led them to do far more than that. A hardy tribe of merchants and fishermen, they soon built trading-ships on the model of their fishing-boats, and, earliest of all nations known to us, went out upon the sea on commercial expeditions. Content at first with short voyages to the Egyptian coast in quest of corn and other commodities, they quickly gained in skill and boldness, and went to more distant shores, planting trading-stations, of which some became famous colonies. Carthage arose thus. Gades, now Cadiz, was a smaller settlement that grew out of the Phœnician visits to Spain in search of silver; and like visits are supposed to have been made, in very ancient times, to Britain for tin and to Prussia for amber. The treasures brought from the far East were given in payment for the produce of the West, and so the seeds of civilisation were planted in new places, while Phœnicia was enriched by her enterprise. Sidon, "the haven of fishermen," gave place to Tyre, greatest among a score of great trading-ports and busy factories. The raw material of other lands was here worked up for foreign commerce, as well as for home use. When Greece was in its infancy, the Phœnician marts were re- nowned for their linen and woollen manufactures—including the Sidonian garments of Homer, dyed with a purple which no other clothmakers could imitate—for their glass wares, and potteries, and trinkets of all sorts. The England of the Old World was at the height of its prosperity when David made a commercial treaty with Hiram, King of Tyre, and when Hiram assisted Solomon in building the Temple at Jerusalem and in extending the trading occupations of the Jews.

That was about a thousand years before the Christian era. Very curious are the records of the commercial rela- tions between the Phœnician and the Jewish kings, Solomon at first recompensing Hiram for his services by an annual payment of twenty thousand measures of wheat and of twenty measures of pure oil, and afterwards by a surrender of twenty cities in the land of Galilee. "And Hiram came out from Tyre to see the cities which Solomon had given him, and they pleased him not. And he said, What cities are these which thou hast given me, my brother? And he

called them the Land of Dirt." The friendship between
the two monarchs lasted, however ; and during a brief period
the Jews vied with the Phœnicians in commercial enterprise.
Solomon established a colony at Ezion-geber, on the Red
Sea, and thence dispatched expeditions, guided by pilots
lent to him by Hiram, to the land of Ophir. He also
organised a trading-fleet to visit Tarshish—supposed to be
Spain—in company with his neighbour's merchant ships.
" Once in three years came the navy of Tarshish, bringing
gold, and silver, and ivory, and apes, and peacocks." Jewish
caravans, moreover, went regularly to Egypt and Arabia,
and there was busy trade, in Solomon's days and afterwards, between Judæa and other parts, until the prosperity
inaugurated by David and his son was overthrown by
Nebuchadnezzar, and the Jews were taken into captivity.

Nebuchadnezzar conquered Tyre as well ; but a new
Tyre was quickly built, and Phœnician commerce lived yet
more vigorously in Carthage. Much of the greatness, too,
of the younger cities of Asia Minor and of the islands in
the direction of Greece, now at the summit of its renown,
was due to Phœnician teaching and example. Carthage,
however, was the chief commercial successor of Tyre until
its destruction by the Romans, and then other ports became
in turn the great centres of trade between Europe and Asia.
Alexandria, Miletus, and Ephesus were successively the principal resorts of merchants during the centuries of Roman
supremacy ; though, in spite of the growth of its younger
rivals, the special advantages possessed by Alexandria fo.
traffic with the East caused it to be an important mart, until.
falling under the curse of Mahometan rule, it was finally
superseded by Venice and Genoa, chief of the trading citie:
throughout the Middle Ages.

The history of the Wandering Jew dates from Nebu
chadnezzar's conquest in the sixth century before Christ.
Whither the ten tribes of Israel wandered, and what became

of them, we know not. Those of Judah, who were taken
captive to Babylon, appear to have found their chief employment in usury, and the lawful and unlawful ways of
banking which ever since have been their favourite pursuits.
When the fragment of the nation returned to Palestine, the
fortunate few retained these callings, and the luckless many
were reduced to a sort of bondage to them. Nehemiah
records the complaints made in his day. "We have mortgaged our lands, vineyards, and houses, that we might buy
corn, because of the dearth. Lo, we bring into bondage
our sons and our daughters to be servants; neither is it in
our power to redeem them; for other men have our lands
and vineyards." Nehemiah did something to remedy this
evil state of affairs. "I pray you, let us leave off this usury,"
he said to his wealthy neighbours; "restore to them, even
this day, their lands, their vineyards, their oliveyards, and
their houses"—certainly a moderate restitution—" also the
hundredth part of the money, and of the corn, the wine,
and the oil, that ye exact of them," and his counsel was
followed. The Jews, whatever their offences against others,
have generally dealt generously with their own people, and
there does not seem to have been very much ground of
complaint against the usurers in the ensuing times; but
banking of a primitive sort continued the chief source of
profit to the merchants, while the mass of the people applied
themselves to agricultural pursuits, and to humble trade
with the Phœnicians and others, who procured for them
such foreign commodities as they were rich enough to
purchase. But it is probable that the most enterprising
Jews never returned to Palestine, and that during the four
or five centuries before the destruction of Jerusalem there
was a constant emigration of Jews, most eager and most
fit to make money, to the more prosperous cities in the
neighbourhood, especially to Tyre and Alexandria. Here
the ancient Rothschilds and Goldsmids found congenial

occupation, profitable to themselves and beneficial to the world. Generally the worst that could be said of them, whether in their own country or in other lands, was that they pursued their business with a zeal that hindered them from fulfilling their other duties to society.

After Titus's great exploit, the Jews wandered perforce in very much larger numbers, sometimes of their own accord, sometimes by compulsion. In the year 130 the Emperor Adrian planted a colony of them in Spain, where they helped to develop the linen manufacture that was there extensively carried on during the later period of the Roman empire. Alexandria and its neighbourhood, however, were the favourite resort of the shrewdest money-makers, as they had been in previous centuries. All through the time of Alexandria's greatness, Jews thronged its streets, and, according to the old historian, were famous "for their egregious cunning in trade, and in the practice of brokerage." As soon as modern commerce began to take firm root in Venice and the other Italian trading towns, the Jews began to be sharers in it, and as it spread through-out Europe, they went with its pioneers. Wherever there was money to be made, the Wandering Jew was to be found.

Shakespeare's " Merchant of Venice" gives us a lively picture of a mediæval Jew-trader, coloured by the hatred with which, till long after Shakespeare's day, the Jews were regarded by nearly all Christians. *Shylock* grows rich by lending money to the adventurous Italian merchant-princes, and has all his evil passions stirred by the contempt that is poured upon him even by the men whom he helps greatly in their speculations—

> " Signor Antonio, many a time and oft
> In the Rialto you have rated me
> About my moneys and my usuries :
> Still have I borne it with a patient shrug,
> For sufferance is the badge of all our tribe.

> You call me misbeliever, cut-throat, dog,
> And spit upon my Jewish gaberdine,
> And all for use of that which is mine own.
> Well then, it now appears you need my help:
> Go to, then. You come to me, and you say,
> 'Shylock, we would have money :' you say so.
> What should I say to you? should I not say,
> 'Hath a dog money?' Is it possible
> A cur can lend three thousand ducats?' or
> Shall I bend low, and in a bondman's key,
> With bated breath, and whispering humbleness,
> Say this :
> 'Fair sir, you spat on me on Wednesday last ;
> You spurned me such a day ; another time
> You called me dog ; and for these courtesies
> I'll lend you thus much moneys?' "

The revenge which Shakespeare makes *Shylock* attempt
to take upon *Antonio*, for the indignities offered by him and
his brother merchants, is unnatural ; but it is true that much
bitter feeling was engendered by the harsh treatment to
which the Jews were subjected in all their adopted lands
throughout the Middle Ages. If they resented this treatment, and retaliated by driving hard bargains with their
allies in trade but enemies in religion, there was considerable
excuse for them. Whatever their private dispositions, however, whatever greed and spite they displayed or cherished
in secret, they were great public benefactors. In every
rising mart of Europe, from Venice up to York, and from
Barcelona to Hamburg, there were plenty of Shylocks to be
spit upon and sponged upon, and to make great wealth for
themselves, notwithstanding their hard usage all through
these bygone centuries. Settling wherever a trade was
growing, they were the chief providers of the money necessary to promote its growth. In times when usury was prohibited among Christians, their usurious ways were tolerated
and even encouraged, because they were indispensable ; and
kings and parliaments, as well as merchants and commercial guilds, experienced their value. Everywhere they

acquired wealth, and the power that comes of wealth. In the twelfth century they were owners of half Paris, and held the reins of nearly all the commerce possessed by France. In spite of laws to the contrary, they served as judges, governors, and ministers of state both in France and in Spain, and that at a period when it was considered a religious duty for all Christians to strike them in the face and stone their houses at Easter. Often their ill-treatment was attended by circumstances showing that their persecutors were adepts in the guile supposed to be peculiar to the persecuted. At the beginning of the thirteenth century Philip Augustus of France exonerated his subjects from all their debts to the Jews, on condition that a fifth part of the money owing was paid into his own coffers ; and his grandson, St. Louis, in order to conciliate his subjects, issued an ordinance, in which it was said, "for the salvation of his own soul and those of his ancestors, he returns to all Christians a third part of what is owing by them to Jews." There were many like instances of eccentric Christian morality and spiritual logic.

The history of the Jews in mediæval England illustrates their history throughout Europe. They came hither more than eleven hundred years ago, and were successful traders among the Anglo-Saxons when our country's trade was in its infancy. About the year 750, the Christians of Northumbria were prohibited from imitating the manners or partaking the feasts of the Jews—a circumstance that shows they must even then have had an influential position in one of the rudest districts of the rude England of that time ; and, oddly enough, we find Jews named among the donors of land to the old Abbey of Croyland in 833. Perhaps, however, they were not very numerous until the time of the Norman conquest, when William brought over many of the Hebrew nation from Rouen, and placed both the old and the new settlers under his especial protection. Most Anglo-

Saxons fell under vassalage to the Norman barons; but,
says the old law, "the Jews and all that are theirs are the
king's." The purpose of this reservation is clear. The
shrewd, money-making ways of the race made them very
serviceable adherents of the monarch. The royal "protection" meant chiefly the exclusive power of fining them;
but even that was to their advantage, as they were saved
from the extortions of greedy barons and jealous burghers,
under which groaned many of their kinsmen on the Continent. For two centuries and more they were enterprising
traders, settled in all parts of England, and useful as money-
lenders, or money-givers under compulsion, to the Anglo-
Norman and the early Plantagenet kings.

There were many noteworthy episodes in their progress
during these two centuries; the progress being one of great
commercial value to the nation, and generally of great profit
to the Jews themselves. Alternately favoured and persecuted, they helped mightily to promote the trade by which
the little island of Britain was destined to make itself a great
nation. The favours, grudgingly accorded, were usually
only such, and of such sort, as would encourage them to
pursue their money-making avocations, and so render their
persecutions profitable. William Rufus is almost the only
monarch who was really friendly to them. London being
their chief place of resort in his day, he assigned to them a
burial-ground, in which they could observe their own rites,
in Cripplegate, just outside the old London wall, and near
to the locality in which they resided, still marked by the
name of Old Jewry; and this was their only place of
sepulchre, until Henry II. allowed them to have a cemetery
in the outskirts of every town in which they dwelt. By that
time they had established considerable colonies in nearly
every English mart, especially in Norwich, Lynn, Lincoln,
Stamford, St. Edmondsbury, and York—towns conveniently
near to the eastern coast, from which was carried on most of

the traffic with the Continent, whereby English wool was exchanged for French and German wine. Their importance may be gathered from the fact that when, in 1188, Henry II. proposed to fit out a crusading expedition, he arranged to collect £60,000 from the Jews, and only £70,000 from all his Christian subjects. The crusade and the tax were both prevented by Henry's death, but a far greater hardship soon fell upon the Jews.

On the accession of Richard Cœur de Lion, in September, 1189, the wealthiest Jews crowded up to London from all parts of the country with rich presents, intended to win the favour of the new king. Their quaint garb rendered them conspicuous among the multitude who made merry on the coronation-day. They were forbidden to enter Westminster Abbey and be actual spectators of the ceremony; but many showed themselves near the doors, and one, driven either by his own curiosity or the mob behind him, passed the threshold. No sooner was this discovered, than he was pushed back and struck by the soldiers keeping guard. A scuffle ensued, in which others of his race were roughly handled, and one or two were killed. The news of this catastrophe, exaggerated as it passed from mouth to mouth, ran like wildfire through the crowd at Westminster and along all the streets of London. A report arose that the king had ordered that all the Jews should be massacred, and the long-suppressed hatred of the Christians made them very willing to obey the mandate. Every Jew found in the streets was slaughtered. An angry mob rushed in the direction of Old Jewry, and every house in which a Jew was known or thought to be was entered, plundered, and burnt, after its inmates had been butchered. No heed was given to the messengers sent by King Richard to forbid the massacre and threaten the culprits with severe punishment. The murderous work lasted through the night, and in the morning hardly a Jew was left alive in London.

The tragedy was repeated at Lynn, at Lincoln, at Stamford, at Norwich, and elsewhere, as soon as intelligence
arrived of the new crusade started in London ; but at York,
where rich Jews were especially numerous, the atrocities were
greatest. There the first account of the doings in London
was brought by a few of the hated race who had managed to
save their lives, and at the same time the king's disapproval
of the massacre was made known. But the good people of the
northern capital were not to be deterred from the pious task
thus suggested to them. The wealthiest Jew of the town
had been murdered in London, but his family and his treasures remained ; and on the night of the 16th of March,
1190, a gang burst into his house, seized the property, and
slaughtered the women and children within it. A general
massacre was planned for the following evening ; but, in the
meanwhile, the Jews sought the protection of the governor,
and were admitted, with as much of their property as they
could bring, into the castle. There, however, they were besieged by the people, headed by the governor, who had
changed his mind, and by the sheriff of the county. The
siege lasted for several days, until at last—a great ransom
having been offered in vain—the fugitives, who numbered
some five hundred men, besides women and children, found
they could hold out no longer. Then a desperate course
was resorted to. " Men of Israel," said the Rabbi, " God
bids us die for the Law, and our glorious ancestors have so
died in all ages. If we fall into the hands of these our
enemies, not merely death but cruel torture awaits us. Let
us, then, return to our Almighty Creator that life which he
gave. Let us die, willingly and devoutly, by our own hands."
A few shrank back, but nearly all agreed. They buried their
gold and silver, and then Joachim, the patriarch of the company, set the example by plunging a sword into his wife's
breast. In a short time all the women and children were
killed, and after that the men stabbed one another—the last

of all being the Rabbi, who, after slaying Joachim, killed himself. Thereupon the two or three dozen who had refused to join in this ghastly enterprise told the tale to their assailants, and offered to become Christians if their lives were spared. The bargain was agreed to ; but directly the gates were opened it was broken, and the residue of the Jews were put to death. A great bonfire was made of all the mortgages and other deeds which the Jews had received from the Christians for money lent to them, and the ring-leaders of the exploit were punished by being bound over to keep the peace in future.

Richard I. was not responsible for these crimes. While they were being perpetrated he was proceeding on his famous Crusade against the Saracens in occupation of the Holy Land—an outburst of religious zeal which contrasts strangely with the persecutions heaped upon the people who claimed Palestine as their rightful possession.

Great, however, as were the hardships of the Jews in England, they suffered less than their brethren in France, and new immigrants very soon made the Jewish quarters as crowded and as busy as they had been. John, both as governor of England on his brother's behalf and as king in his own right, encouraged the Jews ; and, while frequently exacting money from them, treated them with tolerable leniency in other respects. Henry III. was a yet more lenient master. The Chief Rabbi was presented to him on election, and confirmed in his office. While thus counte-nancing their own religion, however, Henry sought by peaceable ways to convert the Jews to Christianity. The Rolls Chapel in Chancery Lane was built in this reign for the use of Hebrew Christians, and other conciliatory acts were adopted by this monarch. He extorted money from them, as his predecessors had done, but not with ruinous violence. Indeed, the marvel is, that the Jews should have been able to bear, and to bear lightly, such heavy burdens as were put upon them. In 1230 a tax, amounting in value to a third of all their movable goods, was levied upon them, in order to prosecute the war with France ; in 1232 another tax, yielding 18,000 marks, was levied ; in 1236 they were forced to contribute 10,000 marks ; and there were several other impositions put upon them. Yet they were able to prosper and grow rich. The daughter of Hamon, a Jew of Hereford, paid as a relief to the king the enormous sum of 5,000 marks ; and one Aaron, of York, asserted that, in the course of seven years, Henry had borrowed from him as much as 30,000 marks. When Henry was at war with his barons, he summoned his Jewish subjects to a special Parliament, six coming from each of the towns in which they were most numerous, and two from each of the other towns—the number of the whole being upwards of a hundred ; and the demand made to this curious assembly was like that made to other and more regular Parliaments. The Jews were called upon to raise 20,000 marks for the sovereign's use in his time of trouble, and they collected it without difficulty.

They had good reason, however, to help the king in his civil war. It was a war which, very helpful in its issues to the English nation, was ruinous to the Jews in England. Having been under the special protection of the Crown since the time of William the Conqueror, they had been able to hold their ground, except during the massacres of 1189 and 1190, against the Church and the people. The struggle for civil liberty, by which Henry III. was sorely harassed, led to their overthrow. Langton and the ecclesiastical authorities, who fought for the people against John and Henry, shared all the popular hatred of the Jews, and even quickened it on religious grounds. Early in Henry's reign Archbishop Langton issued an edict forbidding Christians to furnish Jews with even the necessaries of life ; and the king had to make a counter-edict, enjoining his subjects to disregard the spiritual interdict. All through this reign every kind of outcry was raised against the hated race, and all sorts of persecutions were resorted to. The civic authorities of London, classing together "Jews, lepers, and swine," made it penal for any one to let a house to a Jew out of Jewry, and appointed a frivolous and vexatious tax of threepence-halfpenny on every burial in the cemetery outside of Cripplegate. In 1244 the students of Oxford broke into all the Jewish houses in that city, and did serious damage, alleging that they were being ruined by the exorbitant interest—twopence a week for every pound— charged by the Hebrew money-lenders to whom they resorted; and at another time they publicly alleged, as a ground for their inability to continue their studies, that all their books were in pawn to these same money-lenders. No one saw that all the fault lay with the students who adopted these wasteful ways of procuring cash for their amusements. It is clear, however, that many Jews took an unfair advantage of these Christian follies. When, during the Barons' War, one Abraham, of Berkhampstead, being sent to prison because his wife had ill-treated an image of the Virgin Mary, offered to pay 700 marks for his release, his brethren proposed to pay 1,000 marks that he might be kept in gaol, alleging that his evil practices rendered him a disgrace to the whole community. He was released, however, and rendered efficient service to his liberators by indicating the secret treasures of his rivals of his own faith.

A terrible persecution fell upon the Jews during the last years of Henry's reign. Its immediate cause was a report, true or false, that the Jews of Lincoln had, in 1255, murdered —some said, crucified—a Christian child; and for this offence ninety-two were apprehended, and eighteen were hanged— not after trial, but because they refused to be tried by a jury of Christians. What became of the other seventy-four is not stated. This occurrence, if it had any real foundation, served to stir up the hatred of Christians all through

the kingdom, and, besides suggesting Chaucer's " Prioress's
Tale," gave origin to many popular ballads.   One begins
by telling how a lad was playing with his mates in " Merry
Lincoln " :—

> "Then out and came the Jew's daughter,
>   Said, ' Will ye come in and dine ?'
> 'I will not come in, I cannot come in,
>   Without my playmates nine.'

> "She pulled an apple red and white,
>   To entice the young thing in ;
> She pulled an apple white and red,
>   And that the sweet bairn did win.

> "And she has ta'en out a little penknife,
>   And, low down by her gair [dress],
> She has parted the young thing and his life ;
>   A word he never spake mair.

> "And out and came the thick, thick blood,
>   And out and came the thin ;
> And out and came the bonny heart's blood ;
>   There was no life left in.

> "She laid him on a dressing-board,
>   And dressed him like a swine ;
> And, laughing, said, ' Go now and play
>   With your sweet playmates nine.'

> "She wrapt him in a cake of lead,
>   Bade him lie still and sleep ;
> She cast him in a deep draw-well,
>   Was fifty fathoms deep.

> " When bells were rung and mass was sung,
>   And every lady went home ;
> Then ilka lady had her young son,
>   But Lady Helen had none.

> "She wrapt her mantle her about,
>   And sore, sore 'gan she weep ;
> And she ran into the Jews' castél,
>   When they were all asleep.

" 'My bonny Sir Hugh, my pretty Sir Hugh,
  I pray thee to me speak !'
'O lady, run to the deep draw-well,
  If you your son would seek !'

"Lady Helen ran to the deep draw-well,
  And knelt upon her knee ;
'My bonny Sir Hugh, an ye lie here,
  I pray thee speak to me !'

" 'The lead is wondrous heavy, mother,
  The well is wondrous deep ;
A keen penknife sticks in my heart,
  A word I cannot speak.

" 'Go home, go home, my mother dear,
  Fetch me my winding-sheet ;
And at the back of merry Lincoln,
  It's there we two shall meet.'"

By ballads like these the evil passions of the Christians
were quickened against the Jews, and many murders were
committed in various parts of the country, which the
authorities did not care to punish. Legalised murders were
also frequent, the chief ground of which was the alleged
offence of the Jews in clipping the coin. It is likely enough
that Jews as well as Christians often offended in this way,
but very unequal punishment fell upon them. In 1279—
seven years after the accession of Edward I.—all the Jews in
the kingdom were arrested on one day, on the plea that
they were all implicated in the prevalent falsifying of
money; and, three days afterwards, 293 of those in London,
with three Christians, were drawn and hanged. A great
many executions also occurred in the provinces.

That, however, was only a warning of the vengeance
that was shortly to fall upon the Jews. Edward I. shared
in the hatred with which they were regarded by the people,
and on the 1st of August, 1290, at the request of Pope
Honorius, he issued an edict expelling the whole race from
England. Three months were allowed them for settling

their affairs and gathering together their property; but they were warned that if any one was found in the kingdom after the 1st of November his head would be cut off, license being given to every Christian to play the part of executioner. More moderation was shown by the king, at any rate, than in some other Christian states. The Jews were permitted to carry off all their available property, although outstanding mortgages, and the like, were to be forfeited to the Crown, and ships were to be provided for their conveyance to any destination—not very remote—that they chose. But the promise was badly kept by the people. About 16,000 Jews made ready to depart, and collected in the various eastern ports towards the end of October. Some were properly conveyed to the Continent. Others were taken on board, and then robbed and murdered by the sailors. The captain of one ship, off Queenborough, allowed the Jews to place in his care all their packages—a rich cargo of gold and precious stones—and then, before they had time to accompany their goods, put to sea, mockingly advising them, as he sailed off, to call upon Moses, who had cut a passage for their forefathers through the Red Sea, and who, if they were true children of Israel, would do as much for them. Men, women and children, thus prevented from quitting England within the prescribed time, were left to starve on the shore, or to be leisurely slaughtered by their Christian enemies.

Thus England was rid of the Jews, who, doubtless, often offending, had set its people the best example of money-making, and had rendered many and great services to its commerce. Before that, they had been exiled from France and other states. Two centuries later, their brethren, lodged in Spain for thirteen centuries, were driven out in like manner, and with greater sufferings, by Ferdinand the Catholic. The Jew was again a wanderer, but it is not necessary here to follow his wanderings. Many of the

persecuted race went to Egypt and other parts of the
Levant, and so worked their ways to new homes in Asia and
Africa. Others went to Russia and the still barbarous
countries north, east, and south of Poland. They settled
in great numbers in the remote parts of Europe, until, under
the protection of a revived and better toleration, they were
allowed to turn westward again.

England was the first home opened to them. Some of
the Spanish Jews are supposed to have found a refuge in
England after the banishment of 1492. There is evidence
that a few, at any rate, were settled in the country, and
sharing in its new ways of commerce under the Tudors;
but their presence was first publicly sanctioned by Oliver
Cromwell, though even he could not grant them the liberty
that he and some other enlightened republicans desired.
Harrington, in his "Oceana," gravely proposed that Ireland,
then, as since, a great trouble to England, should be sold
to the Jews, and used by them as a new Canaan. Many of
them settled in the country during the Commonwealth, and
they came yet more abundantly during the reign of
Charles II., and afterwards. In the reign of William III.
it was proposed to revive the old spirit of persecution, and
to raise £100,000 by a poll-tax on the Jews. That project
was abandoned, but their subsequent offer to buy the town
of Brentwood for £500,000, with full liberty of trading
and worshipping there as they liked, was not accepted.
During the last 180 years, however, the Jews have
had liberty of residence in England, and the recent full
concessions of civil and religious liberty that have been
made to them are well known.

A long history might be written concerning their connection with English trade during this later period. True
to their old traditions, they have continued to find in
banking, money-lending, and brokerage their favourite
pursuits. There is no branch of commerce in which they

have not profitably engaged, but the Stock Exchange has always been the great resort of the most enterprising of their number. "The whole people," wrote Addison, in the *Spectator*, "is now a race of such merchants as are wanderers by profession. They are, indeed, so disseminated through all the trading parts of the world, that they are become the instruments by which the most distant nations converse with one another, and by which mankind are knit together in a general correspondence. They are like the pegs and nails in a great building, which, though they are but little valued in themselves, are absolutely necessary to keep the whole frame together." They became far more influential in England shortly after Addison's day. The greatest London Jew of the middle of the last century was Sampson Gideon, son of a West India merchant, and a friend of Robert Walpole. He made a fortune by stock-buying, during the panic caused by the Pretender's Rebellion in 1745, and increased it by shrewd speculations during the next seventeen years. "Gideon is dead," said a letter-writer in 1762, "worth more than the whole land of Canaan." His son, brought up in the Christian faith, became Sir Sampson Gideon Eardley, and his grandson was Baron Eardley. Worthier, if not wealthier Jews, of the next generation, were Benjamin and Abraham Goldsmid. Their father, Aaron, came from Hamburg and settled in London as a merchant about the year 1750. They carried on the business till 1792, and then started as stockbrokers, with Sir Francis Baring for their only rival. They amassed vast fortunes and used them well. By a strange fatality, they both committed suicide, Abraham in 1808, and Benjamin in 1810; but the house that they founded still retains its name for honesty and enterprise.

The house of Rothschild, however, best illustrates the prosperous ways pursued by the Wandering Jew in these more fortunate times. Meyer Anselm, surnamed Rothschild because of the sign of the "red shield" by which his house was marked, was a shrewd broker and money-lender, afterwards a banker, in Frankfort, during some forty years previous to 1812, when he died, leaving twelve thousand florins to his five sons, Anselm, Solomon, Nathan Meyer, Charles, and James, on the condition that they should continue in partnership and spread the ramifications of their house all over Europe. Anselm remained in Frankfort. Solomon established branches in Berlin and Vienna. Charles went to Naples, and James to Paris. Nathan Meyer, the cleverest of the five, chose England for his home. Born in 1776, he settled in Manchester when he was about twenty-two. In 1803 he removed to London, and he spent the next three-and-thirty years in developing the largest branch of the largest private banking-house in the world. "I hope that your children are not too fond of money and business, to the exclusion of more important things," said Thomas Fowell Buxton to him on one occasion; "I am sure you would not wish that." "I am sure I *should* wish that," answered Nathan Rothschild; "I wish them to give mind, and soul, and heart, and body—everything—to business. That is the way to be happy. It requires a great deal of boldness, and a great deal of caution, to make a great fortune; and, when you have got it, it requires ten times as much wit to keep it." Younger members of the house have not quite adhered to the old man's wish; but they have fared none the worse in commerce by failing to make money-getting the sole purpose of their life.

The Wandering Jew—nearly always a trader, and gene-rally a successful trader—is now to be found in every part of the world in which money is to be made. Of the five millions or so that at the present time make up the race, it is supposed that nearly two millions are in Asia and Africa; their settlements extending from China to their own ancient home, and from Alexandria, their first great halting-place, to the Cape of Good Hope. About a million and a quarter are in Russia; and a million, or but little less, in Austria. It is estimated that there are six hundred thousand in Poland, a hundred thousand in France, thirty thousand in Great Britain, seventy-five thousand in the United States, and a goodly number in other parts of America and in the English colonies.

CHAPTER II.

"THE good merchant," says Fuller, "is one who by his
trading claspeth the islands to the continent, and one
country to another : an excellent gardener, who makes
England bear wine, and oil, and spices ; yea, herein he goes
beyond Nature, in causing that *omnis fert omnia tellus.*" If
the Wandering Jew—driven from land to land—has carried
with him special skill in one important branch of trade, and
everywhere found ready pupils in his banking art—merchants
of every other race, by force or choice, have also wandered
to and fro, bearing to each district the produce of other
districts, and offering to each a hundred foreign commodities
in exchange for every article of native produce. Nearly
the whole history of commerce, indeed, is a history of the
ways in which wares have wandered from place to place, to
satisfy the growing needs and varying tastes of every civilised community; so that, as Fuller puts it, Nature is outdone,
and all lands bear all things.

Englishmen, now-a-days, with a thousand apparent
necessaries of life at hand, and a million luxuries to choose
from, can hardly realise the condition of their forefathers
when they were limited to the scanty fruits of their own

home and their own labour. The "good merchant" has
been the prime agent in changing their primeval barbarism
into modern civilisation.

The change began before history, as the silent records
of primitive life, found under old mounds and barrows, testify.
If the theory is true that the ancient Britons, like the Teutons
and Scandinavians who overcame them, as well as the
Greeks and the Romans, are sprung from that old Aryan
race which peopled Persia and India, they must have
brought much rude knowledge of trade from their Eastern
fatherland, and must have acquired much more in the course
of their long wanderings westward. They had a lively
commerce with their kinsmen on the Gallic coast when
Julius Cæsar visited them ; and as soon as they were incorporated in the Roman empire they became sharers in all
the wealth of traffic that Rome gave to her vassals. Trade
was honourable, and, within narrow limits, was abundant,
under the Anglo-Saxons. " I am useful," says a merchant,
in one of their books, " to the king and his nobles, to rich
men and to common folk; I enter my ship with my merchandise, and sail across the seas and sell my wares, and
buy dear things that are not produced in this land, and
bring them with great danger for your good ; and sometimes
I am shipwrecked, and lose all my wares, and hardly escape
myself." " What is it you bring us ?" asks one. " I bring
you," he replies, " skins, silks, costly gems, and gold;
various garments, pigments, wine, oil, iron and brass,
copper and tin, silver, glass, and such like." " Will you
sell your wares here, as you bought them there ?" inquires
the other speaker. " Nay, in truth," answers the merchant,
" else where would be the good of all my labour ? I will
sell them here dearer than I bought them there, that so I
may get some profit, to feed me and my wife and children."
That dialogue shows that the philosophy of trade was
clearly understood in England at least ten centuries ago.

The foreign wares that wandered to England in Anglo-Saxon and Anglo-Norman times, however, were few indeed in comparison with the supply and the variety of our own day. So it is in the case of what are now the commonest articles of food and clothing, as well as with regard to the thousand-and-one luxuries or artificial necessities to which we have grown accustomed.

Beef, mutton, and corn, have of course been of native growth in England from the earliest known times, and the only changes that have occurred in respect of them have resulted from the necessity of going to other lands for the use of the people who have increased faster than the productive powers of the land. More than half our meat is still of native growth, but a million or more cows, sheep, and pigs, are brought over, dead or alive, from the Continent; and among the latest curiosities of the commerce of food are the efforts to introduce into the English market the flesh of beasts still over-abundant in South America and Australia. And considerably more than half the bread now eaten in England is made of foreign grain. Russia, Prussia, Denmark, and Central Germany alternate with the United States and British North America in yielding the chief supply, according to the varying richness of the harvests in the Old World and the New.

Other staples of food have arisen to eke out the necessities of our population. Among these the potato is the most important. It was first brought to Europe about 1550, by the Spanish conquerors of South America, who converted the Indian name of *papas* into *battata;* but very little heed was paid to it till 1586, when Thomas Hariot—one of the unfortunate party with which Sir Walter Raleigh attempted to found his colony of Virginia—returned to England, and wrote a learned account of the botanical and other curiosities of the district he had visited. Here he described the potato as a plant with " round roots hanging together as if fixed on ropes, and good for food, either boiled or roasted, in which way it was commonly used by the natives." A few years later it was recommended by another writer, Gerarde, as an excellent ingredient for " delicate conserves and restorative sweetmeats." "To give them greater grace in eating," Gerarde also said of potatoes, "they should be boiled with prunes." Nearly a century passed before the real value of potatoes was discerned. Hariot, or some of his comrades, brought over a few plants, which were cultivated as rarities. Raleigh, receiving from Queen Elizabeth a grant of land at Youghal, in the south of Ireland, took them to his new home ; and by him, as Sir Robert Southwell said in 1693, some were given to his grandfather, and naturalised in the country to which they were to prove so important an article of diet. But in 1663 the best that Boyle, discoursing to the Royal Society, could say of these Youghal vegetables was, that they were "very good to pickle for winter salads, and also to preserve." A year before that, however, some one else had suggested to the Royal Society that famine might be prevented " by dispersing potatoes throughout all parts of England." The idea, with or without the help of learned men in London, was quickly taken up. Before the end of the seventeenth century the potato had become a cheap luxury all over Ireland, and its cultivation had extended to Scotland and the north of England. Once established as a popular favourite, it quickly became a great staple of food.

Other garden stuffs, some of them hardly less useful, were introduced among us rather earlier. Garden economy, still insufficiently practised in England, was a thing almost unknown in these islands until the Flemish colonists—who came in frequent tides under the Plantagenets, and most abundantly in Queen Elizabeth's reign—set our forefathers a good example of thrift and tact. During the Middle Ages, even a common cabbage was a present fit for a king, only

to be obtained through the intervention of some friend
trading with the Low Countries. The Flemish and Dutch
refugees, however, who fled to England from Philip II.'s
persecutions, brought their habits with them; and carrots,
celery, and a dozen other vegetables, as well as cabbages,
first grown in the neat little gardens that they planted in
Kent, Norfolk, and various parts of the country, were by
them established as common articles of food.

Of other substitutes for bread imported into England,
but not fit for native growth, rice is the chief—a staple
food to a greater number of people than any other grain,
and grown extensively in India from the most ancient
period. It was in early times occasionally brought to
Europe as a curiosity, and as soon as the East India Company became influential, regular trade in it began. But the
Indian merchantmen had better cargoes at command, and
rice was chiefly shipped by them for the use of their sailors
during the passage. About two hundred years ago, however, a vessel coming to England from Madagascar, being
driven by winds upon the coast of Carolina, its captain gave
a little bag of rice-seed to a colonist named Woodward, who
had befriended him. Woodward sowed the seed in some
marsh land, and a good crop resulted; but the colonists
knew not how to clean and prepare the grain for use, and
the rice was neglected. Finding the soil congenial, it continued to grow and spread, so that it covered a wide area
before the residents took any trouble to learn what use they
could make of it. That they at length did; and then they
found themselves possessed of a commodity of great value
in itself, and of greater value in that it grew, almost without
cultivation, in districts too swampy to be made much use of
in any other way. It was principally by help of its rice,
used at home and sent in large quantities to Europe, that
Carolina throve during more than a hundred years, and it
still vies with cotton as a profitable article of trade.

Sugar is another commodity that has wandered from the far East to the far West. Honey was the only sweetening ingredient known in Europe till the last days of the Roman empire, when sugar was introduced as a sweetmeat and a medicinal adjunct, and described as " the Indian salt, in colour and form like common salt ; but in taste and sweetness like honey." It came from India with the spices and other rarities brought by the Oriental traders, but nothing appears to have been known of its production till the eleventh or twelfth century. The Crusaders learnt to like it, and the taste which they encouraged was soon partly gratified by the Arabs and Moors, who planted the sugarcane in Rhodes, Cyprus, Crete, and Sicily, and afterwards in Spain and Portugal. In 1420 the Portuguese introduced it to more congenial soil in Madeira (discovered and colonised by them in the previous year), and in 1503 it was taken by the Spaniards to the Canaries. Thence it was quickly carried to the Spanish and Portuguese settlements in the New World. Hispaniola and Brazil furnished most of the sugar conveyed to European markets until 1641, when its cultivation was established in the English colony of Barbadoes. There it flourished so well, and by that time its value was so well understood, that in 1676 Barbadoes sugar furnished employment to four hundred vessels, with an average burthen of 150 tons a-piece. It soon spread to the other West Indian colonies, and to the Dutch settlement in Guiana. But sugar was a tolerably rare commodity in England till shortly before the year 1700, when some 20,000,000 lbs. were consumed in the country. By 1782 that quantity was multiplied eight times, and it was again doubled by 1840. More than 1.000,000,000 lbs. are now annually consumed in Great Britain and Ireland.

This increase is mainly due to the introduction of new beverages—tea, coffee, and cocoa—into the country. In ancient times the only drink common in the country, besides water, was a poor sort of wine produced from grapes, grown in Gloucestershire and the neighbouring counties. The vine throve better in France, and during the Middle Ages Burgundian wine was almost the principal commodity imported into the country. Beer, now the national beverage, was known to the Anglo-Saxons and occasionally drunk, and even made at home, with wormwood instead of hops, throughout the subsequent centuries. But its use has only been general during the last four hundred years or less. The Flemings were the first hop-growers and the first beer-drinkers, and great was the abuse heaped upon them by the mediæval English for their gross tastes in this respect. According to the old couplet—

> " Hops, Reformation, baize, and beer
> Came into England all in one year ;"

the year being 1524, when Flemish immigrants, settling in Kent, began to cultivate hops in their gardens. Kentish hops, however, soon became famous, and beer quickly grew into favour with the people. There were many, in Queen Elizabeth's day, ready to join in the chorus of the famous old drinking-song attributed to Bishop Still—

> " I cannot eat but little meat,
> My stomach is not good ;
> But sure I think that I can drink
> With him that wears a hood.
> Though I go bare, yet take no care,
> I nothing am a-cold ;
> I stuff my skin so full within
> Of jolly good ale and old.
>
> " Back and side, go bare, go bare,
> Both foot and hand, go cold ;
> But, belly, God send thee good ale enough,
> Whether 't be new or old."

And the liking for beer has hardly lessened, in spite of the wonderful extension in England, during the last two centuries, of a taste for less stimulating drinks. Tea, used from the earliest known times by the Chinese, is mentioned occasionally by mediæval travellers in the East; but only became an article of European trade in the seventeenth century. It first came overland to Russia. We are told of a Russian embassy to Mongolia, which received a present of tea in exchange for its costly gifts of sable furs. The Russians protested against such useless wares, but they took the parcel back to Moscow, where it was so well liked that more was sent for, and thus a trade began. About the year 1610 the Dutch began to trade with China by sea, and small quantities of tea were brought over by them; but it was not known in England long before 1660, when a law was passed by Charles II.'s first Parliament, levying a duty of eightpence on every gallon of tea, chocolate, or sherbet made for sale. In 1661 Pepys wrote in his Diary: "I did send for a cup of tea, a China drink, of which I never had drunk before;" and in 1667: "Home, and there find my wife making of tea, a drink which Mr. Pulling, the potticary, tells her is good for her cold and the defluxions." But Mrs. Pepys was lucky in being able to enjoy her new medicine. In 1664 the East India Company had difficulty in buying thirty-four ounces for a present to the king; and in 1669 we find the Company writing out to its servants in India to "send home 100 lbs. of the best *tey* they could find." In 1678 it imported 4,713 lbs.; but thereby the market was greatly overstocked, and during the following six years only 410 pounds more were brought into the country. Soon after that, however, a regular and steadily-growing trade began. In 1711 the consumption in Great Britain amounted to 142,000 lbs., and in 1781 to 3.500,000 lbs. In 1785 the duty was reduced from 119 to 12½ per cent. on the value, and the consequent reduction of price led to a much greater demand. In that year about 13,000,000 lbs. were consumed; in 1828 about

36,000,000 lbs.; in 1860 about 80,000,000 lbs.; and in 1866 about 140,000,000 lbs.

Coffee-drinking, though a much more modern custom than tea-drinking, began in England a little earlier. It was first practised in Arabia about the middle of the fifteenth century, when the story goes that the chief of a company of dervishes noticed that his goats frisked and played all night long whenever in the previous day they had eaten of a shrub growing wild in the neighbourhood. Finding it difficult to keep his disciples awake during their evening devotions, he prepared a beverage of the leaves or berries of the shrub, and it proved so helpful to the midnight piety of the dervishes, that from that time coffee came into use. The coffee-plant being abundant and easily cultivated, the new beverage soon became a favourite all over Arabia. Great opposition was offered to it by many good Moslems, who urged that it was an intoxicating drink quite as bad as the wine forbidden in the Koran, and numerous raids were made upon the coffee-houses; but the very fact of its serving as, in some sort, a substitute for the juice of the vine tended to make it popular. It reached Constantinople about 1554, and was of universal use in all Mahometan countries before the close of the sixteenth century. So essential was it deemed to domestic happiness that a Turkish law recognised a man's refusal to supply his wife with coffee as sufficient ground for her claiming a divorce. About the year 1600 it began to be talked of in Christendom as a rare and precious medicine. In 1615 it was brought to Venice, and in 1621 Burton spoke of it, in his "Anatomy of Melancholy," as a valuable article which he had heard of but not seen. In 1652, Sir Nicholas Crispe, a Levant merchant, opened in London the first coffee-house known in England, the beverage being prepared by a Greek girl brought over for the work. Other coffee-houses in abundance were soon opened. In William III.'s and Queen Anne's days they were the great places of resort

for wits, beaux, fops, gallants, wise men, and fools, and as
such are amply described in the *Spectator* and other works
of the time. And coffee was not merely an excuse for social
intercourse : its first drinkers in England knew how to
drink it. Pope says :—

> " For, lo ! the board with cups and spoons is crowned,
> The berries crackle and the mill goes round ;
> On shining altars of Japan they raise
> The silver lamp ; the fiery spirits blaze ;
> From silver spouts the grateful liquors glide,
> While China's earth receives the smoking tide.
> At once they gratify their scent and taste,
> And frequent cups prolong the rich repast."

The growing demand for coffee, of which more than
30,000,000 lbs. are now annually consumed in Great Britain,
caused the plant to be cultivated in other districts as well
as Arabia, where it is indigenous and thrives best. At a
very early date the Dutch began to grow it in Java and
their other East Indian possessions, and they were unintentionally the causers of its introduction to the New World.
In 1690 some seeds were brought from Mocha to the Botanic
Garden at Amsterdam, and from the produce of these seeds
a single plant was, in 1714, sent as a present to Louis XIV.,
and by him treasured up in Paris. In 1717 a Frenchman
named Déclieux obtained a plant raised from one of its
seeds, and carried it to Martinique. The ship was weather-
bound, and before the Atlantic was crossed the crew were
in grievous trouble for want of water. There was water on
board, but the captain, anxious above all things to preserve
his treasure, doled it out in meagre quantities to the men,
while he nourished the coffee-plant without stint. And the
plant made a good return for the care bestowed upon it.
From its seeds, we are told, have descended all the coffee-
trees now abounding in the West Indies and Brazil.

Few wandering wares have a more curious history than
tobacco, one of the many commodities that the New World

has given to the Old in exchange for the many that have
been sent to it from this side of the Atlantic. The Spanish
conquerors of San Domingo were not long in learning from
their native subjects the use made by them of the prolific
weed, which they styled *tobako*, and which all the world now
knows by the same name. The conquerors of other districts
found the same weed, under different titles, in favour with
the Indians, and it soon came to be equally in favour with
Europeans. In 1559 it began to be cultivated in Lisbon, and
about that time the French ambassador in Portugal—from
whose name, Nicot, has come its scientific name of *Nicotiana*
—sent some seeds to Catherine de' Medici. Its cultivation
spread rapidly over the southern and central parts of Europe,
and across the whole breadth of Asia. Before 1600 it was
known in Java, China, and even in Japan, and everywhere
known as tobacco; though it is probable that in many parts
the plant had previously existed as a useless weed, and that
only its cultivation and employment as a narcotic had been
learnt from the Red men of the West Indies and their conquerors. We hear nothing of it in England till 1586, when,
along with the potato, it was introduced by Raleigh's would-
be colonists of Virginia. It was described by Hariot, whose
allusion to the potato has been already quoted :—" There is
an herb," he says, " which is sowed apart by itself, and is
called by the inhabitants *uppowoc*. In the West Indies it hath
divers names, according to the several places and countries
where it groweth and is used. The Spaniards generally call
it *tobacco*. The leaves thereof being dried and brought into
powder, they are wont to take the fume or smoke thereof, by
sucking it through pipes made of clay into their stomach and
head, from whence it purgeth superfluous phlegm and other
gross humours, and openeth all the pores and passages of
the body. This *uppowoc* is of so precious estimation among
them, that they think their gods are marvellously delighted
therewith ; whereupon sometime they make hallowed fires,

D

and cast some of the powder therein for sacrifice. We ourselves, during the time we were there, used to suck it after their manner, as also since our return, and have found many rare and wonderful experiments of the virtues thereof, of which the relation would require a volume by itself. The use of it by so many of late, men and women of great calling, and some learned physicians also, is sufficient witness."

The use of it certainly became rapidly prevalent in England. Many stories are told of Sir Walter Raleigh's own exploits with his pipe, and of the pleasure taken by great courtiers, as well as common folk, in the new luxury provided for them. Before many years were out, Edmund Spenser, in his "Faerie Queene," spoke in praise of the "divine tobacco," and other champions were not wanting. Ben Jonson, on the other hand, was one of its first public opponents. Nearly every one of his early plays has in it a smoker or two—always a fop, a knave, or a fool. King James I.'s aversion to it is well known. In his famous "Counterblast," written in 1619, he denounced smoking as "loathsome to the eye, hateful to the nose, harmful to the brain, dangerous to the lungs, and, in the black stinking fume thereof, nearest resembling the horrible Stygian smoke of the pit that is bottomless." One of the arguments against it, to which he attached most weight, was that it was wicked and disgraceful for civilised Christians to borrow anything from barbarous heathens—an argument that would apply equally well to the potato and half-a-thousand other useful commodities brought into the country. "Have you not, then reason," he asked, "to forbear this filthy novelty, so basely grounded, so foolishly received, and so grossly mistaken in the right use thereof—sinning against God, harming yourselves both in your person and in your goods, creating thereby the marks and notes of vanity upon you?" That was on a par with Pope Urban VIII.'s order excommuni-

cating every one who took snuff in church. But the
smokers smoked on, and became every year more
numerous.

At first the demand for tobacco in England was met
by supplies of the article brought from America by way
of Spain and Portugal, or of the coarser produce of the
European tobacco-fields. It even began to be cultivated
in England, and yet more in Ireland. As soon as Virginia
was really colonised, however, in James I.'s reign, a direct
trade was started. For a long time tobacco was the only important produce of Virginia, and large quantities of it were
annually shipped to the mother country. In the colony itself it served as money. The fine for absence from church
was a pound of tobacco, and slander of a clergyman had
to be atoned for by a payment of 800 lbs. Innkeepers
were forbidden to charge more than 10 lbs. for a dinner, or
more than 8 lbs. for a gallon of strong ale. In vain King
James, in 1622, ordered the Virginians to breed silkworms,
and set up silk works, as "a rich and solid commodity,
preferable to tobacco." In vain his son, Charles I., in 1631,
bade them send home " some better fruit than tobacco and
smoke," and so avoid "the speedy ruin likely to befall the
colonies, and the danger to the bodies and manners of the
English people, through the excessive growth of tobacco."
The trade was too profitable and too much patronised by
the English to be given up. In 1628 the annual produce
of Virginia, containing 3,000 inhabitants, was reckoned at
412,500 lbs. Other American colonies, Maryland especially,
soon followed the same traffic. In 1740 at least 200
British ships were constantly engaged in the collection of
tobacco, and the annual total of their cargoes exceeded
18,000,000 lbs. Liverpool and Glasgow owed much of
their progress as great commercial towns—cotton being
then hardly known in America—to the tobacco trade, and
the trade still thrives, in spite of other and more important

rivals. The United States now send to England about 40,000,000 lbs. of tobacco, and some 20,000,000 lbs. come from other parts of the world. Of this quantity, however, hardly more than two-thirds is for home consumption. The national revenue derived from the heavy duties levied on tobacco amounts to nearly £6,000,000 a year.

Tobacco, looked upon as a sort of food by many, and as a poison by others, is by some regarded as a medicine. The history of the introduction of some other and more legitimate medicines into England is very curious. Let quinine serve as an instance.

The cinchona plant, called *kina* or *kinken* by the Indians, had grown wild in some elevated parts of Peru long before the valuable properties of its bark were known. An old fable says that they were first discovered by some natives, who perceived a sick lion gnawing at the stem and chewing the bark, and that this curious phenomenon caused them to use it in like manner when attacked by fever. A more probable story is that the Jesuits of Loxa, anxious to understand the botanical and medicinal properties of the various plants in their new home, tasted this plant along with the rest, and that the accident of its being first given to an invalid, and helping to cure him, led to its employment in cases of fever and ague. A third story is that the Countess Chinchon, whose husband was Viceroy of Peru early in the seventeenth century, was the first to test it; and that, being cured by it, she brought some to Europe and dispensed it to her friends. Nothing is certain, however, except that it began to find favour in Spain about the year 1640, and that ever since that time it has been regarded as one of the most valuable of medicines. It was procured and exported by the Jesuit missionaries, and largely used by the Catholics, although for many years opposed by the Protestants on religious grounds. In 1726 La Fontaine made it the subject of an epic poem; but not till a later day was it known by Europeans that the bark bought from the Indians, who gathered it in forests rarely visited by white men, came from a tree almost unrivalled in the exquisite beauty of its leaves and the delicious fragrance of its flowers. In the course of his long and famous voyage of scientific research in the equatorial regions, lasting from 1735 to 1743, La Condamine visited Loxa and collected some plants to transfer to Paris, but they were washed overboard on the passage; and in 1771 Jussieu took a similar disaster so much to heart that he is said to have thereby lost his reason. Quite recently some specimens have been reared at Kew; but the plant can only grow naturally within precise limits of latitude, and varies in size, according to the locality, from a high tree to a diminutive shrub. Even in Peru, since the increased demand for the bark for use on this side of the Atlantic, it has been gathered so recklessly, from trees young as well as old, that there was good ground for fearing, not only that the augmented price would put it out of reach of ordinary patients, but that before long it would be altogether extinct.

This serious danger has been fortunately removed. In 1839 Dr. Forbes Royle urged the importance of transplanting the Peruvian bark to India, as being necessary for the adequate supply of a drug indispensable in the treatment of Indian fevers. In 1852 this was attempted under the direction of the East India Company, but the experiment failed as signally as all earlier efforts to introduce it into Europe. In 1859, however, a new attempt was made by Mr. Clements Markham, with the assistance of Lord Stanley, then Secretary of State for India, and this time with success. Mr. Markham had to overcome many obstacles incident to the labour of exploring a large and not easily-accessible district in search of the best varieties, and of collecting a sufficient quantity of seeds and plants in opposition to the jealousy of the residents, who, though reckless in their

treatment of the cinchona, were loth to assist in the formation of a trade which they deemed detrimental to their interests. Once, with no food but some parched maize, he was
for eleven hours in the saddle, riding quickly over a rugged
country, and in intense cold, which he dreaded less for
himself than for the young plants that were in his keeping.
Many difficulties had to be undergone before the various
pots and parcels could be brought in good condition to the
Peruvian coast, and thence taken across the Pacific to India,
where another series of difficulties had to be contended with
before suitable soil and climate could be found. Nearly
three years were spent in the whole business. In the
northern highlands of India, however, and especially among
the Neilgherry Hills, the cinchona now flourishes; and the
greatest benefits, both to rich and poor, are likely to spring
from Mr. Markham's energy in finding a new home for the
best of all known febrifuges.

Turning from food and kindred articles to clothing and
the commodities necessary for its improvement, we find
that quite as great benefits have been effected by wandering
wares and the traders who have transported them from one
country to another. Wool, of course common wherever
sheep are found, furnished material for the garments of our
forefathers from the time of the Roman conquest, and a
rude sort of manufacture prevailed in the country during
the ensuing centuries. But during the Middle Ages the best
clothing came from Flanders, whither England sent its wool,
to take back so much of it as was required in a more available shape. A large section of the history of commerce
down to the sixteenth century concerns this traffic. It was
not till near the period of Queen Elizabeth that woollen
manufacture became important, and then the change was to
a great extent due to the settlement of Flemish Protestants
in England, who brought with them their skill in weaving
and the other branches of cloth-making. Since then we

hear little of the importation of woollen goods, and still less of the exportation of raw wool to be made up abroad. In 1739 it was reckoned that a million and a half of persons —nearly a fifth of the whole population—were engaged in woollen manufacture. From the commencement of its colonies, England clothed its colonists as well as itself, and even before that a small foreign trade in woollen wares had begun. About a century and a half ago it was found that the raw material possessed by the country was insufficient for the needs of the factories, and more had to be obtained from other districts; and this trade has made wonderful progress during the last hundred years. In 1771 the quantity of foreign wool brought into the country, chiefly from Spain, was under 2,000,000 lbs.; in 1801 it exceeded 7,000,000 lbs.; in 1831 it was nearly 32,000,000 lbs.; and in 1860 it exceeded 115,000,000 lbs., besides about 30,000,000 lbs. which came here to be sent at once to other parts.

The sources from which this vast supply—to which must be added more than 100,000,000 lbs. of home-grown wool —has been derived have varied strangely. In 1800 the imports from Spain were fourteen times as great as those from Germany; in 1840 the imports from Germany were seventeen times as great as those from Spain. In 1807 Australia sent us its first cargo of wool, weighing 245 lbs. In 1840 the quantity had risen to 10,000,000 lbs., and in 1860 to 60,000,000 lbs. It is now not far short of 100,000,000 lbs.

The history of this Australian wool trade is very note-worthy. In 1793 it occurred to Captain John M'Arthur, then stationed with his regiment in Sydney, that the Australian climate was well adapted for the production of merino sheep; but the colony had nothing but an inferior Bengal breed, useful only for food, and there was great difficulty in obtaining any other. At length, in 1797, Captain

M'Arthur conveyed to Sydney three rams and five ewes
of pure merino stock, and, mixing with them seventy of the
native sort, applied himself zealously to sheep-rearing. In
1803 he came to England, bringing with him samples of his
wool, which he recommended both to a committee of cloth-
manufacturers and to the Government as being "in softness
superior to many of the wools of Spain, and certainly equal
in every valuable property to the very best procured from
thence." Some fun was made about his "wool-gathering"
theories; but his samples and his arguments gave satisfaction to competent judges, especially as Europe was then
harassed by Napoleon's wars, and there was constant risk of
a stoppage of the supply derived from Spain. M'Arthur's
modest request of a grant of 10,000 acres of grazing land
to be assigned out of the unoccupied territory, with thirty
convicts to serve as shepherds, was acceded to; and George
III., who took a lively interest in the matter, gave him
several fine merino sheep, chosen from his flock at Kew.
He returned to Australia, and in 1807, when the little stock
with which he had begun to work ten years before had
increased to 4,000, he sent home his first bale of wool.
During the next seven-and-twenty years he rode his hobby
steadily and with wonderful success. He died in 1834,
worthily honoured as "the father of the colony," and in
that year the shipment of Australian wool to England—a
great part of it drawn from his own great and well-ordered
sheep-runs—was nearly ten thousand times as great as that
which he first made. He had plenty of followers. Squatters
spread over vast tracts of New South Wales, Victoria, South
Australia, and Tasmania, and, mightily enriching themselves,
have succeeded in adding immeasurably to the wealth o
the huge Australian commonwealth; while their produce
has been of hardly less value to the mother country—and
not to her alone. America now imports large supplies of
Australian wool, all of which, till lately, were obtained by way

of England, and spanned two-thirds of the globe in its transit, though now a shorter route, across the Pacific, is being established.

Another sort of wool comes to England from America, and has begun to be naturalised in Australia. The large alpaca sheep of Peru yields longer, softer, and more lustrous wool than any other animal of the tribe. Its softness and lustre made shrewd manufacturers anxious to use it; but the very length of the hair, sometimes extending even to forty-two inches, was an obstacle. The machinery commonly used by the woollen manufacturers was not fitted for it, and it was tangled and broken in the working. The few parcels brought to England were accordingly rejected, and, thrown away as useless, lay idle in the Liverpool warehouses till 1834, when Mr. Titus Salt—a young farmer, whose father was a woolstapler in Leeds, and who himself now settled in Bradford as a spinner—began to devise means for getting over the difficulty. One episode in his adventures was characteristically described by Charles Dickens. "A huge pile of dirty-looking sacks," he said, "filled with some fibrous material which bore a strong resemblance to superannuated horsehair, or frowsy, elongated wool, or anything else unpleasant and unattractive, was landed in Liverpool. When these queer-looking bales had first arrived, or by what vessel brought, or for what purpose intended, the very oldest warehouseman in Liverpool docks couldn't say. There had once been a rumour—a mere warehouseman's whisper—that the bales had been shipped from South America on spec., and consigned to the agency of C. W. and F. Foozle and Co. But even this seems to have been forgotten, and it was agreed upon by all hands, that the three hundred and odd sacks of nondescript hair-wool were a perfect nuisance. The rats appeared to be the only parties who at all approved of the importation, and to them it was the very finest investment for capital

that had been known in Liverpool since their first ancestors
had migrated thither. Well, those bales seemed likely to
rot, or fall to the dust, or be bitten up for the particular
use of family rats. Brokers wouldn't so much as look at
them. Merchants would have nothing to say to them.
Dealers couldn't make them out. Manufacturers shook
their heads at the bare mention of them; while the
agents of C. W. and F. Foozle and Co. looked at the bill
of lading, and once spake to their head clerk about
shipping them to South America again. One day—we
won't care what day it was, or even what week or month
it was, though things of far less consequence have been
chronicled to the half minute—one day, a plain, business-
looking young man, with an intelligent face and quiet,
reserved manner, was walking along through those same
warehouses at Liverpool, when his eyes fell upon some of
the superannuated horsehair projecting from one of the
ugly, dirty bales. Some lady rat, more delicate than her
neighbours, had found it rather coarser than usual, and had
persuaded her lord and master to eject the portion from
her resting-place. Our friend took it up, looked at it, felt
it, smelt it, rubbed it, pulled it about; in fact, he did all
but taste it, and he would have done that if it had suited
his purpose—for he was 'Yorkshire.' Having held it up
to the light, and held it away from the light, and held it in
all sorts of positions, and done all sorts of cruelties to it,
as though it had been his most deadly enemy and he was
feeling quite vindictive, he placed a handful or two in his
pocket, and walked calmly away, evidently intending to
put the stuff to some excruciating private tortures at home.
What particular experiments he tried with this fibrous substance I am not exactly in a position to relate, nor does
it much signify; but the sequel was, that the same quiet,
business-looking man was seen to enter the office of C. W.
and F. Foozle and Co., and ask for the head of the firm.

When he asked that portion of the house if he would accept eightpence per pound for the entire contents of the three hundred and odd frowsy, dirty bags of nondescript wool, the authority interrogated felt so confounded that he could not have told if he were the head or tail of the firm. At first he fancied our friend had come for the express purpose of quizzing him, and then that he was an escaped lunatic, and thought seriously of calling for the police ; but eventually it ended in his making it over in consideration of the price offered. It was quite an event in the little dark office of C. W. and F. Foozle and Co., which had its supply of light (of a very inferior quality) from the grim old churchyard. All the establishment stole a peep at the buyer of the 'South American stuff.' The chief clerk had the curiosity to speak to him and hear him reply. The cashier touched his coat tails. The bookkeeper, a thin man in spectacles, examined his hat and gloves. The porter openly grinned at him. When the quiet purchaser had departed, C. W. and F. Foozle and Co. shut themselves up, and gave all their clerks a holiday."

It was in 1835 that Mr. Salt made that purchase. He put it to such good use that in 1853 the imports of alpaca wool, chiefly for his own use, greatly exceeded 2,000,000 lbs.; and his business had become so large that in that year he built the famous Saltaire Mills, near Bradford, with a town around them able to hold five thousand workpeople. His new commodity found favour for ladies' dresses, umbrellas, and a dozen other useful articles, and the trade with Peru became so extensive that the Australians began to covet a share in it. In 1858 Mr. Charles Ledger carried 276 alpacas, llamas, and vecuñas to Sydney. The animals throve well in New South Wales, and already they furnish a considerable portion of the wool taken from these varieties of the sheep, and collected for the English market.

The oldest rival—or, rather, the material made of it

being so different, the oldest associate—of wool in English manufacture of clothing is linen. The use of flax, known to the ancients, was encouraged in all parts of the Roman empire, and not forgotten by its sometime subjects after Rome was overthrown. But linen was not made extensively till late in the Middle Ages, and then the chief seat of its manufacture was the same industrious little district of Flanders which formerly made all the woollen clothing for Europe. Diaper (cloth d'Yprès) came from Yprès, and cambric from Cambray. In 1445 the price in England of fine linen for altar-cloths and surplices was eightpence an ell. There was not then much demand for it for commoner uses; but soon after that, the growing refinement—which caused even peasants to be dissatisfied with nothing but coarse woollen garments worn both day and night, and made them wish for under-clothing and bed gear—led to extension of the trade. More linen was brought from abroad, until Flemish and Huguenot refugees in the sixteenth and seventeenth centuries brought their skill with them to England, and flax-spinning began to be considerable in our island. An old staple of trade from Ireland to England was flax, and its manufacture was carried on to some extent in the sister island from very early times. The first man who made it important, however, was Louis Crommelier, a Huguenot, who migrated to Belfast after the Revocation of the Edict of Nantes. Ireland had 50,000 acres of flax in cultivation in 1812; 110,000 in 1826. The area, partly in consequence of the potato famine, had sunk to 58,000 in 1847; but by 1853 it had risen to 170,000, and in 1864 it exceeded 300,000 acres. Linen manufacture was not introduced into Scotland till the early part of last century. In 1745, 165,760 lbs. of flax were imported by Dundee; fifty years later the quantity was nearly forty times as great, and since then Dundee, like Leeds, has grown steadily as a great centre of the trade.

To feed this trade the increased production of Ireland has proved quite inadequate. To the 10,000,000 lbs. or more, now annually brought from Ireland, are added some 20,000,000 lbs. imported from foreign countries, three-fourths coming from Russia, and much of the rest from Egypt.

The raw cotton now brought into the country is seven or eight times as great in value as both the flax and the wool imported for manufacturing purposes, and exceeds them yet more in quantity. Two centuries ago, however, there was hardly any cotton manufacture in England, and ninety years ago it was hardly one two-hundredth part as great as now. The plant has been cultivated and has yielded material for clothing from the earliest known times in India, where the trade is still carried on with very little change from the methods that prevailed three thousand years ago; and calicoes from Calicut were occasionally conveyed to Europe by the merchants of Tyre and Alexandria, and in later days by those of Venice. The establishment of the East India Company rendered easier the bringing of cotton goods to England, and soon cotton itself began to be brought in small quantities, and worked up at home. Manchester, still the centre of this manufacture, has the credit of beginning it. " They buy cotton wool in London, that first comes from Cyprus and Smyrna," wrote Lewis Roberts in 1641, " and at home work the same, and perfect it into fustians, dimities, and other such stuffs, and then return it to London, where the same is vended and sold, and not seldom sent into foreign parts." Bolton and other towns soon took up the trade, and prospered by it. It made the wealth which Humphrey Chetham, first of the great Manchester merchants, used so worthily in founding Chetham College. It made but slight progress during a century, however; and some time afterwards the chief cotton manufacturers were Huguenot exiles, who in 1676 began to follow their callings in London and other towns on the Thames, and that in spite of opposition which in the end helped to drive nearly all the trade from the south of England into the Lancashire district in which it had been started. Great resistance was offered to it by the manufacturers of woollen, linen, and silken goods, who imagined that it would ruin their own trades. They encouraged riots in the streets of London and in country towns, and they procured the passing of arbitrary laws in Parliament. In 1712 an excise duty of threepence was set on every square yard of calico made in England; in 1714 the duty was raised to sixpence; and in 1721 cotton goods were absolutely forbidden, a penalty of £5 being incurred by every wearer of them, while every seller was rendered liable to a fine of £20 for each offence. In 1736 the manufacture of calicoes was permitted, with a cotton woof, provided the warp was linen, and in 1774 the production and selling of every kind of "painted, stained, and dyed stuffs, made wholly of cotton," were made lawful; but this removal of the old restrictions benefited chiefly the manufacturers of the north, who had carried on their work in spite of laws to the contrary, and to whom wonderful facilities for extending it were just commencing with the importation of new supplies of cotton to Liverpool and Glasgow.

Columbus found the cotton plant growing almost wild, and its produce used for clothing by the natives in the West Indies; and Cortes, the conqueror of Mexico, sent to Charles V. "cotton mantles, some all white, others mixed with white and black or red, green, yellow, or blue; waistcoats, handkerchiefs, counterpanes, tapestries, and carpets of cotton," which, both in workmanship and in colour, were declared to be superior to the European manufactures of that time. But the cotton wealth of America was for a long time neglected by its conquerors. The cotton goods brought by the East India Company from its possessions, and the raw cotton brought from Turkey and Asia Minor to be worked up in England, met all the demand that was made till early in the eighteenth century. Then a trade began with our West Indian colonies, some of which found cotton almost as profitable a production as sugar. In 1743 Jamaica was reported to yield the best cotton in the world, and soon afterwards the Bahamas were famous for their growth of the kind now known as "sea island."

The rise of the cotton trade of the United States may be traced to some royalists who took shelter in the Bahamas during the War of Independence, and who, in 1786—as soon as it was safe for them to return to their own country—took with them some sea-island cotton to Georgia, and there found that its dry and sandy coast line was excellently adapted for the growth of the plant. Two years before that, in 1784, when a trading vessel from the United States arrived at Liverpool, eight bales of cotton included in its cargo were seized by the Custom-house authorities, on the ground that this could not be a native production, and therefore was contraband; but England was not much longer in igno-rance of the cotton-producing powers of the United States. Very soon it became the chief source of supply, although it would be a mistake to suppose that the opening-up of this new trade was in any direct way a cause of the new energy in cotton manufacture that was at this time being developed in England. In 1786, the year in which the sea-island variety was first planted in Georgia, about 20,000,000 lbs. of cotton were brought into the English market—a fourth from Smyrna and Turkey, nearly a third from the British West Indies, more than a third from the French, Spanish, and Dutch colonies, and a tenth from Brazil. That was more than five times as great as the quantity imported twenty years before; and cotton would have come in yet larger supplies, as the demand for more arose, from the older sources, if the United States had not shown themselves able to compete with them. That they did, however, and before long they acquired the lion's share of the quickly-growing trade. In 1791 they exported — nearly all to England — 189,316 lbs. of cotton ; in 1800, 17,789,803 lbs. ; in 1810, 93,874,201 lbs. ; and in 1820, 127,860,152 lbs. Of the latter quantity, 90,000,000 lbs. were sent to England, which received a third as much from its West Indian colonies, and a like quantity from other sources, the total import being 152,829,633 lbs. Those figures show how vast was the increase of the cotton trade in the course of five-and-thirty years. It continued to grow as rapidly down to 1860, when the civil war in America helped to bring about a crisis from which there has not yet been complete recovery. The imports, nearly eight times as great in 1820 as they were in 1786, were nearly ten times as great in 1860 as they were in 1820. In 1860 nearly 14,000,000,000 lbs. were brought into the country—considerably more than two-thirds from the United States, about a seventh from the East Indies, and most of the rest from Egypt and Brazil. And the cotton thus imported is nearly trebled in value by the process of its conversion into marketable commodities. The cotton goods manufactured in England in 1760 were worth £200,000 ; those of 1860 were worth £85,000,000, and that in spite of a vast reduction—in some cases to nearly a twentieth—in the price charged for the articles produced. Cotton is the most stupendous of all the wares that have wandered into England, and the new wares into which it is converted by British industry now wander into every quarter of the world. India, which taught us the trade, and America, which provides its staple, are alike, to a great extent, clothed by us.

In comparison with cotton, silk is an insignificant commodity ; but its commercial value is great, and its history is curious. Like so many other wares that have now been naturalised in Europe, it came to us from Asia. Alexander the Great is supposed to have first brought some garments made of it from Persia into Greece; and from that time the apparel that had during a long previous period been a badge of luxurious wealth among Oriental nations, came into vogue, first in Greece and afterwards in Rome. It is said that the Emperor Aurelian, who died in 275, had to deny his wife a silk robe because of its high price; but in later generations its use became more frequent. In 555 some monks, who had been in India, represented to the Emperor Justinian "that the Romans need not any longer be obliged to purchase raw silk of the Persians, nor of any others; for, having lived long in a country called Lerinda, they now assured him that, although the origin of raw silk was till now a secret from the West, it proceeded from certain worms taught by Nature to spin it out of their own bowels; and that, though it was impracticable to bring those worms so far alive, yet it would be easy to procure their bags, which would produce the worms." Their proposal was accepted, and thus the silkworm was brought westward as far as Constantinople, and from Constantinople it was taken to Greece.

The trade grew slowly during the Middle Ages. In 790 Charlemagne sent as a present to Offa, King of Mercia, two silken vests. But Constantinople, Greece, and the far East were the only sources from which silk was derived till 1130, when Roger II., King of Sicily, having conquered Athens, Corinth, and Thebes, took home with him some Greek prisoners, who not only introduced the silkworm, but also taught the natives how to spin and weave its fibre. So incensed at this were the Venetians, who had hitherto had a monopoly of the commodity through their Oriental trade, that in 1148 they made war with the Sicilians on account of it. Palermo silk-working prospered, however, and the trade soon extended to the south of France, to Spain, and to other parts, whither the Venetians went to collect both the raw material and the stuffs, for distribution in all the countries with which they dealt. A company of Silk-women, devoted to the manufacture of the precious article, was established in London in the fifteenth century, and by an Act of Parliament passed in 1455, "upon the heavy complaint of the women of the mystery and trade of silk and thread workers in London, that divers Lombards and other foreigners enriched themselves by ruining the said mystery," it was directed "that no wrought silk should be brought into England by way of merchandise for five years to come." In 1489 there was no silk manufacture in France; but the trade began in that country a little later, and there it made far more rapid progress than in England, attaining a pre-eminence that has lasted to the present day. It was the French Protestant refugees, settling in Spitalfields and elsewhere after the Revocation of the Edict of Nantes, in 1685, who enabled this country to make the first important advance upon the slight achievements of the old mystery of Silk-women. In 1553 Sir Thomas Gresham sent from Antwerp to King Edward VI. what Stow, the historian, calls "a great present," a pair of long Spanish silk stockings; "for you shall understand," he adds, "that King Henry VIII. did wear only cloth hose, or hose cut out of ell-broad taffeta, unless that by great chance there came a pair of Spanish stockings out of Spain." It was also a matter strange and important enough to be recorded by sober historians, that a pair of silk stockings was worn by Queen Elizabeth in 1561; but these, and all the gay apparel in which her courtiers and those of the two Jameses and the two Charleses delighted, came from the Continent.

The foremost names in the history of English silk manufacture are those of Sir Thomas Lombe and his brother John, of Derby. In 1715 John Lombe went to Leghorn, then the busiest city in Italy, and a great centre of the silk trade, peculiar machinery being there employed, the secret of which was jealously guarded from strangers. "One of his first movements," says his biographer, "was to go as a

visitor to see the silk works; for they were occasionally
shown under very rigid limitations, such as that they would
be seen only when in motion—the multiplicity and rapidity
of the machinery making it impossible then to comprehend
them—and the spectator was also hurried very rapidly
through the place. At first young Lombe thought he
could have accomplished his object in this way, by going
again and again under different disguises. One time he
was a lady, another a priest. He was as generous, too, with
his money as he could be without exciting suspicion. But
it was all in vain; he could make nothing of the hurried
glimpses he thus obtained, and every effort to see the
machinery put in motion, or at rest, failed. He now tried
another course. He began to associate with the clergy,
and, being a well-educated man and of liberal tastes, he
succeeded in ingratiating himself with the priest who acted
as confessor to the proprietor of the works. And there can
be no doubt of the fact that the priest's assistance was
obtained by Lombe. Neither do we think there can be any
doubt of the means by which that assistance was won.
Hardly any bribe could be too great that enabled the young
adventurer to succeed in his object. A plan was now designed, and put into execution, for young Lombe's admission
into the works. He disguised himself as a poor youth out
of employ, and went to the directors with a recommenda-
tion from the priest, praising his honesty and diligence,
and remarking that he had been inured to greater hardships
than might be supposed from his appearance. Lombe was
engaged as a boy to attend a spinning-engine called a
'filatoe.' He had now evidence of the sufficiency of his disguise, was accommodated with a sleeping-place in the mill;
in a word, his success was, as it were, at once secured. But
even then he had an arduous and most hazardous task to
perform. After he had done his day's work, the secret work
of the night had to begin, and if discovered in that employ-

ment!—he must often have shuddered at the possibility. Even the few appliances he required were an additional source of danger. It appears that there was a hole under the stair where he slept, and there he hid his dark lantern, tinder-box, candles, and mathematical instruments. And now the work went rapidly on. Drawing after drawing was made from different parts of the machinery, and handed over to the priest, who called occasionally to inquire how the poor boy got on. The priest handed the drawings over to the agents of the Messrs. Lombe, who transmitted them to England piecemeal in bales of silk; and thus at last every portion of the machinery was accurately drawn, and the secret a secret no longer. Lombe stayed at the mill until a ship was ready to place the suspected out of reach. No sooner was he on board than suspicion was aroused, and an Italian brig dispatched in pursuit, but Lombe was not captured, and returned safely to England. He died at the age of twenty-nine, and there is a tragical story told of his death, which is likely enough to be true. It is said that the Italians, when they heard of the whole affair, sent over a female to England to poison him. Lombe had brought over with him two Italians, who were accustomed to the manufacture he had risked so much for. The woman succeeded, through the means of one of them, in administering a deadly poison."

Sir Thomas Lombe, the elder brother, was more fortunate. In 1719, with help of the information thus diligently acquired, he set up a great silk-throwing machine on the Derwent, which was one of the wonders of the day. "This amazingly grand machine," according to contemporary testimony, "contains 26,586 wheels and 97,746 movements, which work 73,726 yards of organzine silk thread every time the water-wheel goes round (being thrice in one minute), and 318,504,960 yards in one day and night. One water-wheel gives motion to all the other movements, of which any one may be stopped separately, without ob-

structing the rest. One fire-engine conveys warm air to
every individual part of this vast machine, containing, in all
its buildings, half a quarter of a mile in length." Sir Thomas
Lombe received a patent from George I., and so highly was
his silk machine thought of, that in 1732, when the patent
had expired, Parliament voted him a sum of £14,000, "as
a consideration for the eminent services he had done, in
discovering, in introducing, and bringing to full perfection,
at his own expense, a work so useful and beneficial to this
kingdom." The reward was well earned. His enterprise,
and that of others like him, had so promoted the silk manufacture of England, that at this time it was thought to be
the best in Europe. " In Italy itself," wrote a traveller in
1730, " the silks of English manufacture are most esteemed,
and bear a greater price than those of Italy; so that at
Naples, when a tradesman would highly recommend his
silk stockings, he protests they are right English." From
that time silk manufacture became an important occupation
in England, and, though surpassed by that of France, it has
steadily progressed during the past century and a half. In
1860 the raw silk imported and worked up in this country
was worth £6,471,000, the manufactured goods imported in
the same year being valued at £3,344,000.

Closely connected with the materials for clothing, and
especially with silk and cotton, are dyes; concerning which,
from the primitive woad, with which the ancient Britons
stained their bodies, down to the magenta and other colours
with which modern fashion is humoured, much curious information abounds. It will be sufficient here to mention
the two most important, indigo and cochineal.

Indigo—prepared from the juice of a shrub, of which
there are about one hundred and fifty varieties growing freely
all round the equinoctial line—was known to and valued
by the civilised nations of the East; but, though accurately
described by Marco Polo in the thirteenth century, and

soon afterwards brought westwards, it was not made much
use of in Europe till the seventeenth. Even in 1705 it
was spoken of as a mineral. Before it could find favour
in Christendom it had a hard battle to fight with the older
woad. In 1577 the German Diet denounced it as the devil's
dye—"pernicious, corrupt, and corrosive;" and the dyers
of the Nuremberg district were bound by most solemn oath
never to employ it in their work. In 1580 it was similarly
condemned by the English Parliament, and commissioners
were appointed to visit all places where it was likely to be
found, and to destroy both it and logwood. In 1598 the
French authorities resorted to equally severe measures for
keeping it out of the busy district of Languedoc. Prejudice,
however, was gradually overcome. In 1631 the Dutch
brought seven vessels full, weighing 333,545 lbs., from the
East Indies, and after that an extensive trade was carried
on by them, until they were superseded by the English. In
1779 the East India Company began to encourage its production. Civil servants were assisted in establishing factories, and private adventurers were allowed to engage in
the trade. Though the plant grows readily, it is easily in-
fluenced by a change of weather, and the extraction of the
dye is liable to disastrous accidents. Vast fortunes were
made, and vast fortunes were sometimes lost, in the business.
In 1795, however, the produce of the country amounted to
about 3,000,000 lbs. In Bengal and Bahar, to which the
Indian trade is now chiefly confined, some 10,000,000 lbs.
are now annually produced by 50,000 families, upon some
1,200,000 acres of land. Nearly two-thirds of this quantity
are brought to England, half for home use and half for exportation. Indigo is also cultivated in Java and Manilla,
in Egypt and Senegal, and in Guatemala and Caraccas;
but the produce of all these districts together is hardly
more than a fourth as much as that of India, and is inferior
in quality.

Cochineal, on the other hand, though first brought from India, now comes almost entirely from America. It was highly prized by the Romans, and revived as an article of trade by the Arabs and Moors. The splendid use made of it by the Mexicans, at the time of the Spanish conquest, attracted the attention of Europeans; and in recent generations a vast demand for it has arisen, corresponding with the increased quantity of cloth to be dyed. About seventy thousand curious little insects, akin to the ladybird, have to be gathered from the cactus trees on which they fix themselves, and to be baked or boiled, to make a pound of cochineal; and England imported from Mexico, Central America, and Brazil 1,569,120 lbs. in 1844, and 3,131,184 lbs. in 1855. It is said of Linnæus that, in 1756, he obtained with great difficulty a plant covered with the insects, in order to study its characteristics with care. The plant arrived while he was delivering a lecture, and, before he could have it safely housed, his gardener, supposing it to be infested with a blight likely to spread to other treasures, succeeded in destroying every one of its parasites.

Cochineal and indigo, besides being useful in other ways, help to convert the simple textile fabrics, which they colour, into hundreds of new wares, designed to please the taste and serve the special purposes of their buyers. In the same way every other ware, brought into or produced in the country as raw material, takes countless shapes; and the result of all is the manufacture of articles, a mere catalogue of which would more than fill a volume, and of which even a brief description would crowd a library. From pins, pens, and pans, up to steam-engines, iron churches, and portable docks—like that lately built in London and conveyed to Bermuda—there is a wonderful array of wandering wares, useful and ornamental, necessary and fantastic, each one with a curious history, and all contributing to swell the glory of trade as a prime agent in the progress of civilisation. Further reference to them here need not be attempted.

There is one wandering ware, however, which stands apart from all the rest, and which has connected with it too much strange incident and painful romance to be overlooked. Trading in all else that the world produces, men have not scrupled to trade in one another, and have not yet grown honest enough altogether to eschew the traffic. Slavery is almost as old as humanity, and it is hardly to be wondered at that it should have prevailed in ancient times, when men were split up into thousands of small communities, ever at war with one another, and each anxious to bring its rivals into bondage and to make them useful as bondmen. But the worst form of it is of tolerably modern growth, and through nearly three centuries had England for its chief caterer.

The cruelties practised by the Spaniards upon their Indian subjects in the New World, and their prompt effect in exterminating the poor wretches in some districts, and in greatly thinning them in all the rest, are well known. Very soon it became necessary to import fresh slaves; and even Las Casas, the great champion of the Indians, saw no harm in subjecting African negroes to the treatment from which he sought earnestly to save the aborigines of the New World. The African slave-trade was begun by the great and good Prince Henry of Portugal, whose agent, Gonzalez Baldoza, brought home, in 1442, ten negroes captured by him in the course of a voyage, and they served as a curious present to Pope Martin V. Immediately a Portuguese association was formed for trading in negroes. In 1444 two hundred were procured, and before long the annual average was raised to seven or eight hundred. They were at first made use of in Portugal and its near dependencies. As soon as Portugal had possessions in America they were conveyed thither; and, when these possessions were sufficiently stocked, the Portuguese gladly sold their human wares to the Spanish colonists. In and near the year 1539, from ten to twelve thousand negroes were sold annually in the slave-market of Lisbon. Thus the trade had grown very considerable before the English began to supersede the Portuguese in conducting it.

That beginning was made by Sir John Hawkins, an enterprising Plymouth merchant, who became famous as a sea-captain, and did good service to his country in the Armada fight in 1558, and in many other ways. Trading with or on behalf of his father, William Hawkins, to the Canaries, he was then, according to his first biographer, "amongst other things, informed that negroes were very good merchandise in Hispaniola, and that store of negroes might easily be had upon the coast of Guinea." While he was thinking of devoting himself to this new trade, a countryman, John Lock, visited the coast of Guinea in 1554, and there bought five negroes, described by him as "people of beastly living, without God, law, religion, or commonwealth," whom he brought to England. But this importation did not prove profitable, and slave-buying seems not to have been repeated by Englishmen till 1562, when Hawkins set out on his first voyage. At Sierra Leone, we are told, "partly by the sword, and partly by peaceable means, he got into his possession three hundred negroes at the least, besides other merchandises which that country yieldeth." Crossing the Atlantic, he found a ready market for his slaves, and he returned to England with such good store of wealth that he resolved to continue the business on a more extensive scale. In that he was only hindered by the jealousy of Philip II. of Spain, who, not objecting to traffic in slaves, objected to its profits falling into the hands of foreigners, and saw shrewdly that, if the English once fell into the habit of visiting the West Indies for any purpose at all, they would soon attempt to make them their own. Therefore he angrily complained to Queen Elizabeth of Hawkins's proceedings; but Elizabeth, while promising that they should not be repeated, so heartily approved of them—or, rather, of the profit to be derived from them—that she entered into a sort of partnership with Hawkins and enabled him to go clandestinely on another slave-trading expedition. That he did in 1564. There was an exuberant piety about him and his associates, which contrasts very strangely with their unholy work. They spent two months in slave-stealing—the Africans being now unwilling to sell their kinsmen along the Guinea coast—"going every day on shore to take the inhabitants, with burning and spoiling of their towns." Once the negroes retaliated and attempted to surprise some of the English while they were on shore; " but," says one of them, " God, who worketh all things for the best, would not have it so, and by him we escaped without danger." Again, the vessels having a slow passage to the West Indies, there was scarcity of water. "This pinched us all," it was said, "and that, which was worst, put us in such fear, that many never thought to have reached the Indies without great dearth of negroes and of themselves; but the Almighty God, which never suffereth his elect to perish, sent us the ordinary breeze." Hawkins and his comrades really thought that in promoting the slave-trade they were fulfilling a divinely-appointed mission. They made money by it, at any rate, and were highly commended on their return to England. Hawkins was knighted by Queen Elizabeth, his crest, aptly chosen, being a " demi-Moor, in his proper colour, bound and captive."

Hawkins's later exploits and those of his successors in the trade need not be detailed. It flagged for a time, but was vigorously resumed as soon as the southern portions of what are now the United States began to prosper and to call for slaves. A hundred years ago—and down to 1805—about 100,000 negroes were annually exported from Africa to the West Indies—38,000 to the English islands, 31,000 to the

French, 25,000 to the Portuguese, 4,000 to the Dutch, and
2,000 to the Danish. Occasionally they found their way to
England. A newspaper advertisement of 1769 runs thus:—
"At the Bull and Gate, Holborn, a chestnut gelding, a tun
of whiskey, and a well-made, good-tempered black boy."
Another, of the same year, was :—" To be sold, a black girl,
the property of J. B., eleven years of age, who is extremely
handy, works at her needle tolerably well, is of an excellent
temper and willing disposition. Inquire of Mr. Owen, at
the Angel Inn, behind St. Clement's Church, in the Strand."

Happily, however, trade in slaves has now almost died
out. Bristol and Liverpool grew rich by it ; but it was prohibited by the British Parliament in 1807, Denmark and
the United States having previously condemned it ; though
the condemnation of the latter country was of small effect,
while slavery prevailed at home and there were English
ships to supply the market. A further triumph was gained
by the law emancipating all slaves in our colonies, in 1834 ;
and the like excellent result of the late American civil war
has brought the traffic very nearly to a close.

CHAPTER III.

FAIRS.

The Place of Fairs in Commercial History—Their Origin—Early English Fairs—Winchester Fair—St. Bartholomew Fair—The Fair at Beaucaire —The Leipzig Fairs and their Book-trade—The Russian Fair at Nijnii Novgorod—Indian and Arabian Fairs.

WARES generally wander now—when they can be said to wander at all—to settled marts, ready all the year round to receive them, and with permanent provisions for their re-ception and exchange for other wares; and much more commonly, instead of wandering in search of buyers, they are bought before they leave their starting-place, and, though they travel half across the world, do so because it is known that at their destination prompt use will be made of them. But in the old stages of commerce, and in many nations which still follow the old ways, it was, and is, quite different. Before the requirements of foreign powers were understood, or could be measured with any precision—when each district knew little more than that it had certain commodities which it desired to sell somewhere, and that it needed certain other commodities which must, if possible, be obtained from some place or other—all trade was very much less certain than it has now become. The first steps towards lessening the uncertainty were made in the establishment of fairs.

Fairs were held thousands of years ago, and are still held in the East, of vastly greater importance than any that have prevailed in our own country; but there is no record of their beginning, and we can only infer that it was sub-stantially the same as that of the smaller fairs about whose history we do possess details. It is even probable that they had some sort of a religious origin, akin to that which is clearly traceable in the fairs of Christendom. "In the beginning of Holy Church," it is written in an old legend, "it was so, that people came at night-time to the church with candles burning. They would wake and come with light toward the church in their devotions. But after, they fell to lechery and songs, dances, harping, piping, and also to gluttony and sin, and so turned the holiness to cursedness. Wherefore holy fathers ordained the people to leave that waking"—a term still retained in the Irish *wakes*— "and to fast at even." The evening fasts, however, were nearly as unprofitable, in a religious point of view, as those formerly held at night-time. The people who assembled in the churchyards soon turned their meetings into opportunities for amusement, and laid the foundations of those periodical fairs which, despite all the opposition of the clergy and other lovers of good order, have held their ground almost to the present day.

But the fairs, if in them praying soon gave way to playing, were from the first put to another use. Bringing together the inhabitants of different villages and parishes who had few other opportunities of meeting, they afforded facilities, of which advantage was promptly taken, for interchanging local produce and manufactures ; and soon prudent traders from a distance saw the benefit of bringing other wares for sale, or for barter, in lieu of the native wares. In this way fairs became markets, and thus acquired an importance, which lasted long and proved very serviceable to the advancement of commerce. They served also as sources of revenue to the Crown, or to the Lord of the Manor in which they were held. We read in "Domesday Book" of one fair in Bedfordshire that yielded £70 a year to Edward the Confessor by way of toll, and of another at Taunton which produced about fifty shillings.

Every important district of England soon had its annual fair, to which all the neighbours brought their money, and traders from all parts brought their commodities; or to which the traders brought the money, and the residents brought the wool and other produce that they had been storing up during the previous months. So it was, for instance, in the neighbourhood of Leeds, at which during many centuries the merchants of Hull and other ports each year met the farmers and peasants of Lancashire and Yorkshire, and large supplies of wool and sheep-skins were obtained for transmission to the great manufacturing towns of Flanders, where they were worked up, and in large quantities sent back as clothing for sale in the localities from which they had first come.

Occasional fairs were also held. Thus, in 1245, Henry III., with the avowed object of making money out of the tolls, appointed a fair to be held at Westminster; and ordered all the traders of London to close their shops and bring their wares to it, and all other fairs throughout the kingdom were to be suspended during fifteen days, that there might be no hindrance to its success. Matthew Paris, however, records that it failed through badness of the weather. Rain fell in torrents during the whole fortnight; the dealers had to stand all day in the mud, with the wind and rain beating upon them, waiting in vain for customers, while their goods rotted in miserable tents. In 1249 there was another great fair ordained, and with like failure. "In this year," says an old historian, "the citizens of London, at the request of his Lordship the King, not compelled and yet as though compelled, took their wares to the fair at Westminster, on St. Edward's Day; and also the citizens of many cities of England, by precept of his Lordship the King, repaired thither with their wares; all of whom made a stay at that fair of full fifteen days, all the shops and warehouses of the

merchants of London in the meantime being closed." Again
the weather was unfortunate, and the merchants suffered
great loss; "but the King did not mind the imprecations
of the people."

Winchester Fair was a great centre of trade during
several centuries. Winchester, now interesting for its anti-
quities, has lost the supremacy in commercial as well as
in political affairs that it once held among towns out of
London. In it the Roman colonists established the first
rude cloth manufacture of which England can boast, and
it continued to be for a long time the chief resort of dealers
in wool and woollen goods. License to hold, on St. Giles's
Hill, an annual fair, in which wool was the staple commodity, and in which commerce had precedence both of
religion and of sport, was granted to the bishop of the
diocese by William the Conqueror; and its duration, at first
limited to one day, was gradually extended, until, by a
charter of Henry II., it was allowed to last sixteen days.
During that period the shops of Southampton as well as
Winchester were to be closed, and all wares sold within a
radius of seven miles outside of the fair were to be forfeited
to the bishop. Tolls were established on every bridge and -
roadway, and the revenue thus levied on the goods taken
to the fair, and on the persons going to sell, was very considerable. The great common was divided into temporary
streets—the Drapery, the Spicery, the Pottery, and so on.
On St. Giles's Eve—the eve of the fair—the mayor and
bailiffs of Winchester went out of office, and surrendered
the keys of the city to the bishop, who appointed his own
functionaries for the time being, and thus the Church had,
for the busiest fortnight in the year, exclusive control over
the commerce of the district. One object of this ecclesiastical
control, ostensibly at any rate, was a desire that the trade
might be done honestly and in a Christian spirit; but the
object was not always attained. In that famous old allegory

of the fourteenth century, "The Vision of Piers Plough-
man," Covetousness says :—

> " To Wye and to Winchester
> I went to the fair,
> With many manner merchandise,
> As my master me hight ;
> But it had been unsold
> These seven years—
> So God me help—
> Had there not gone
> The grace of guile
> Among my chaffer."

The grace of guile abounded here as in other places ;
but Winchester Fair long had supremacy among the markets
of England, even after Winchester itself had lost much of
its commercial importance. Two circumstances led to its
decline. The first was the transference, near the time of
Edward III., of the woollen trade from Exeter, Southampton, and other southern ports, to Hull, Boston, and
other ports on the eastern coast. The other was the commencement, at about the same time, of the annual visit,
paid by the Venetian traders' fleet to England. The fleet,
laden with precious wares from all lands, to be exchanged
for English wool, generally halted at Southampton. Thither,
and to the neighbourhood, flocked the merchants who had
hitherto gone to Winchester; and there, during the stay of
the Italian visitors, a great irregular fair was held, which
thus came to be of far greater commercial value than old
Winchester Fair.

Almost the longest-lived, and certainly the most notable
of the English fairs, was that of St. Bartholomew, held in
Smithfield. Smithfield was veritably a smooth field, when
Rahere, the king's jester, became a monk, and obtained
from Henry I. permission to build thereon a priory consecrated to St. Bartholomew, and to hold an annual fair upon
the saint's day, the day before, and the day after. Wool was
from the first the chief commodity sold here, and foreigners

came from distant parts to be present at the great cloth-fair of St. Bartholomew; but very soon the sheep from which the wool was taken, as well as other animals, came to be sold at Smithfield, and this branch of trade survived all the rest. The Smithfield cattle-market, altered from its original condition, in being made a permanent instead of an occasional institution, was only abolished a few years ago.

The importance of the fair in Queen Elizabeth's time may be understood from a proclamation, issued in 1593, ordering the suspension of its holiday-making in consequence of the plague then raging in London, but sanctioning the wholesale trade, as a thing too essential to be checked even for fear of pestilence. " Whereas there was a general resort of all kinds of people out of every part of her nation to the said fair," the queen here says, " in the usual place of Smithfield there shall be no manner of market for any wares kept, nor any stalls or booths for any manner of merchandise or for victuals suffered to be set up; but the open space shall be only occupied for the sale of horses and cattle, and of stall wares—as butter, cheese, and such like—in gross and not by retail, and for the vent of woollen cloths, kerseys, and linen cloth, to be all sold in gross and not by retail—the same shall be all brought within the close of St. Bartholomew's; and the sale and vent of leather shall be kept in the outside of the ring of Smithfield, as hath been accustomed, without erecting of any shops or booths for the same or for any victualler or other occupier of any wares whatsoever."

Five years after that, Paul Hentzner, a shrewd German came to London, and went to the fair. " It is worthy of observation," he said, "that every year, upon St. Bartholomew's Day, when the fair is held, it is usual for the mayor, attended by the twelve principal aldermen, to walk in a neighbouring field, dressed in his scarlet gown, and about his neck a gold chain, to which is hung a golden fleece, and,

F

besides, that particular ornament which distinguishes the
most noble Order of the Garter.   When the mayor goes out
of the precincts of the City, a sceptre and sword and a cap
are borne before him, and he is followed by the principal
aldermen—himself and they on horseback.   Upon their
arrival at a place appointed for that purpose, where a tent is
pitched, the mob begin to wrestle before them, two at a
time, and the conquerors receive their prizes from the magis-
trates.   After this is over, a parcel of live rabbits are turned
loose among the crowd, which are pursued by a number of
boys, who endeavour to catch them, with all the noise they
can make.   While we were at this show, one of our company had his pocket picked of his purse, which, without
doubt, was so cleverly taken from him by an Englishman,
who always kept very close to him, that he did not perceive
it."   Paul Hentzner was struck, not by the serious commercial value of the fair, but by its humorous and vicious
aspects ; and both these are shown with wonderful precision
in Ben Jonson's comedy of "Bartholomew Fair," written in
James I.'s time.   Ben Jonson, always more of a moralist
than a comic writer, paints a lively picture of London's way
of holiday-making at the time of its great holiday ; and
from that day till 1840, when the fair was put an end to, its
progress and its decline as a centre of popular amusement,
healthy and unhealthy, may be clearly traced.   Some two
hundred years before that it had ceased to be a centre of
trade, though trade lasted longer here than at most other
English fairs.

A hundred years older than St. Bartholomew Fair, yet
still full of life and importance, is the great French fair,
held between the 22nd and the 28th of July at Beaucaire, a
little town on the Rhone, and not far from its entrance into
the Gulf of Lyons.   Founded in 1217, this fair was once
without an equal in Europe.   Merchants from Marseilles
and other ports on the Mediterranean came hither with rich

stores of all the wealth brought from East, West, North, and South by the trading-fleets of Venice and her rivals. To meet them, came traders from all the inland towns, silk-mercers from Lyons, wine-dealers from Mâçon and Dijon, and representatives of every mart and factory that had any-thing to buy or sell. A century ago the average attendance was 100,000, and the wares that changed hands were worth more than 150,000,000 francs. At the present day the commercial value of the fair is hardly a fifth as great, but still some 50,000 persons assemble to buy and sell and make merry with their friends ; soldiers come from Nîmes and Tarascon to keep order, and fair-law, which was once nearly the same all over Europe, is dispensed by the prefect of the department.

More important are the great fairs of Leipzig, famous resorts for trade in everything, but having books for their special commodity. Leipzig furnishes a signal instance of the way in which fairs help to enrich the locality in which they are held, and to benefit all the world. An old Slavo-nian village, which received its name from the lime-trees—*lipsk*—that grew around it, Leipzig was made a chartered town by Margrave Otho the Rich, who fortified it, and granted a license for the holding of two fairs every year—one at Easter and one at Michaelmas. That was in the twelfth century. In 1458 a New Year's fair was also authorised, and the three fairs were confirmed by the Emperor Maximilian in 1507, eight days being appointed as the limit of each, though they generally lasted for three weeks or more. They soon became great centres of resort—the Easter fair being the busiest—for traders of every land and in every ware. Cloth goods, glass, and leather from Saxony and the States of the Zollverein ; cottons, woollens, and hardwares from England ; silk, shawls, lace, and jewellery from France ; glass, plated goods, and broadcloths from Austria ; cloth-work and the like from Switzerland ; toys from Nuremberg;

furs from Russia; and articles from the distant East, from
America, and from Australia, here still change hands as
they have done for seven centuries; and the famous city
is thronged by representatives of nearly every country
in the world during its busy holiday-time. The fair has,
like all others, decayed since railways have begun to open
up new ways of commerce; but some 40,000,000 lbs. of
goods, of all sorts not including books, are now bought and
sold in the three fairs of each year, and the value of the
trade done at Easter is said to exceed £3,000,000.

The book-trade of Leipzig stands by itself. Frankfort
had an ancient fair, vieing in importance with that of
Leipzig; and thither from 1473, if not earlier, the booksellers of Antwerp, Paris, Basle, and other great printing
places, went to sell their wares. In 1486, however, the
Archbishop of Mayence established a censorship of the
press throughout his see, and this proved so vexatious to
the booksellers who sought buyers in Frankfort, that they
transferred their market to Leipzig, and made use, especially,
of its great Easter fair. The fame of the Leipzig University,
founded in 1409, and soon a great seat of learning and free
thought, greatly helped their traffic. Their first coming
seems to have been in 1545. In 1589, 362 new works were
offered for sale, and in 1616 that number was exactly
doubled. The special business done in fair-time naturally
encouraged the establishment of permanent shops and
printing-presses in Leipzig. In 1616 there were fourteen
booksellers and printers in the town, Frankfort having eight,
Nuremberg seven, and Jena only four. The local traders
in that year produced 153 new books, while 57 were brought
from Venice, 47 from France, 38 from Holland, 22 from
Switzerland, and 4 from England. The Thirty Years' War
checked the trade, both in books and in all other articles,
for a time, but it revived and made steady progress with the
restoration of peace. The new books sold at the fair in

1716 were 558 in number. In 1789 they had risen to 2,115, more than a seventh being produced in the town. Soon after that Napoleon's wars caused fresh confusion; but the taste for literature was by that time too strong to be suppressed, and the fair prospered in spite of the terrible three days' battle at Leipzig in October, 1813, when Napoleon was totally defeated by the allied armies under Schwartzenberg. In 1814 the number of new books brought out at the fair was 2,529; in 1830 it was 5,926. It now varies from 8,000 to 10,000. The trade, however, is no longer limited to fair-time. All important publishers in Germany, and many in other countries, have agents at Leipzig, and consign to it large quantities of their new books as they appear, ready for sale at any period of the year. Wholesale traffic is still chiefly carried on at fair-time, when booksellers from all parts meet together and take counsel concerning the progress of their trade. Since 1834 Leipzig has had a handsome Book Exchange, and in the town there are now about 120 publishing-houses, and 260 printing-presses, 14 of which are worked by steam.

As we travel eastward we find fairs more numerous and more antique in their character. A great Russian fair is now held during six or eight weeks each autumn at Nijnii Novgorod, whither it migrated from Makarieff in 1817. This famous market began at Kasan, when it was the Tartar capital, and, after many centuries' existence, was removed to Makarieff, about fifty miles from Nijnii, in 1648. At that time the fair lasted five days, and was the principal meeting-place of caravans coming from the far East, and of merchants from Russia, Germany, and other districts of the West. It grew with the growth of trade. In 1750, for the accommodation of its visitors, the Government built a huge bazaar, comprising 800 temporary shops. These being soon filled to overflowing, the Emperor Alexander caused a new bazaar, with 1,400 compartments, to be erected;

but even this space was insufficient, and 1,800 outside
sheds had to be put up. All these being made of wood
and canvas, a spark set them all on fire in August, 1816,
just before the close of the fair; and, instead of causing
the old site to be re-covered, the emperor transferred the
fair to Nijnii Novgorod, an old, but till then an insignificant town, conveniently placed at the junction of the Oka
and the Volga, and easy of access to the White Sea, the
Gulf of Finland, and the Caspian.

Here a vast stone town was erected, containing twenty-
five hundred shops, each with a sleeping-apartment attached
to it, and provision was made for less securely-built sheds
outside. Five thousand or more shops are now used by the
250,000 or 300,000 persons who flock to the fair from all
quarters; and during the few weeks of their attendance the
fair-city contrasts strangely with the bleak desolation that
prevails throughout the months before and after. Thirteen
gay covered streets furnish a promenade nearly thirty miles
long. "The shops, generally very handsome," says a traveller, "extend, in some instances, from street to street, so
as to have two fronts. They present nothing of the confusion of a fair. The goods of every kind are as neatly
arranged as in the shops of a large capital. The tea quarter
is one of the most interesting in the fair, not only from the
number of Chinese seen in it, but also on account of the
large demand for the article. The Russians are, after the
English, the most inveterate tea-drinkers in Europe, and the
tea sold at Nijnii is said to be the finest imported from
China. It is certainly the most fragrant and perfumed, and,
therefore, to the English palate generally, perhaps not so
agreeable. It is introduced into Russia by Kiatka, on the
frontiers of China, a very insignificant place, and separated
from it and the Chinese town of Mamaia by a small brook.
At this first depôt it is exchanged for goods, and is thence
transported, partly by land and partly by water, to Nijnii.

From 90,000 to 100,000 chests are annually imported. Half of these remain in Siberia, and reach Moscow by sledges during the winter, while the remainder are sold at this fair. Next in importance is the quarter of the Persians, situated in a suburb on the opposite side of an arm of the Oka, in which are sold costly shawls, carpets, and silk pieces. Then there is the quarter for the dealers in skins and furs. Here the outside garment of nearly every beast that claims the Arctic Circle for a home may be seen, from a sable to a bear; and a pelisse of the choicest skins of the latter will fetch as much as £500. Near this is the quarter for the sale of Siberian iron—a perfect metal town. One may walk for nearly half a league surrounded by every species of bar-iron, palisades, pots, agricultural and other instruments." Goods worth from £7,000,000 to £8,000,000—about three-fourths of them being Russian—are sold annually at this monster fair; and it differs from most other fairs in being a market for sober trade, in which no provision is made for the amusement of the visitors, tea being the most exciting beverage, and the goods offered for sale the only sight, provided.

With most of the thousand and one fairs that are held in the districts east and south of Nijnii Novgorod, in India and on to China, in Persia and down to Arabia, it is different. Here, generally, the old religious associations of the fair are strictly maintained. "The Arabian Nights' Entertainments" show how closely trade and religion are blended; and the vivid pictures there presented are true of earlier and of later times, of Brahmin as well as of Moslem lands. At Hurdwar, "the gate of the Ganges," hundreds of thousands of pilgrims assemble to perform their devotions by the sacred river, and use their meeting for carrying on a lively trade, apparently identical in manner with that which prevailed long before the Christian era; and it is the same at Mecca. Piety and profit go hand in hand, and the profit, at any rate, is great.

These religious fairs mainly help to keep in vigorous condition the primitive trade which is in vogue among millions
of people, and it is hardly altered in character by the large
admixture of Manchester and Birmingham goods with the
native wares, that are fashioned and disposed of in ways
that were old when Manchester was a bog and Birmingham
a marsh.

CHAPTER IV.

THE SINEWS OF TRADE.

Money—Primitive Banking—Athenian Money-lenders—Jews and Lombards—Early English Bankers—Sir William de la Pole and others—The Goldsmiths as Bankers—George Heriot—The Rise of Regular Banking—Origin of the Bank of England—Its Operations and History—Bank-note Forgers and their Punishment—Joint-Stock Banks—Private Bankers—The Woods of Gloucester—Smith, Payne, and Smiths—Jones, Lloyd, and Company—Joseph Denison—The Scotch Banks and their Specialities—Coutts; Drummond; and Herries—Modern Trade in Money.

"A SIMPLE invention it was," says Mr. Carlyle, "in the old-world grazier, sick of lugging his slow ox about the country till he got it bartered for corn or oil, to take a piece of leather, and thereon scratch or stamp the mere figure of an ox, *pecus*, put it in his pocket, and call it *pecunia*, money. Yet hereby did barter grow sale ; the leather money is now golden and paper, and all miracles have been out-miracled ; for there are Rothschilds and English national debts ; and whoso has sixpence is sovereign, to the length of sixpence, over all men—commands cooks to feed him, philosophers to teach him, kings to mount guard over him, to the length of sixpence." The first use of money marks an epoch in the history of commerce—is, indeed, the beginning of commerce as we now understand the term, and in all its subsequent progress has served as its pivot or fulcrum. If money is "the sinews of war," it is that because, in a much more real sense, it is the sinews of trade.

The banker's calling is both new and old. As a distinct branch of commerce, and a separate agent in the advancement of civilisation, its history hardly extends over three

hundred years ; but, in a rude and undeveloped sort of way,
it has existed during some dozens of centuries. It began
almost with the beginning of society. No sooner had men
learnt to adopt a portable and artificial equivalent for their
commodities, and thus to buy and sell and get gain more
easily, than the more careful of them began to gather up
their money in little heaps, or in great heaps, if they were
fortunate enough.   These heaps were, by the Romans,
called *montes*—mounds, or banks—and henceforth every
money-maker was a primitive banker.   The prudent farmers
and shopkeepers in out-of-the-way villages, who now lock up
their savings in strong boxes, or conceal them in places
where they are least likely to be found by thieves, show us
how the richest and most enterprising men of far-off times,
whether in Anglo-Saxon or mediæval Britain, ancient Greece
and Rome, China or Judæa, made banks for themselves
before the great advantages of joint-stock heaping up of
money were discovered.   When and in what precise way
that discovery was made antiquarians have yet to decide.
It is enough for us to know that everywhere, as soon as
commerce and patriotism had engendered enough fellow-
feeling and community of interest among groups of men
and sections of society, banking began to pass out of its first
rude stage, and to advance towards the condition in which
we now find it.

Perhaps Jews and Greeks set the example to the modern
world.   Every rich Athenian had his treasurer or money-
keeper, and whenever any particular treasurer proved himself a good accountant and safe banker, it is easy to understand how, from having one master, he came to have several,
until he was able to change his condition of slavery for the
humble rank of a freedman, and then to use his freedom to
such good purpose that he became an influential member of
the community.   Having many people's money entrusted to
his care, he received good payment for his responsible duty,

and he quickly learned to increase his wealth by lending out his own savings, if not his employers' capital, at the highest rate of interest that he could obtain. The Greek bankers were chiefly famous as money-lenders, and interest at thirty-six per cent. per annum was not considered unusually exorbitant among them. For their charges they were often blamed by spendthrifts, satirists, and others. "It is said," complains Plutarch, "that hares bring forth and nourish their young at the same time that they conceive again; but the debts of these scoundrels and savages bring forth before they conceive, for they give and immediately demand again; they take away their money at the same time as they put it out; they place at interest what they receive as interest. The Messenians have a proverb: 'There is a Pylos before Pylos, and yet another Pylos still.' So of the usurers it may be said, 'There is a profit before profit, and yet another profit still;' and then, forsooth, they laugh at philosophers, who say that nothing can come out of nothing!"

The Greek bankers and money-lenders, those of Delos and Delphi especially, are reported to have used the temples as treasure-houses, and to have taken the priests into partnership in their money-making. Some arrangement of that sort seems to have existed among the Jews, and to have aroused the anger of Jesus when he went into the Temple of Jerusalem, "and overthrew the tables of the money-changers, and said unto them, It is written, My house shall be called the house of prayer; but ye have made it a den of thieves."

Bankers' or money-changers' tables were famous institutions all over the civilised world of the ancients. Livy tells how, in 308 B.C., if not before, they were to be found in the Roman Forum, and later Latin authors make frequent allusions to banking transactions of all sorts. They talk of deposits and securities, bills of exchange and drafts to order, cheques and bankers' books, as glibly as a modern mer-

chant. But these things were nearly forgotten during the
dark ages, until the Jews, true to the money-making propensities that characterised them while they still had a
country of their own, set the fashion of money-making and
of banking in all the countries of Europe through which they
were dispersed.

Their first customers and their first disciples were the
Italian merchants who made Venice, Florence, and Genoa
great during the Middle Ages. Shakespeare's picture of the
relations between *Shylock* and *Antonio*—historically true,
in its broad outline at any rate, like everything else in the
writings of our great dramatist—has already been referred
to. The young Italian merchants, however, soon became
formidable rivals of the older Jewish traders. In England,
under the Plantagenets—and it was the same in all the
mediæval states of Continental Europe—Jews and Italians
settled themselves as traders in everything, but especially in
money, wherever any sort of fruitful commerce was carried
on. The kings of England used them as cashiers, pawnbrokers, and the like, until their own subjects were sufficiently trained in monetary arts to take their place ; and
the royal examples were followed by all manner of folk who
had need of gold, and credit enough to obtain it. Old
Jewry and Lombard Street still mark the districts in London
that were frequented by these foreigners between the twelfth
and the fifteenth centuries. Therein, and in the Old Jewries
and Lombard Streets of York, Hull, Bristol, Exeter, and
other trading towns, were hoarded up the treasures for which
monarchs often pawned their crown jewels and crown lands,
once or twice even their crowns themselves, and for which,
yet more frequently, gay courtiers and spendthrift noblemen
were willing to pledge their trinkets and mortgage their title-
deeds.

The Jews and Lombards in England, however, were
only bankers in the sense of money-lenders, and the Eng-

lishmen who succeeded them were of the same character
down to the seventeenth century. The first great English
banker, in this limited acceptation of the term, was Sir
William de la Pole, a famous merchant in Hull before he
was a banker, and styled *mercator noster* in the charters by
which Edward III. made recompense for the great services
done by him to the Crown and the State. Needing, for the
prosecution of his fighting in Scotland and France, more
money than Parliament was willing to grant, Edward borrowed from De la Pole, and, through him, from scores of
other merchants. "Know," it was written in one of ·
Edward's charters, issued in 1339, while he was in France,
"that our faithful and well-beloved subject, William de la
Pole, presently after our coming to the parts on this side
the sea, hearing and understanding that our affairs were,
for want of money, very dangerously deferred, and being
sensible of our wants, came in person unto us, and to us
and our followers made and procured to be made such a
supply of money that by his means our honour hath been
preserved. The said William undertook the payment of
great sums for us to divers persons, for which he engaged
himself by bonds and obligations, and if he had not done
so we could not by any means have been supplied, but
must necessarily, with a great deal of reproach, have abandoned our journey and designs." That is only one of many
documents extant, showing in what way William de la Pole
acted as banker to King Edward III. He lent him all his
own money, and all that he could borrow from other rich
men, and added to his rude but efficient services as banker
services equally rude but equally efficient, as paymaster-
general and chief commissariat officer to the army, collector
of the King's rents, and purveyor to the Court. For the
sums which he had advanced, and for the interest due to
him thereupon, he was generally repaid by a grant of
customs and excises, either in all England or in certain

parts of it, the whole proceeds of which he was authorised to appropriate until his charges were defrayed.

What Sir William de la Pole was to Edward III. Sir Richard Whittington was to Henry IV. and Henry V., and Sir Thomas Gresham to Edward VI. and Queen Elizabeth, and these famous men were only representatives of an irregular class of bankers, who enriched themselves and added greatly to the wealth and welfare of England during a dozen generations. All merchants were then to some extent bankers, but the trade of banking in its primitive condition was especially a part of the goldsmith's calling. This was only natural when gold was money much more exclusively than it is now. The Goldsmiths' guild in London was started early in the twelfth century, if not sooner, although its first extant charter was granted by Edward III., in 1327. Its members were great money-lenders and pawnbrokers, until the company, like the other old City charities, gave way as an active commercial agency to other associations better fitted to meet the needs of the time.

The work of the goldsmiths as bankers is well illustrated in the career of George Heriot, the worthy founder of Heriot's Hospital, in Edinburgh, and the "jingling Geordie" of Sir Walter Scott's "Fortunes of Nigel." Heriot, born in 1563, rose from small beginnings to be the greatest gold-smith and jeweller in Edinburgh, while James I. of England was still only James VI. of Scotland. His shop, adjoining St. Giles's Kirk, existed till 1809. It was only about seven feet square, but large enough to hold the honest tradesman and the great customers who came to it to buy trinkets, or to pawn them for money to be spent in new luxuries. One of his best customers was King James, famous for his love of extravagant finery. The story goes that once, when Heriot had gone to Holyrood House to show some new treasure that he had for sale, he found the king warming himself before a perfumed fire, which he praised for its sweetness. "Ay, ay," answered the king, "and it is costly." Heriot replied that if the king would go to his shop he would show him one yet costlier. "Indeed, and I will," exclaimed the monarch; but when they had reached the goldsmith's booth, King James found only a few poor flames flickering in the forge. "Is this, then, your fine fire?" he asked. "Wait a little," answered the merchant, "till I get. the fuel;" and then, opening his strong box, he took from it a bond for £2,000 which he had lent to the king, and threw it among the embers. "Now," he asked, "whether is your Majesty's fire or mine the better?" "Yours, most certainly, Master Heriot," was the answer.

If that anecdote is true, Heriot could afford thus to humour his royal patron. He grew rich by selling jewellery to James and his wife, Anne of Denmark; and if the payment was slow, it was heightened at last by the interest charged for the delay. Wealth came to him in yet greater abundance when, immediately after his sovereign's accession to the English throne, he followed him to London and set up a large shop, "foranent the New Exchange," where he became the most notable of the irregular bankers then to be found in London.

The next King of England unintentionally increased the banking occupations of the goldsmiths. The Royal Mint, then within the precincts of the Tower of London, had long been used by the merchants as a place of safe custody for their surplus money, till 1640, when Charles I., sorely in need of funds with which to raise an army against the rebellious Scots, took possession of about £200,000 then lodged with the Master of the Mint, regardless of the indignant complaints made by the owners. From that time the Mint ceased to be employed as a bank of deposit, but the troublous state of the country—just entering upon civil war—rendered something of the sort more necessary than ever. The example of one or two who entrusted their

savings to the goldsmiths, accustomed to the guardianship
of large amounts of treasure, was quickly followed by others.
Country gentlemen, also, many of them far away from their
homes, and in constant risk of losing all the property that
they had about them, adopted the same course, if they did
not do more, and employed the goldsmiths as attorneys, to
collect as well as to lock up their rents.   This new arrangement found favour the more rapidly through the willingness
of the goldsmiths to pay interest for the money placed in
their hands; and long before the time of the Restoration
they found themselves placed in a position very similar to
that of private bankers of the present day.   Some of them,
indeed, were actually founders of banking-houses that now
exist.   William Wheeler, one of the number, left his shop
in Fleet Street, next door to Temple Bar, to his son-in-law,
Francis Child, known—probably because he was the first to
throw aside the goldsmiths' trade, and make banking his
only business—as "the father of the profession," and the
same site is still occupied by the establishment which he
made famous. James Hore, or Hoare, settled first in
Cheapside, and afterwards in Fleet Street, was, in like
manner, the builder up of the business that yet bears his
name.

    That improvement upon the old arrangement was not
altogether beneficial. Giving paper bonds for the vast sums
of money that they received, just as they had been in the
habit of receiving paper bonds for the money that they lent,
the goldsmiths soon had half of the actual coin of the land
in their keeping, and the paper equivalents for it, issued
by them, came to be everywhere used as money ; thereby
inordinate power was placed in their hands, and great risk
was incurred by those who made them their cash-keepers.
The money entrusted to them was often lent out by them
at high rates of interest, and if they failed through their over-
speculation, their clients were the chief sufferers.   It was

partly to lessen this danger, and to provide merchants with a safe means of investing their capital, and with a trustworthy machinery for lending and borrowing money, that the Bank of England was started in 1694.

Venice had had a public bank since the latter part of the twelfth century; one had been established in Genoa in 1345; and others were opened at Amsterdam, Hamburg, and Rotterdam early in the seventeenth century, in each of which private speculators, in return for special services rendered to the State, in lending it money and collecting its revenues, received from it special privileges and protection in their financial relations with their fellow-citizens. The Bank of Amsterdam was most prosperous when William III. became King of England, and from it William Paterson to a great extent derived the suggestions which he offered to Parliament in 1591. In that year, Paterson— a merchant whose philanthropy and political wisdom were greatly in advance of his own interests, and who, accordingly, became a pauper through his desire to benefit others—was examined before the House of Commons as to the best way of collecting and managing public loans, the National Debt being then a new thing, and its amount of £3,000,000 being apparently an overwhelming burthen to the country. He proposed that, in lieu of the occasional and unsettled mode of borrowing hitherto adopted by the Government, a fixed sum of £1,000,000, at six per cent. interest, should be subscribed by a corporation of merchants, and converted into a permanent fund, to be employed partly in meeting the pressing claims upon the State, and partly in forming a public bank, " to exchange such current bills as should be brought to be enlarged, the better to give credit thereunto, and make the said bills the better to circulate." The suggestion was demurred to by Parliament, and the old straggling ways of public borrowing continued. " When the Treasury was empty," as Macaulay says, " when the

taxes came in slowly, and when the pay of soldiers and
sailors was in arrear, it was necessary for the Chancellor of
the Exchequer to go, hat in hand, up and down Cheapside
and Cornhill, attended by the Lord Mayor and by the
aldermen, to make up a sum by borrowing £100 from this
hosier and £200 from that ironmonger," and for these
paltry loans he had to pay such interest as spendthrifts now
pay to extortionate Jews upon accommodation bills. The
National Debt was thus raised from £3,000,000 to
£6,000,000 in three years; and in 1694 the Government
found itself in such embarrassment that it was forced to
adopt Paterson's project substantially, though not quite as
he planned it, for a Bank of England. To all who joined
in raising a fund of £1,200,000, permission was granted to
form themselves into a company, with power to deal in bills
of exchange, bullion, and forfeited bonds ; and, contrary to
the expectations of its enemies, who combated the proposal
zealously both in Parliament and in the Cabinet, the money
was collected and the Bank was established in the course of
ten days. Thereby, and through the persistent advocacy of
one great man, whose greatness is now almost forgotten,
England, then perplexed with a costly war, was saved from
bankruptcy, and an entire and most beneficial revolution was
effected in the financial history of the country.

For two-and-thirty years the Bank of England had temporary lodging in the old Grocers' Hall, in the Poultry.
There the business was conducted, in one long room, by
the directors and fifty-four subordinates. " In one of my late
rambles," wrote Addison, in 1711, " I looked into the great
hall where the bank is kept, and was not a little pleased to
see the directors, secretaries, and clerks, with all the other
members of that wealthy corporation, ranged in their several
stations, according to the parts they act in that just and
regular economy." The "just and regular economy" has
grown with the rapid growth of the Bank in subsequent

years. In 1736 it had a house of its own in a modest structure set up in Threadneedle Street, and the building has been added to from time to time till its present proportions have been attained. It now covers an area of 124,000 square feet, and gives employment to more than a thousand clerks, distributed over some two hundred offices and apartments. It has ten country branches, giving occupation to about a hundred and fifty other clerks. The governor, deputy-governor, and twenty-four directors, who manage this great machinery, so manage it as by it to regulate, to a very great extent, all the commercial affairs of England, and even of every other country. The Thursday meetings in the famous Bank Parlour test and register the financial barometer of the whole world ; and their decisions have vastly more influence upon the happiness and activity of men than any resolutions of cabinet councils, or any proclamations of kings or emperors.

Four great duties are performed by the Bank of England. It has the custody of about £23,000,000 in gold coin and bullion ; it manufactures and keeps in circulation about £38,000,000 in bank-notes ; it has the management of the National Debt, now amounting to £740,000,000 ; and it serves as the collecting-house and centre of distribution for the country's revenue and expenditure, being some £70,000,000 a year. Each duty involves an immensity of detail, and has to be fulfilled with a nicety that can hardly be conceived.

The coin and bullion are, of course, the property of individual owners, who choose this as the safest resting-place for their wealth. The bullion sent from Australia or any other part of the world, if not required for manufacturing purposes, can, as soon as it has been purified and assayed to the sovereign standard of twenty-two carats, be either sent to the Mint, there to be coined into money, or lodged in the Bank. The Mint returns £3 17s. 10½d. for each ounce of gold handed to it; but the delay that occurs before the coinage is completed makes it cheaper to dispose of the bullion at once to the Bank, which immediately pays at the rate of £3 17s. 9d. for each ounce deposited. The bullion so received is stowed away in bars, each weighing about 16 lbs., and worth about £800, until occasion arrives for turning it into current money. The relative amount of coin and bullion, as well as the quantity of both sorts of gold in the Bank, is of course for ever fluctuating; but the average of both is between £22,000,000 and £23,000,000. Counting rapidly through ten hours every day, a man would be occupied for nearly three years in counting that number of sovereigns. In the Bank, however, the counting is done by machine. The weight of any given number of sovereigns is known, and to count a thousand or a million is as easy as to count five. It is only necessary for accuracy in the calculation that the coin shall be of proper weight, and as this is also, on other grounds, very necessary, every sovereign is periodically tested by a weighing-machine, which is a marvel of ingenuity and accuracy. This machine was invented by Mr. Cotton, a Bank director, in 1844. It is a square brass box, at the top of which is a long trough, filled with sovereigns, which drop one after another upon a balance, carefully guarded from currents of air and everything that can vitiate the process. If the coin is of correct weight it falls into one box, if it is faulty it is jerked into another. Since 1844 not a single error has been found in the working of this machine. Twelve of them are in constant operation at the Bank, and they weigh about 50,000 gold pieces every day.

That is the only mechanical process to which gold money is subjected at the Bank, its manufacture being carried on at the Mint; but paper money is all made in Threadneedle Street. About 220,000 quires of paper, carefully prepared in Hampshire, are consumed each year in the printing of bank-notes, of which an exact equivalent for the gold bullion stowed away is kept in circulation, with the addition of £15,000,000 for which there is no actual gold security. That sum represents an accumulation of debts due to the Bank by the Government, amounting to about £11,000,000, and a sum of £4,000,000 for which the Bank holds Government securities. The £15,000,000 represent all the paper currency of the country in lieu of which the Bank does not issue actual coin or bullion ; and the interest upon this floating money pays all the expenses of the Bank, and reduces the taxation necessary to meet the national expenditure.

It was, as we have seen, mainly to relieve the State of the embarrassments caused by its debt that the Bank of England was established. The National Debt, amounting to some £6,000,000 when the Bank was started, has grown mightily since then. Every great war has added to it. The ten years' strife with France and Spain, ending with 1750, caused an addition of £31,500,000 ; and the expenses settled upon posterity by the fighting of the next seven years amounted to nearly £60,000,000. The American war, prior to 1786, cost about £90,000,000 ; and the long and ill-managed war with France under George III. and Pitt, fruitful in domestic misery of every sort, causing starvation to the poor and poverty to the rich, increased the debt by £600,000,000. When peace was declared in 1815, it amounted to £861,000,000, and the retrenchments of more than half a century have only reduced it by a quarter. The bulk of this debt is known as Consolidated Stock, or Consols, of which there are some 270,000 holders, for each of whom a separate account has to be kept, and interest reckoned up and paid every half year. All this business, complicated by frequent transfers, has to be conducted by the Bank of England, which receives in payment for the trouble £300 for every £1,000,000 of debt. The payment covers all losses through accidents and fraud. The defalcation of Astlett cost the Bank £340,000, and its losses by the frauds of Fauntleroy were still greater.

The operations of the Bank in collecting and distributing the national revenue are quite as complicated. All the receipts of tax-gatherers, and all the proceeds of custom and excise duties, and other sources of revenue, find their way into the Bank; and, in return, it has to meet the demands of all the public departments for their several expenses, these demands being frequently made long before the funds to meet them have been received. In 1810 the nation's account with the Bank was overdrawn some £16,000,000, and in 1814 the balance on the wrong side amounted to £30,000,000.

Being thus the banker of the nation, the Bank of England is also the banker of all other bankers, each of whom keeps an account with it, and draws from it each day so much money as is required for the day's transactions. The mighty establishment, moreover, acts for private individuals as other bankers do. It keeps some 5,000 private accounts for millionaires, merchants, and shopkeepers.

The stages by which this wonderful advance upon William Paterson's project have been reached are curious and instructive. The history of the Bank of England, which has been told in lengthy volumes, and need here be only very briefly referred to, includes nearly the whole financial history of England during the last hundred and seventy years. With every great war, with every administrative change, and with every commercial crisis, it has been intimately connected. Its success was not achieved without many hard struggles, and its prosperity has kept even pace with the prosperity of the nation.

Its first difficulties arose from the opposition of other banking corporations, of which many were started while it was in its infancy, some to cause serious injury by their bad trading, and consequent loss to those who entrusted their money to them. For selfish reasons, but also for the benefit of society, the directors of the Bank obtained, in 1709, an Act of Parliament forbidding the establishment in England of any joint-stock banks of issue in which there were more than six proprietors. With private bankers they did not interfere; but its monopoly of public banking helped their corporation to make great progress in wealth and influence during the eighteenth century. The wars that were then plentiful also enabled it to assume immense importance as agent for the National Debt, and for irregular loans that were gradually absorbed in the debt. The great war with France, however, involving constant drains on the Exchequer, which the Bank had to meet, brought it to the verge of bankruptcy; so much gold being required by the Government, that hardly any was left for the use of merchants and the public. In October, 1795, the directors informed Pitt that they could not hold out much longer, and other messages followed, till February, 1797, when the Bank was authorised by the Privy Council to refuse cash payments for its notes, or the issue of any coin in sums larger than twenty shillings. In the following May an Act was passed enforcing that resolution, and sanctioning an almost unlimited supply of notes. The arbitrary law lasted for four-and-twenty years, and by it the bank-notes were depreciated in value more than a fourth; that is, all creditors of the State were compelled to accept fourteen or fifteen shillings for every pound owing to them. A better state of things began with Sir Robert Peel's Act of 1819, which still allowed the Bank to issue as many notes as it chose, but compelled it to exchange them for gold on demand, and thus virtually prevented it from giving out more than the public were willing to take at the full price of their equivalent in bullion. The Bank Charter of 1844 completed the reform, or, at any rate, brought it to its present condition, by limiting the quantity of paper

money issued in excess of the amount of gold held by the
Bank to £15,000,000, which the State is pledged to make
good in case of need.   Opponents of the Charter, however,
urge with much force that this paper currency of £15,000,000
is either too great or too small; that either it should be
done away with altogether, and gold be made the only legal
money, or that it should be made sufficiently large to meet
the growing requirements of commerce, and in that case be
taken out of the hands of the half public and half private
Bank of England, and controlled only by the functionaries
of the State.

Many stories are told of frauds upon the Bank of England.   The first forger of bank-notes was Richard William
Vaughan, a linendraper, of Stafford ; and though his offence
was soon detected, in 1758, he had many imitators.   During
the thirty years previous to 1832, when capital punishment
for forgery was abolished, 1,816 men were convicted of the
crime, and of these 628 were hanged.   The horror caused
by these executions was found to have only the effect of
making forgery more common, as many victims of the fraud,
with clear proof against the culprits, chose to suppress it
rather than cause their death.   There was quaint sarcasm in
the words with which one judge concluded his remarks in
passing sentence of death upon a man who had uttered a
spurious one-pound note : "And I pray that, through the
mercy and moderation of our blessed Redeemer, you may
there receive that mercy which due regard for the paper currency of the country forbids you to hope for here."   Since
1832 forgery has been very much less frequent, this being
partly due to the cessation of one-pound notes, and the
greater care taken in the manufacture of those of higher value.

The Bank's losses are not all through forgery.   In 1740 a
rich director took home a £30,000 note, with which to pay
for an estate he had bought.   He placed it carelessly on a
table, and thence it mysteriously disappeared.   It could no-

where be found, and, thinking it must have fallen into the fire, he obtained next day a duplicate note from the Bank, pledging himself to restore the original if he could find it, or to supply the money should it be presented for payment by any one else. Nothing was heard of it for thirty years, when, to the amazement of the Bank authorities, it was handed across the counter by a man who stated that he had received it from abroad in a lawful way, and who thus appeared to have a legal claim to the money. In the end, it was found that the document had really fallen upon the fire, but, without being burnt, had been taken up by the draught, and had lodged in a corner of the chimney, where it was discovered and stolen by a builder employed in partly pulling down and repairing the house. The director to whom it had been given had died long before, and the Bank was unable to make good in law its claim upon his executors for a return of the value of the duplicate handed to him.

Great as it is, the Bank of England is now only the greatest unit in a vast machinery of banking. Its chief rivals are the joint-stock banks, of which the London and Westminster Bank, founded in 1834, through the enterprise of John William Gilbart, is the oldest and most important. But private banking has advanced steadily since the days of Sir Francis Child. There are now more than a hundred private banks in London. In England there were, out of London, hardly a dozen banks in 1750; in 1793 there were more than four hundred, and now there are about eleven hundred.

The histories of some of these establishments aptly illustrate the general rise of banking. Almost the oldest was a bank in Gloucester, founded in 1716 by James Wood, a chandler and grocer, who added money-holding and money-lending to his trade in soap and sugar. At one counter of his shop the retail business was carried on, and at another the banking was attended to; and both throve so well that his grandson, the notorious miser Jemmy Wood, who died in

1836, was worth more than £1,000,000. Most of that fortune was wasted in litigation among his kinsmen; and the bank, passing into the hands of a company, throve all the better without him.

In like manner, the London house of Smith, Payne, and Smiths owes its origin to the enterprise of a Nottingham draper, who, early in the eighteenth century, began to serve both himself and his customers by holding for them their gains, to be prudently invested, and returned with interest when they asked for it. " I will take care of your money," the eldest Smith used to say to the farmers of the neighbourhood, "and will also keep an account of your market transactions, and you can draw your cash, or get goods from me, whenever you like." In that way he did good service to his neighbours, and, in the end, closing his draper's shop, amassed much wealth as a banker. His son carried on the business in Nottingham, and extended it to Lincoln and Hull, where the establishments still exist. His grandson found a shrewd London partner in Mr. Payne, and with him founded the central bank in Lombard Street, now with few rivals in the skill and greatness of its operations.

Another house, that of Jones, Loyd, and Company, lately merged into the London and Westminster Bank, had a kindred origin. Old Jones was a thriving man of business in Manchester, adding trade in money to his trade in cotton and woollen goods. Mr. Lewis Loyd was a dissenting minister, who fell in love with and secretly married the daughter of the half-banker, and who afterwards, to make peace with his father-in-law, left the pulpit for the counting-house. The business in Manchester became great, and when Mr. Loyd brought it to London it soon assumed vast proportions. The son of Lewis Loyd, the dissenting minister, is the present Lord Overstone.

Other great banks arose in Manchester, Liverpool, and the neighbouring towns, in ways akin to that followed by

Jones, Loyd, and Company, some of them ultimately planting themselves in London, and making it the centre of a busy network of monetary trade spreading all over the kingdom. Half-a-dozen rich banking-houses and two or three peerages have grown out of the enterprise of the brothers Heywood, who began as Liverpool merchants more than a century ago, and of their family connections, the Milnes and the Pembertons. One ally of some of the Heywoods was Joseph Denison, born at Leeds in 1726. His parents, it is said, were too poor to send him to school, but he taught himself to read and write ; and, having too much ambition to be satisfied with an errand-boy's work in Leeds, made his way to London with a carrier's wagon, sometimes riding, and sometimes trudging by the horse's side. In London he obtained a subordinate place in the counting-house of John Dillon, a merchant, in St. Mary Axe. There he worked up to a partnership, and at length, John Dillon failing, he began business for himself, taking his old master as his clerk. In 1775 the Heywoods established their bank in Liverpool, and employed him as their agent in London. Here, again, he steadily pushed himself into the topmost place, bequeathing, in 1806, the senior partnership in the house of Denison, Heywood, and Company, besides more than £1,000,000 in land and money, to his son, William Joseph Denison, who died worth something like £3,000,000. His daughter, also, had a sufficient dowry to make her a fitting wife for a marquis; and the beggar-boy of Leeds became grandfather to the first Lord Londesborough.

The banking of Scotland has a history in some respects different from that of England. Its origin, however, was the same, and George Heriot, of Edinburgh, who has been already referred to, had many predecessors, contemporaries, and followers, who grew rich, as he did, by money-lending and a rude sort of bill-discounting. One of the most notable of these, living in Heriot's day, was George Hutcheson, a

notary of Glasgow, who received money on deposit, paying
for it a small interest, and lending it out at higher rates
on mortgage to landed proprietors in the west of Scotland. His floating cash he kept in a large oaken chest,
secured by double locks, in a vault of his strong house near
the Tolbooth. He died rich in 1639, and left his wealth to
found the hospital that bears his name. In 1695, a year
after William Paterson, the Scotchman, had started the Bank
of England, John Holland, an Englishman, succeeded in
establishing, on Paterson's model, the Bank of Scotland;
but, unlike the Bank of England, it promptly began to open
branches in various parts of the country, and this innovation
has given a special character to Scotch banking. In Scotland, moreover, there was no bar, as in England, to the
formation of other public banks; and, accordingly, it had
formidable rivals in the Royal Bank, founded in 1727, in
the British Linen Company, dating from 1746, in the Dundee
Banking Company, begun in 1763, and in the Perth Banking
Company, three years younger—the first two having their
headquarters in Edinburgh, and numerous country branches.
All were empowered to issue unlimited supplies of notes,
generally of the value of twenty shillings, and all granted
interest on the balance of current accounts, however small;
an arrangement which tempted fishermen, peasants, servants,
and other humble capitalists to make use of them. While
the Bank of England was almost exclusively the treasure-
house of the rich, the great Scotch banks did something like
the work of modern savings-banks and friendly societies.
" Half-yearly or yearly," it was said in evidence before the
House of Lords, in 1826, "these depositors come to the
bank, and add the savings of their labour, with the interest
that has accrued upon the deposits, to the principal; and in
this way it runs on accumulating at compound interest, till
the depositor is able either to buy or build a house, or till
he is able to commence business as a master in the line in

which he has hitherto been a servant. A great part of the
depositors in our banks are of that description, and a great
part of the most thriving of our farmers and manufacturers
have arisen from such beginnings." To that prudent and
most beneficent arrangement the Scotch banks added another of equal value. " There is also," it was stated in the
report just quoted from, "one part of their system which
has had the best effects upon the people of Scotland, and
particularly upon the middle and poorer class of society, in
producing and encouraging habits of frugality and industry.
The practice referred to is that of ' cash credits.' Any person who applies to a bank for a cash credit is called upon
to produce two or more competent sureties, who are jointly
bound, and, after a full inquiry into the character of the
applicant, the nature of his business, and the sufficiency of
his securities, he is allowed to open a credit, and to draw
upon the bank for the whole of its amount, or for such part
as his daily transactions may require. To the credit of the
account he pays in such sums as he may not have occasion
to use, and interest is charged or credited upon the daily
balance, as the case may be. From the facility which these
cash credits give to all the small transactions of the country,
and from the opportunities which they offer to all persons
who begin business with little or no capital but their character
to employ profitably the minutest products of their industry,
it cannot be doubted that the most important advantages
are derived by the whole community."

The wise management of its public banks offered some
hindrance to the progress of private banking in Scotland.
Many great bankers, however, arose in Edinburgh, Glasgow,
or elsewhere, and thence have come some of the most notable now existing in London. The house of Coutts is as
old as the Bank of Scotland, in which Thomas Coutts was
one of the first shareholders. Patrick Coutts, his kinsman,
was a merchant who dealt in serges and bills, and his son

John turned the bill-discounting into banking proper. John Coutts's four sons, Patrick, John, James, and Thomas, greatly extended its operations. Two of the brothers remained in Edinburgh, where their bank passed ultimately into the hands of Sir William Forbes, till 1838, when it was amalgamated with the Union Bank of Scotland. The other two came to London, where they entered into partnership with George Campbell, a goldsmith-banker in the Strand, and from 1760 Thomas Coutts, the youngest and most enterprising of the four, was the chief manager of the business. His history and the history of his bank are too well known to need repeating here.

Thomas Coutts soon made for himself a profitable and aristocratic connection, but his clients were chiefly Whigs and Radicals. George III. banked with him till his connection with Sir Francis Burdett, his son-in-law, brought him into disfavour with the Tory monarch. His near neighbour and rival, Andrew Drummond, at Charing Cross, had the patronage of the Tories. Another great private bank for the aristocracy, that of Herries, Farquhar, and Company, in St. James's Street, was started at about the same date, by Sir Robert Herries, another Scotchman, and a famous tobacco-merchant, who was for some time connected with Sir William Forbes and the Edinburgh offshoot of the first Coutts's bank.

Concurrent with the growth of these and other West End houses, has been the progress of the chief City banks during the last hundred years or more. The vastness of their aggregate transactions is shown by the fact that at the Clearing House, where representatives of the chief banks meet every afternoon, to exchange the drafts received by each one upon every one of the others during the previous day, the amount thus negotiated often exceeds £10,000,000.

The Bank of England, the hundred and more joint-stock banks, and the thousand and more private banks in

Great Britain, which act as cash-keepers for merchants and
capitalists, large and small, by no means exhaust the list of
traders in money. Money is now much more than gold.
" Credit," as Daniel Webster said, " has done more a thousand times to enrich nations than all the mines of all the
world." Every actual pound that passes from hand to
hand means scores or hundreds of pounds in trade and daily
life. Everything which has an exchangeable value—lands,
goods, muscles, and brains alike—can have its value stated
on paper, which, if not quite as safe as a bank-note, is safe
in honest hands, and can be, to a great extent, protected
from dishonesty; and all this paper can be traded with.
The trade forms a wonderful development of modern commerce, and gives employment to all the stock-dealers, bill-
discounters, loan-contractors, and the like, who are more
or less of bankers, but also very much more than bankers.
Stupendous businesses, like those of the Rothschilds, the
Barings, and the Goldsmids, are of this sort, and their vastness cannot be estimated. Millions of pounds, on paper,
pass from hand to hand each hour of every day in London,
and Capel Court and Lombard Street are but two notable
limbs, out of thousands, through which the sinews of trade
pass to give life and vigour to the whole world.

CHAPTER V.

POLITICS IN TRADE.

Political Interference with Commerce—Native and Foreign Merchants in Mediæval England—"The Emperor's Men" and the German Steelyard in London—Flemish and French Traders in London—The Venetian Trading Fleets—Flemish Immigrants in England under the Plantagenets—Their Services to Trade—Edward I.'s "Charta Mercatoria"—The Commercial History of Flanders—Bruges and Ghent—Jacob van Arteveldt—The Commercial Greatness of Antwerp—The War of the Netherlands with Philip II.—Flemish Immigrants in England in Elizabeth's Reign—Their Good Work—The Huguenots as Traders—Their Settlement in England after the Revocation of the Edict of Nantes, and its Beneficial Effects on English Trade—The Puritans, and the English Colonisation of America—The Origin and Growth of the East India Company—The Opium Monopoly—Political Services of Merchants—The Greshams—Jacques Cœur Colbert—Growth of Free-Trade Principles—War and Commerce—The Commercial Results of English Wars—The Sufferings caused by the Great War with France—Commercial Treaties—The Methuen Treaty and the Cobden Treaty—Cobden's Services to Commerce.

POLITICAL interference, which has caused the Jews to be wanderers on the face of the earth, and given them an exceptional place in the history of commerce, has, during the same long period, had many other noteworthy results. Free-trade is only a very modern word, and intelligent understanding of the thing is yet more modern. Nation cannot trade with nation, even now, without hindrances or stimulants that are alike at variance with the best commercial interests of the whole world; but the hindrances and stimulants that now prevail among most civilised communities are slight indeed in comparison with those that existed in former times. Trade flourished in spite of them, sometimes in consequence of them; but the successive

occasions of their removal are so many epochs in the progress of intelligence and of the truest wisdom.

Their history in England bears close resemblance to
their history in all other countries. In early centuries, when
foreign commerce was slight, the political interference was
chiefly local. Each town and each trade sought to benefit
itself, and obtained from lords of the manor, sheriffs, and
other authorities special privileges in the way of tolls and
the like ; but foreign trade, being only of slight importance,
rarely met with much opposition. Indeed, the first instances
we have of the dealings of kings and statesmen with foreign
trade show nothing but a desire to protect and encourage it.
Before the Norman Conquest, and for some time after it, the
merchants of other nations were freely admitted into the
country, and often special facilities of trade seem to have
been afforded them. They were only looked upon as
enemies when native merchants began to be able to do the
work that foreigners had hitherto done for them, and when
native manufacturers began to seek public assistance in their
efforts to produce at home the clothing and other commodities that had previously been made abroad.

The first foreign merchants of importance who settled
in England or visited it periodically came from Germany.
Ethelred the Unready gave them peculiar advantages in
London. "The men of the Emperor who come in their
ships," according to a law of his time, "are law-worthy, like
ourselves :" traders of other nations being subject to more
or less heavy tolls and taxes. And their privileges lasted
long. "Let there," wrote Henry II. to Frederick Barbarossa,
in 1157, "be between ourselves and our subjects an in-
divisible unity of friendship and peace, and safe traffic of
merchandise." German dominion then extended from the
shores of the Adriatic to the shores of the Baltic and
the German Ocean. While Venice and other Italian towns
were becoming great by the industry of their citizens, in

H

bringing into Europe the treasures of the East, and establishing a new centre of commerce, which was to surpass in
value and influence those of the ancient world, many of the
northern cities of Germany began to follow their example
and share its benefits. Traffic on the sea led to inland
commerce, and gradually and steadily trade advanced north-
wards, having Augsburg for some time as its headquarters,
and eventually turning Lübeck, on one side of Denmark,
and Hamburg, on the other, into enterprising ports. From
these and other northern towns came the " Emperor's men "
to England, long before the Venetian merchants established
any considerable trade by sea with this country, and they
continued their dealings after they had practically thrown
off the imperial yoke, and established that famous commercial democracy known as the Hanseatic League.

The Hanse was started in the middle of the twelfth century, through the necessity of co-operation among the northern
ports for repressing piracy, but the civil war that soon began to
desolate Germany, and the lack of all good government consequent on the rival claims of two nominal emperors, made it
easy, if not necessary, for the trading towns, in 1241, to form
themselves into a sort of republic. In that way the League
changed its character, and grew rapidly. In 1360 sixty-six
cities belonged to the confederacy, and it had commercial
branches in every town of importance in northern Europe.

The branch in London had its home in the old Steelyard, whose site is now covered by the Cannon Street Railway
Station. Here the *Gilhalda Teutonicorum* was established
in very early times, as a sort of hotel in which German
merchants could reside and warehouse their goods. In
Richard II.'s reign this first building was found too small
for its inmates, and a second one, adjoining it, was added.
A third house was found necessary in the time of Edward
IV., and soon afterwards the three buildings, with perhaps
some others, were surrounded by strong walls, which often

the London 'prentices, jealous of the prosperity of the foreigners within, attempted to break through. "Within this structure, partitioned into separate cells," says Werdenhagen, the historian of the Hanseatic League, "the residents lived under strict regulations. They had a common table, and were probably then, as well as subsequently, divided into companies, each having its master and associates. All were obliged to remain single : any one who married an Englishwoman lost his *hanse*. For the sake of good order, no housekeeper, not even a bedmaker, was allowed. As it was necessary for them to become more united and able to resist the attacks of the London mob, none of the residents, or, at least, none who belonged to the council of commerce, were allowed to sleep out of the Steelyard. No less strict was the prohibition against communicating to the English anything which passed in the establishment. The direction was vested in an alderman and two deputies or co-assessors, with nine councilmen, who composed together the chamber of commerce. These persons assembled every Wednesday, in summer at seven, in winter at eight o'clock in the morning, to deliberate on general affairs, the authority of the alderman being usually undisputed. He it was who decided what ventures should be undertaken, and how those under him should employ their talents. All negotiations with foreigners were conducted by him, and it was for him to communicate with the similar *hanses* in other parts of Europe, so as to bring about a common course of action, and secure the interests of all."

That picture of a little colony of foreign traders in the heart of London, bound together by the closest ties, and intimately connected with similar and often larger associations in nearly every important town of Europe, is very curious. The merchants of the Steelyard held their ground for very nearly five hundred years. Prospering greatly themselves, they did much in teaching the English how to prosper in commerce. Welcomed at first because of the Continental and Asiatic produce which they brought over in little trading-fleets, they earned the enmity of their pupils as soon as those pupils were able to do without them. The City guilds, which still live as dinner-eating and charity-dispensing corporations, were framed partly on the model of the *hanse* in the Steelyard, and, while they were powerful agents of English trade, used some of their power in attempting to suppress their rival. Mobs assailed it times without number, and fair means and foul of all sorts were resorted to for its subversion. Its charters were rescinded by Edward VI., but restored by Queen Mary, and it was only finally abolished near the end of Queen Elizabeth's reign.

These German merchants helped to supply England with every kind of produce for which there was a market, but, especially, when corn was scarce in England, with corn grown in Prussia, Russia, and the adjoining countries. Wine from Burgundy was brought over by Flemish and French traders, and particularly by an annual fleet of Lorraine boats, which, all through the Plantagenet times, made their way from the Moselle to the Thames, and being allowed to anchor off Queenhithe for forty days, during which time their owners were subject to heavy restrictions, they were then sent back with such native produce as they could obtain in exchange. These fleets, however, were far less important than those which, during the fourteenth and fifteenth centuries, arrived from Venice, then at the height of its greatness.

A great company of trading-vessels, known as the "Flanders fleet"—other fleets being dispatched for other parts—left Venice every year, laden with silks, satins, damasks, cottons, and various other costly gear, as well as spices, saffron, camphor, and a hundred other articles brought from the East. It halted and traded at the ports of Greece, Italy, and Spain, as it passed through the Mediterranean, gaily and proudly, even as *Antonio's* argosies—

> " With portly sail,
> Like signiors and rich burghers of the flood,
> Or, as it were, the pageants of the sea,
> Did overpeer the petty traffickers,
> That curtseyed to them reverence,
> As they flew by them with their woven wings ; "

and then sailed up to the English coast. The Downs being reached, the fleet broke up for a time, some vessels anchoring off Southampton, Sandwich, Rye, and the chief towns on our southern shore ; others going to the principal Flemish ports, and all making busy trade with the native merchants who were eagerly awaiting their arrival. As soon as the valuable cargo had been exchanged for English wools and Flemish clothing, with a large supply of gold to make up for the difference in the worth of the commodities given and taken, the vessels met again ; and the fleet, after nearly a twelvemonth's absence, returned to Venice, there to prepare for the next year's voyage.

These visits of the Venetian merchants were of great service to England in times when native vessels could very rarely brave the perils of the long voyage to the Mediterranean ; but very soon they began to provoke opposition. Over and over again we find records of quarrels upon land, and sometimes we 'read of battles on the sea, caused by the jealousy of English traders or the greed of English pirates. Protection was accorded to these foreigners, though less complete than in the case of the German merchants ; but the local authorities of London and the other towns often sided with the people. Many complaints of ill-usage by the law, and of the perversion of law to their disadvantage, were made by the Venetian voyagers and their agents settled in England during the fifteenth century, and at length the foreigners were forced to abandon a custom, which, if it was very beneficial to our forefathers, was yet more beneficial to themselves. The last Venetian trading-fleet that visited our shores came in 1532.

Venetians and other Italians, however—Lombards especially—who, in the course of their dealings, had made England their home, remained after the change had taken place. Coming most plentifully at about the time of the expulsion of the Jews, they carried on the irregular banking and money-lending work, in which the Jews had been proficients. Lombard Street in London succeeded Old Jewry as the centre of trade in money ; and every important town had its Italian quarter, the residence of men whose services were welcome to war-making kings and spendthrift courtiers, as well as to enterprising merchants, during the Middle Ages. But they were Christians, though foreigners, and therefore not regarded with such hatred as was heaped upon the Jews. They, or their descendants, became naturalised, and by marriage, and in other ways, gradually blended with the native population.

The blending was yet more thorough in the case of another race of foreigners who settled in England, and the advantages resulting from their settlement were greater. While trading energy was being shown in the growth of great ports on the Continent, from Venice round to Lübeck, special aptitude in manufactures was being acquired by the hardy little family of Flemings, or Netherlanders, subject sometimes to France and sometimes to Germany. This aptitude began to be displayed about the middle of the tenth century ; and, soon after that, Flanders commenced to be famous for its making-up of woollen clothing, the raw material for which was mainly obtained from England, abounding in wool, but not then skilled in its manufacture. The skill was not properly developed till the time of the Tudors ; but wise efforts to promote it were made very soon after the Norman Conquest. In 1100 a great number of Flemings, driven out of their own country by disastrous floods, were allowed by William Rufus to settle in Cumberland, where, in the course of the next ten years, they formed so large a colony that violent complaints were made by the natives. Thereupon they, or most of them, were transplanted to Pembrokeshire and Herefordshire by Henry I., who designed to use them as a barrier for the southern English against Welsh marauders. They served that purpose, and did much more. Joined by tide after tide of their countrymen—whom oppression at home induced to seek a home elsewhere—they gradually spread over the south-western parts of England, giving a new life to Bristol and the other towns of that district. Giraldus Cambrensis speaks of them as "a people notably skilled both in cloth-making and in merchandise, ever ready with any labour to seek for gain by sea or land." Both kinds of skill, but especially the former, were turned to the benefit of England. Factories of a rude sort were set up in various parts of the country, from Cornwall up to Cumberland, for manipulation of the native wool. The Flemings settled in England instructed their new neighbours in the arts that had hitherto been chiefly confined to Flanders ; and woollen cloths, especially of the coarser sort, gradually came to be made at home instead of abroad. Winchester, the centre of a primitive cloth-manufacture that had been maintained since Roman times, lost some of its renown, and was soon surpassed by Bristol in the west, and by Norwich, Lincoln, Hull, Beverley, and York, in the east. "All the nations of the world," said Matthew of Westminster, "are kept warm by the wool of England, made into cloth by the men of Flanders."

To bring over the men of Flanders and employ them in working-up the wool of England, in England itself, was the constant effort of the wisest of our Plantagenet kings. The commercial legislation of four centuries gives frequent evidence of this, though it was often attempted in foolish

ways, and yet more often resented by the native workmen
in various parts of the country. A constant war was going
on between the statesmen in Westminster and the citizens
of London upon this question. The laws enacted in favour
of the foreign workmen were counteracted by civic regulations to their disadvantage, and much litigation and many
frays were the result. It was the same in other parts.
Thomas Blanket, for instance, one of three Flemish brothers
who were the chief promoters of cloth-making in Bristol, was
in 1340 ordered by a local court to pay a heavy fine " for
having caused various machines for weaving and making
woollen cloths to be set up in his houses, and for having
hired weavers and other workmen for this purpose;"
and the fine was only remitted by a special injunction
from Edward III. The inducements held out by that
monarch's agents to the Flemings whom they invited to
settle in England are quaintly set forth by Fuller : "Here
they should feed on fat beef and mutton till nothing but
their fulness should stint their stomachs. Their beds should
be good, and their bedfellows better—seeing that the richest
yeomen in England would not disdain to marry their
daughters unto them—and such the English beauties that
the most envious foreigners could not but commend them."

Edward III. was a famous patron of English manufacture, and of the foreign commerce that was necessary to its
healthy growth ; but he only followed in the steps of his
grandfather. Edward I.'s *Charta Mercatoria*, granted in
1303, was the Magna Charta of trade, often abused and
violated, yet an abiding bulwark of commercial liberty, the
basis of a slowly-developed system of free trade. It enacted
that " the merchants of Germany, France, Spain, Portugal,
Navarre, Lombardy, Florence, Provence, Catalonia, Aquitaine, Toulouse, Flanders, Brabant, and of all other foreign
parts, who shall come to traffic in England, shall and may
safely come with their merchandise into all cities, towns, and

ports, and sell the same, by wholesale, as well to natives as to foreigners. And," it was added, "the merchandise called merceries "—miscellaneous haberdasheries of all sorts, toys, trinkets, and the like—" as also spices, they may likewise sell by retail. They may also, upon payment of the usual customs, carry beyond sea whatever goods they buy in England, excepting wines, which, being once imported, may not be sent abroad again without the special license of the king. Wherefore all officers in cities, towns, and fairs are commanded to do sure and speedy justice to all foreign merchants, observing these three points especially—first, that on any trial between them and Englishmen, the jury shall be one-half foreigners, when such can be had ; secondly, that a proper person shall be appointed in London to be judiciary for foreign merchants; thirdly, that there shall be but one weight and measure throughout the land." The duties levied in return for these privileges were not very exorbitant, but sufficient to yield an important revenue to the Crown all through the ensuing times.

It was by virtue of that charter that the Venetian and other trading-fleets paid their annual visits to England. But the traders who benefited most by it, after the English themselves, were the Flemings. Notwithstanding the constant emigration of this hardy little race to our own country and elsewhere, there were plenty of people left at home to promote the commercial welfare of the province. The story of their enterprise, and of that of their neighbours the Dutch, furnishes a striking episode in the romance of trade, as well as some curious illustrations of the effects of political interference with commerce.

Flanders entered early on its career of prosperity, which was not a little due both to its physical and to its political disadvantages. Subject to frequent inundations of the German Ocean, the inhabitants were forced to use all their energies in raising barriers against these encroachments ; and

those energies, once stirred up, found expression in other
ways of overcoming nature, or turning the difficulties offered
by it into profitable channels. Alarmed, also, by the frequent wars of their great neighbours, France, England, and
Germany, which threatened over and over again to reduce them to slavery, they developed a spirit of freedom,
which took effect in commercial enterprise as well as in political independence. Bruges, their ancient capital, founded
as early as 760, was built on or near the ruins of an older
town—then a port—which the primitive residents had made
a thriving seat of trade before the Norsemen devastated it.
Charlemagne planted the surrounding country with a colony
of Saxons, under an Earl of Flanders, some forty years later,
and from that time it made steady progress. The forests
were soon partly cleared, and a portion of the wood was
used, with other material, to construct sea-walls ; canals
were cut, whereby bogs were reclaimed and the habitable
ground was made very much more extensive.

In the tenth century Flanders began to be famous as a
country of weavers carrying on a lively trade with France ;
and about the year 960 its Earl, Baldwin III., a wise pioneer of free trade, conferred on it great benefit, by establishing annual fairs and weekly markets—"without any tolls
being demanded for goods either imported or exported,"
says the old historian—at Bruges, Courtray, Ypres, and
several other towns. The result was that commodities of all
sorts poured into Flanders, and that merchants of every
nation enriched themselves and it by the traffic that ensued.
The policy of free trade was not always adopted. Earls
and countesses sought often to increase their wealth by heavy
taxes ; and in 1252, especially, the Hanse merchants had to
protest against the exorbitant duties levied by the famous
Countess Margaret. Their complaint was listened to, and
in 1262 Bruges was made one of the four great staples of
the Hanseatic League. Thenceforth it prospered more than

ever. English wool and Russian hemp, as well as linen from the nearer region of Belgium, were brought into it in vast quantities—a great part to be made into clothing in the neighbouring towns ; and to be exchanged for these materials, and for other produce, came large supplies of silk, spices, and the manifold treasures of the East, with which the Venetian galleys were laden. Bruges—though now an inland town—was connected with the ocean by a broad canal, and thus it became a busy mart for traders by both sea and land. Its burghers grew rich, and were proud of their wealth. When Philip the Fair of France went to visit it, his wife, who accompanied him, exclaimed, " I thought I was the only queen here ; but, judging from the apparel of those I see around me, there must be many wives of kings and princes present !"

Philip the Fair, notable for his unfair efforts to wrest from our Edward I. his appanage of Guienne, made like attempts to bring Flanders, nominally his fief, under actual subjection to him. He twice made a prisoner of its earl, and he led an army into the province in 1302. But the traders showed themselves better warriors than the soldiers. On the field of Courtray a powerful army was so utterly defeated, that the burghers carried back as trophies the gilt spurs of 4,000 knights, slain or taken capt' e. That victory led to other fighting, during the following century, in which the people of Ghent were leaders.

Ghent, though not quite as old as Bruges, was prosperous enough in 879 to yield rich booty to the Danes whom Alfred the Great drove from the English coasts. While Bruges rose to eminence as a city of merchants, Ghent attained equal renown as a city of manufacturers. In it chiefly congregated—though they were also abundant and wealthy in Dendermonde, Oudenarde, Yprès, and Lille— the clothworkers who furnished Bruges with its principal staple. In the fourteenth century its walls measured nine

miles round, and Froissart, writing about the year 1400, said
that it would require an army of 200,000 men to besiege
it. 80,000 men able to bear arms were inside, and these
hardy weavers were, during the Middle Ages, the main
champions of democracy, therein surpassing their neighbours
of Bruges, whom they rivalled in haughty bearing towards
both friends and foes. In 1350 the burgomasters of
Bruges, Ghent, and Yprès went to Paris, to render homage
to their nominal master, John II., on his accession.
Greater favours than French courtiers deemed proper were
shown to them, but with these they were not satisfied.
Entertained once at a sumptuous feast, but not provided
with cushions to their seats, they folded up their costly
cloaks, placed them on the hard benches while they ate,
and left them there when they retired. A messenger ran
after them with the garments, but they refused to receive
them. "We Flemings," they said, "are not in the habit of
carrying away our cushions after dinner!"

Perhaps the burgomasters had only gone to Paris that
they might display their proud spirit of independence. A
little while before, they had been at open war with France.
Jacob van Arteveldt, the brewer of Ghent, and the most
powerful man in Flanders—of whom Froissart said that
"there never was in Flanders, nor in none other country,
prince, duke, or other that ruled a country so peaceably or
so long"—had in 1337 become a strong ally of Edward III.
in his designs upon France. While the Earl of Flanders
sided with his feudal lord, Philip VI., the burghers joined
with Van Arteveldt in his adhesion to Edward. They lent
him money, provided food and passage for his troops, and
welcomed him as King of France, during nine years. In
1346, however, Van Arteveldt proposed that the Earl,
whose authority none recognised, should be formally
deposed, and that Edward the Black Prince should be set up
in his stead. Bruges and Yprès assented to the proposal; but

it was rejected by the democrats of Ghent, who feared with good reason that they would thus be taking to themselves a master far more dangerous than their hereditary ruler. Jacob van Arteveldt went himself to argue with them. " He saw," writes Froissart, "such as were wont to make reverence to him turn their backs to him. He began to doubt, and as soon as he had alighted he closed fast his gates, doors, and windows; and scarcely was this done when the street was full of men, especially of the smaller handicrafts. He went at length to a window with great humility, saying, with fair words, 'What aileth you?' They cried, 'We will have an account of the great treasure of Flanders, which you have sent to England?' He wept, and promised an account if he were allowed time to make it. In vain did he remind them truly, 'I governed you in peace and rest. In the time of my governing ye have had all things as ye could wish—corn, money, and all other merchandise.' He drew in his head, and tried to steal through a back door into an adjoining church. Four hundred men got into the house, and pursuing him, slew him without mercy ere he could reach the sanctuary."

It was four years after that, that the Flemings made their show of homage to King John. But they continued their alliance, at a safe distance, with his enemy, and rendered many services to the English during the long wars that ensued. The strife was in one way of advantage to them, as it left them in practical independence. The independence, however, was shown in much jealousy between the towns, Ghent being always the most violent in its democracy. The heavy taxes exacted in more submissive parts of the French dominions, nominal or real, were here bluntly refused, and during a long period the citizens were their own masters. Their boldest and most turbulent leader was Philip van Arteveldt, son of the demagogue murdered in 1346, and under him and his successors the Flemings made war and peace, fought, and signed treaties, and (more than all) advanced in trade and wealth, regardless alike of the authority of the French monarchs and of their own weak rulers, who were the vassals of France. A change of rulers, which took place in 1369, however, produced momentous results a century after its occurrence. In that year Margaret, the heiress of Flanders, was married to Philip, Duke of Burgundy; and by this alliance the little province was brought under the same government as the other states of the Netherlands, and eventually became the scene of other fightings, in which the citizens of Antwerp and Amsterdam were sometimes rivals, and sometimes associates, with those of Bruges and Ghent.

The northern provinces of the Netherlands rose to wealth and importance in ways similar to those that prevailed in Flanders. All were granted in early times to petty princes, earls or counts, in or near the reign of Charlemagne, and afterwards became great through the manufacturing and trading enterprise of their inhabitants, whereby the power of their hereditary lords—themselves aggrandised by it—was rendered insignificant. Antwerp, a town as early as 517, but of small account during many centuries, owed much of its prosperity to its fortunate situation on the Scheldt, which enabled it in the end to absorb much of the commerce that had hitherto passed through Bruges. The English merchants have the credit of being its first great patrons. It was for a long time the chief resort on the Continent of the old Company of Merchants of the Staple—an attempt to imitate in a small way the commercial machinery of the Hanseatic League — and it was afterwards the chosen port of the Society of Merchant Adventurers, a younger and more energetic English trading corporation. "When Philip the Good, Duke of Burgundy," says an old writer, "first granted privileges to this company in the year 1446, there were but four merchants in the city of Antwerp, and only six vessels, merely for river navigation; but in a few years after the company's settling there, the city had a great number of ships belonging to it, whereby it was soon much enlarged." Amsterdam, also, during the fifteenth century, made great progress as a trading town. Both it and Antwerp fared so well that they coveted the greater wealth that still belonged to Bruges, and their desires were gratified by a curious train of circumstances.

The Netherlands had formed part of the vast territory of the Dukes of Burgundy for rather more than a century, when the last Duke, Charles the Bold, ruined by his own ambi-tion, died in 1477, leaving as heiress an only daughter, Mary. This princess was married to the Archduke Maximilian, who became Emperor of Germany in 1493, and thus the old appanage of France was transferred to the dominion of her great rival on the Continent. The Flemings, at any rate, gained nothing by the change. Accustomed to manage their own affairs, with little interference from earl, duke, or king, they resented the sterner authority that was now forced upon them. The traders of Ghent and Bruges headed a rebellion, in which nearly all the Flemish towns took part, while Antwerp, Amsterdam, and the northern districts sided with Maximilian. Terrible sufferings to the people en-sued during the years of strife, and irreparable injury was inflicted upon their commerce—one cunning device, attributed to their rivals in Antwerp, being most productive of damage. In 1482 Maximilian caused the canal which connected Bruges with the sea to be blocked up at Sluys, and thereby the trading-ships of all Europe, that had been wont to visit the capital of Flanders, were compelled to shape their course to Antwerp and Amsterdam. From that time the prosperity of all the Flemish towns began to decline, and Antwerp succeeded Bruges as the great emporium of the world's commerce.

The supremacy of Antwerp hardly lasted for a hundred

years; but till near the close of the sixteenth century it was
without a rival. Most of the Flemish merchants migrated
to it from Bruges, and nearly all the foreigners who had
hitherto made Bruges their centre of trade with every part of
Europe. These foreigners were said, in 1560, to number
more than a thousand. Every nation had here its factory or
little colony of merchants. Frenchmen, Englishmen—among
whom were old Sir John Gresham and his famous son
Thomas—Spaniards, Portuguese, Italians, Germans, Danes,
and even Turks, settled in the town and crowded its bourse,
the first exchange set up in Europe. Two thousand loaded
wagons from France, Germany, and Lorraine passed each
day through its gates, and the merchant ships that
bartered their foreign wares for this inland produce
were more than could be counted. Often 250 vessels
might at the same time be seen loading or unloading
at her quays. Ludovico Guicciardini's account of our own
share in this commerce is precise. "To England," he says,
"Antwerp sends jewels and precious stones, silver bullion,
quicksilver, wrought silks, gold and silver cloth and thread,
camlets, grograms, spices, drugs, sugar, cotton, cummin,
galls, linens (fine and coarse), serges, tapestry, madder, hops
in great quantities, glass, salt, fish, metallic and other
merceries of all sorts, arms of all kinds, ammunition for war,
and household furniture. From England Antwerp receives
vast quantities of fine and coarse draperies, fringes, and
other things of that kind, to a great value, the finest wool,
excellent saffron in small quantities, much lead and tin,
sheep and rabbit skins without number, and various other
sorts of fine peltry and leather, beer, cheese, and other
provisions in great quantities, also Malmsey wines, which
the English import from Candia. It is marvellous to think
of the vast quantity of drapery imported by the English into
the Netherlands, being undoubtedly, one year with another,
above 200,000 pieces of all kinds, which, at the most

moderate rate of 25 crowns per piece, is 5,000,000 crowns; so that these and other merchandise brought by the English to us, or carried from us to them, may make the annual amount to be more than 12,000,000 crowns "—about £2,400,000—" to the great benefit of both countries, neither of which could possibly, or not without the greatest damage, dispense with their vast annual commerce."

The vast annual commerce was not dispensed with, but increased with the increase of wealth that it helped to produce. Before long, however, England had to seek other marts, and Antwerp lost its pre-eminence as a centre of trade. In it, as in Bruges and Ghent, a spirit of political freedom had kept pace with commercial enterprise; and a new power in national life, the spirit of religious freedom, had lately grown out of the teachings of Luther and his fellow-workers. Antwerp, able to buy with its wealth a large measure of political freedom for its citizens, suffered less than many other parts of the Netherlands in which Lutheranism was adopted, during the long persecutions by which Charles V. sought to restore the country to Catholicism; but soon after Philip II.'s accession, and the harsher measures to which he and his great agent, the Duke of Alva, resorted, even Antwerp ceased to be safe. The story of the great struggle that ensued, in which the brave little race of Netherlanders fought single-handed—until England joined in the war, and contributed its great Armada fight —against Spain, and Germany, and Rome, the huge machinery of political and religious tyranny that Philip wielded, is well known. Freedom, against the world's expectations, triumphed, and the Netherlands entered on a new era of prosperity. But Antwerp suffered by the strife. Sacked in 1567, and again more ruinously in 1585, its commerce was forced into new channels, Amsterdam taking its place on the Continent, but not a little of its greatness being transferred, with the men who fled from the dangers that harassed them at home, to London. In 1567 Sir Thomas Gresham, then at the head of the English merchants in the Nether- lands, was asked by the Protestants, of whom there were forty thousand in Antwerp alone, whether they would find welcome and peace in England. His answer induced great multitudes of them to cross the Channel, and the result was an immediate stimulus to English prosperity.

Many Flemings and Dutchmen, however, had crossed before. The earlier immigrations from the Netherlands, that have already been referred to, were insignificant in com- parison with those that began very shortly after Queen Elizabeth's accession. Many English Protestants had taken refuge in the Low Countries from the persecutions of Mary, guided by her husband Philip. As soon as Philip's rule in England was over, and his fanaticism began to work upon the Netherlands, the English returned, and with them came great numbers of their new friends. In 1561 a goodly band crossed over to Deal, whence they spread to Sandwich, Rye, and other parts of Kent. Others joined them in ensuing years, or went elsewhere, everywhere to be encouraged by Elizabeth and her statesmen, and nearly everywhere to be welcomed by those among whom they settled. One stream passed westward from Deal and the Kentish coast, another stream passed westward from Yarmouth and the Norfolk coast. Wherever they settled they made cheerful homes, and worked hard for their own and their neighbours' good. In their gardens they cultivated many vegetables new to England, or hitherto very scarce—carrots, celery, and cabbages among the number. They were skilled car- penters, and all branches of the building trade were much improved by them. Cutlery, clock-making, felt hat manu- facture, and other trades, were introduced by them ; and in others, like pottery, they taught much better ways of working than were before known in the country. More than all, they were weavers, and they greatly developed every sort of workmanship in wool and flax. In Maidstone they started thread manufacture, still known there as "Dutch work." The lacemakers of Alençon and Valenciennes transferred their calling to Cranfield, in Bedfordshire, whence it extended to Buckinghamshire, Oxford, Northamptonshire, and other counties. Others went to Devonshire, and Honiton lace soon became famous, many of the best makers of it at the present day showing their Flemish ancestry in their names. Norwich and London were their chief places of resort. In 1570 there were about four thousand natives of the Low Countries in the former city, and between seven and eight thousand in the latter. In 1588 there were thirty-eight Flemish merchants trading in London, and rich enough to subscribe £5,000 towards the defence of England against the Spanish Armada.

They even went to Ireland, then a scene of so much turmoil that few Englishmen ventured to stay in it, except as soldiers. "I caused," wrote Sir Henry Sidney, the wise Lord-Deputy of Ireland during many years, and the father of Sir Philip Sidney, in a letter to Sir Francis Walsingham, "I caused to plant and inhabit about forty families of the reformed churches of the Low Countries, flying thence for religion's sake, in one ruinous town called Swords; and, truly, sir, it would have done any man good to have seen how diligently they wrought, how they re-edified the quite spoiled old castle of the same town, and repaired almost all the same, and how goodly and cleanly they, their wives, and children lived. They made diaper and ticks for beds, and other good stuffs for man's use, and as excellent leather of deer-skins, goat and sheep fells, as is made in Southwark." It is mainly to the energy of the Flemish refugees in its northern counties that Ireland owes the development of its flax cultivation and linen manufacture.

Antwerp never recovered from the injuries that fell upon its commerce in consequence of the strife between the

Netherlanders and Philip II. ; but Amsterdam succeeded to its greatness as a Continental mart. Soon becoming the capital of the new Dutch Republic, it became yet sooner the great storehouse of Europe for corn, wine, and a hundred other commodities, and it grew with the growth of enterprise by which the hardy Hollanders, holding their own in the world of politics, became formidable competitors of the English in trade and colonisation in both the Indies.

Emigrants from the Netherlands continued to flock to England, and they came very numerously after their country had given William of Orange to ours as king. But the only parallel to the settlement of Dutch and Flemish Protestants in England under Queen Elizabeth is in the case of the French Protestants who began to cross the Channel shortly before the accession of William III. In 1598 Henry IV. of France had issued the celebrated Edict of Nantes, conferring liberty of conscience to Protestants, and that wise measure, joined with other good and patriotic measures of Henry and his minister Sully, had borne rich fruit in the rapid development of trade and manufacture throughout the country. A large share of the new energy had been displayed by the Huguenots, forced to find in commerce the occupation from which in politics they were debarred by feudalism and Catholicism, and they had been worthily protected herein by Richelieu and Colbert, the good geniuses of Louis XIII. and Louis XIV. But in 1685, two years after Colbert's death, the Edict of Nantes was revoked. Bigotry had for a time a semblance of triumph, and Jesuits were able to boast that heresy was in a fair way of being rooted out of France. The real effect was far otherwise. Nothing but injury was done to the nation which refused to find room for its most industrious and worthiest members ; and they, only strengthened in their love of liberty, were forced, amid terrible sufferings, to take refuge in countries willing to receive them and the arts that they brought with them.

About a hundred thousand French outcasts—some ten thousand from Rouen alone—settled in England, and wonderful benefits to our commerce resulted from their coming. The great numbers who found poor homes for themselves in Spitalfields and elsewhere made silk manufacture for the first time an important trade in England; and a great stimulus was given by them to all sorts of workmanship in linen and cotton. The making of buttons, and a hundred small articles of great value in the aggregate. was introduced by them. Beaver hats, which had hitherto been all brought from France, were now made in Wandsworth, and had to be bought there for the Continental dandies who loved them as much as they hated their makers. Glass manufacture, till now hardly known in England, save in its simplest and coarsest branches, was soon turned by the Huguenot refugees into a great staple of English produce. It was the same with paper-making. Among others who followed this trade was Henri de Portal, whose ancestors had been leaders of the Albigenses, and sturdy Protestants for centuries. He set up a paper manufactory at Lavenstoke, on the Itchin, in Hampshire, and managed it so well that he was chosen to furnish the peculiar material required by the Bank of England for its bank-notes, and the monopoly is still possessed by his descendants.*

No later instance of religious persecution equal to that which fell on the French Protestants in 1685 has occurred; but there have been cases quite as memorable of the influence, direct or indirect, of politics upon commerce. The minor persecution which troubled the English Puritans during the years previous to 1685, and which caused many

---

* It is hardly necessary to refer the reader for further information touching these refugees to Mr. Smiles's instructive and interesting work on "The Huguenots in England."

of them to quit their country shortly before the Huguenots came into it, was not designed with any reference to trade, but has had commercial results unparalleled in modern history. The first English colonists in America, the planters of Virginia in the reign of James I., went thither only with the healthy wish to improve their condition by cultivating the rich lands then lying almost waste. Their success, not very great at first, tempted others to follow their example; but the real beginning of prosperity to what are now the United States dates from the settlement of the "Pilgrim Fathers" in Massachusetts. The little group of fugitives from religious tyranny who crossed the Atlantic in the *Mayflower*, in 1620, were pioneers of other groups, who soon made New England a worthy rival of the old England from which they were outcasts for conscience' sake. "The land is weary of her inhabitants," it was said, in a significant Puritan tract, "General Considerations for Planting New England," published in 1649, "so that man, which is the most precious of all creatures, is here more vile and base than the earth they tread on; so as children, neighbours and friends, especially of the poor, are accounted the greatest burdens, which, if things were right, would be the highest blessings. Hence it comes to pass that all arts and trades are carried on in that deceitful manner and unrighteous course as it is almost impossible for a good upright man to maintain his charge and live comfortably in any of them." Therefore tide after tide of Puritans, Independents, Quakers, and others—among the rest, those other persecuted Christians, the Catholics who founded Maryland—crossed over to America, and there managed "to live comfortably," though with not quite as much freedom from "deceitful manner and unrighteous course" as they arrogantly professed. Zeal in money-making went hand in hand with zeal in religion; but though attended by some ugly circumstances, it mightily helped on the growth of young colonies, and even ugly circumstances in the religious zeal led to the same end. Milton's discovery that "New Presbyter is but Old Priest writ long," was as true in America as in Europe. The men who quitted their English homes to secure for themselves liberty of conscience were not inclined to grant liberty of conscience to one another. Despicable squabbles and small tyrannies prevailed, which caused much bitterness among the colonists, and threatened to ruin their prosperity. But the effect was different. There was room enough for all in the splendid country to which they had gone, and the only issue of the religious quarrels was that each petty sect branched off into a petty colony of its own, leaving vacant space enough, as was supposed, to separate it for ever from its rivals. Thus all the land was dotted with thriving little settlements, which soon throve so well that the vacant spaces were filled up; but by that time they had learnt wisdom, and were ready to enter into friendly relations, in spite of their religious differences, and the result was the establishment of a body of united colonies, so powerful that it was able to baffle the commercial tyranny of England, and, shaking off its allegiance, but very little of its sympathy, to reshape itself as a body of United States. Other causes, of course, tended to build up this mighty nation, greater now in number of inhabitants and fourteen times greater in extent of land than the nation that gave it birth; but not a little is the result due to that desire of truly carrying on "all arts and trades" which actuated the "Pilgrim Fathers," and has actuated all their descendants and followers.

The relationship between politics and trade is shown yet more notably, though very differently, in the history of another great outgrowth of English commercial enterprise. In our intercourse with India they have gone side by side, sometimes as rivals, sometimes as allies, but always together, during three centuries. When Sir Francis Drake,

first of all Englishmen, visited the East Indies, in 1579, in
the course of his famous voyage round the world, his double
object was to make private war against Philip II., on
religious and political grounds, and to wrest from him some
of those commercial gains which his Portuguese subjects
had begun to derive from intercourse with Asia and its
southern islands, just as his Spanish subjects had for a longer
time been growing rich through trade and colonisation in
America and the West Indies. Shortly after his return, in
1580, from his three years' voyage, bringing with him booty
worth £47 for every £1 spent upon the expedition—most
of it, it is true, obtained on the Chilian and Peruvian coasts
—and while every tongue was eloquent concerning the
prowess and the value of his exploits, it was proposed by
Queen Elizabeth's Government to found "a company of
such as should trade beyond the equinoctial line," with
Drake for its life-governor. That project was not entered
upon till after Drake's famous career was over; but it took
shape in the formation of the East India Company, which,
after nine years of deliberation, and a trial voyage made by
Captain Lancaster, as agent for some London merchants,
was incorporated by Queen Elizabeth in 1600. Captain
Lancaster conducted its first trading voyage, begun in the
spring of 1601, and, in spite of many mishaps, made a good
beginning of the great work to be done by it. He made
political alliances and commercial treaties with the kings of
Sumatra, and brought home substantial proof of both, in the
costly presents sent by the native monarchs to Queen
Elizabeth, and in the great stores of spices and other articles
bought from the people for his employers. The policy
initiated by him has been maintained to the present day,
with a result far more wonderful than the wildest enthusiast
could have dreamt of nine generations ago. Affording
political support to local potentates, in return for trading
privileges, the East India Company, reshaped and expanded

several times before its abolition in 1858, first gained a
footing on the southern islands, and then advanced upon the
mainland. The power that it gained over the natives, and
which was strengthened even by the efforts of French and
Dutch rivals to weaken it, soon turned Hindoo and Moslem
princes into vassals, and from vassals they became subjects ;
so that now a vast territory, eight times as extensive, and five
times as populous as Great Britain and Ireland, has been
made subject to the English Crown, and at the present time
receives from England about £40,000,000 worth of goods,
in return for which it sends back commodities worth nearly
£60,000,000. All this vast empire has grown out of Sir
Francis Drake's shrewd enterprise, and the enterprise which
it aroused in later men, using commerce as the instrument
of politics, and politics as the instrument of commerce.

But the result has not been altogether satisfactory.
Many dark pages occur in the brilliant history of English
aggression in India. Lust of power and lust of wealth
prompted many famous exploits, and the evil wrought by
them cannot be wiped out by the valour and perseverance
that brought them to a successful conclusion. The tem-
pering of both politics and commerce with philanthropy
in our management of Indian affairs is only a modern
institution, and it is not yet complete. Illustrations of the
misuse of mere political power, for which terrible retribution
appeared in the mutiny of 1857, need not here be given.
One illustration of political interference with commerce—
that furnished by the history of the opium trade—will
suffice.

Opium is an old product of India, and, almost from
the commencement of British rule, officials were allowed
to cultivate and trade in it ; but it was not much thought
of till a century ago. In 1773 it was converted into a
Government monopoly, and the sale was encouraged in
various ways, in order that the profits might swell the

revenue; the chief market being in China, whither the obnoxious drug was sent, not only to meet the existing
demand, but, as far as possible, to foster it. In 1797
poppy-growing was forbidden in any part of India, except
Bahar and Benares, and there only in a limited area.
About 100,000 acres are now appropriated to it; money,
at the beginning of the season, being advanced by
Government to the cultivators, and the balance of their
wages, if any is due, being paid at the close. In 1796 the
Emperor of China prohibited the use of opium in his
dominions; but, by help of armed vessels, which conveyed
it to the coast, and of confidential agents on land, who
received and distributed it, the authorities were evaded;
and in China the annual consumption rose in forty years
from 1,000 to 27,000 chests. About ninepence per lb.
is paid by Government for the production of the opium,
and it charges about three shillings for preparing and packing it for the market. It is then conveyed to Calcutta,
where it is sold to the merchants at prices varying from
seven shillings to a guinea, the average being twelve shillings per lb. The merchants' profits, and the cost of
shipping it to China, raise that average to a guinea, and the
price is further vastly increased by the dealers who retail it
in that country. The profits of the Indian Government upon
this trade add from £4,000,000 to £5,000,000 a year to
the revenue; and, to protect the traffic, more than one war
with China has been entered upon. That a commodity so
objectionable should be heavily taxed, in preference to any
other and more useful produce, cannot be complained of;
but that its consumption should be encouraged, as has been
and still is the case, solely for financial ends, is as wrong as
it is foolish.

Other instances of monopolies, and of kindred inter-
ferences of politics with trade in special articles, will hereafter be given, as well as illustrations of the way in which

particular traders have, wisely or unwisely, sought to promote their own callings, or commerce as a whole, by help
of politics. Some of these cases are very noteworthy, as
showing both the political importance of commerce, and the
bearing of commerce upon politics.

The services rendered by Sir William de la Pole to
Edward III. have been already referred to. Yet greater
were the services rendered by the Greshams to their sovereigns and their country. Sir Richard Gresham, the father,
residing often in Antwerp, acted as political and financial
agent to Henry VIII. and Edward VI. in the Netherlands,
besides being equally useful in London. He negotiated
public loans, and fulfilled many of the duties both of Chancellor of the Exchequer and of stockbroker to the Crown.
He boldly resented many arbitrary measures proposed by
King Henry and Cardinal Wolsey affecting himself and his
brother merchants, and was the first exponent, though
naturally only in rude ways, of the modern principles of
free trade.

Therein, and in all the other wise views that he held,
he was followed and surpassed by his son, Sir Thomas
Gresham, whose public life began in Edward VI.'s reign.
There was need at that time of an honest man to act as
adviser to the sovereign. Edward's mode of borrowing
money, or, rather, that of the foolish statesmen who guided
him, may be gathered from an entry in the royal journal,
dated April the 25th, 1551 : " A bargain made with the
Fulcare," we read—these Fulcare being the famous Fuggers
of Augsburg—" for about £60,000, for the deferring of it ;
first, that the Fulcare should put it off for ten per cent. ;
secondly, that I should buy 12,000 marks' weight of silver,
at six shillings the ounce ; thirdly, that I should pay
100,000 crowns for a very fair jewel, four rubies (marvellous big), one orient and great diamond, and one great
pearl." Against that mode of borrowing money, now aban-

doned by kings, and adapted only for the most foolish
spendthrifts, young Gresham stoutly protested. "To be
plain with your Grace, according to my bounden duty," he
wrote to the Duke of Northumberland in August, 1552,
"verily, if there be not some other way taken for the payment of his Majesty's debts, but to force men from time
to time to prolong it; I say to you, the end thereof shall
neither be honourable nor profitable to his Highness. In
consideration whereof, if there be none other ways taken
forthwith, I most humbly beseech that I may be discharged
of this office of agentship : for, otherwise, I see in the end
I shall receive shame and discredit thereby, to my utter
undoing for ever; which is the smallest matter of all, so
that the King's Majesty's honour and credit be not spoiled
thereby, and specially in a strange country." The straightforward and patriotic young merchant was not allowed to
resign the office of financial agent at Antwerp, in which he
succeeded his father; and, though his advice was not always
taken, he managed by it, and still more by his own good
sense and tact in doing the business entrusted to him, very
greatly to improve the pecuniary condition of the English
Crown. Three weeks before his death, King Edward rewarded him with a grant of land, saying, "You shall know
that you have served a king!" He also served two queens
as well. With Mary he had not much favour; but to
Elizabeth he was an excellent and trusted adviser during
twenty years. Dying in 1579, he left the royal exchequer
in a far more prosperous condition than it had ever been
before; and if his commercial services were thus important
to the State, his political influence was no less valuable
to the general well-being of trade. The Royal Exchange
which he built, and which helped not a little to concentrate
the forces by which London has become the greatest mart
in the world, was only one of the many benefits that he
conferred on commerce.

A far more striking instance of merchants' service to their country occurs in the history of Jacques Cœur, who lived more than a century before Sir Thomas Gresham. Born a few years before 1400, he was the son of Pierre Cœur, a goldsmith or fur-dealer, of Bourges, a quaint old city right in the centre of France, just half-way between Paris and Lyons. In Bourges, Jacques Cœur became a great trader, and that town was, all along, the centre of the commercial relations which he established with every district of France ; but the ancient port of Marseilles afforded greater facilities for extending his operations to foreign countries, and that was his chief place of business during more than twenty years from 1429 or 1430. Marseilles, founded by a Greek colony in the sixth century B.C., had continued to be a trading town in all later times, but was greatly surpassed by the younger Mediterranean marts of Venice and Genoa. Jacques Cœur revived its greatness. Every year he sent a trading-fleet of ten or twelve ships all round the Mediterranean, to exchange the wares of France for spices, silks, and all the costly articles brought from the East. He was the first Frenchman who established commercial dealings with Egypt, and thence he obtained rich stores of articles, for which he found a good and ready market in his own and other lands. At one time, it was said, he had three hundred agents in various parts of the world, and "As rich as Jacques Cœur" became a proverb. He also obtained from Charles VII. a grant of the mining districts around Lyons, and thence extracted so much wealth that the common people believed him to be an astrologer, possessed of the secret of the philosopher's stone. The French monarch appointed him Master of his Mint, first in Bourges and afterwards at Paris. He was also made *Argentier*, or treasurer to the Crown.

Charles VII. then had need of an *argentier*. He himself was so poor that, on one occasion, having nothing for dinner, he was glad to accept from Jacques Cœur a present of a cooked loin of mutton and two fowls. The Duke of Bedford, as regent for Henry VI., was then in possession of the greater part of France, and the poor vacillating heir of the house of Valois starved in Bourges, till Joan of Arc, manlier than all his warriors, led the revolution by which his kingdom was won back for him from the English. The bold merchant was his chief agent in completing the change which the bold maiden had begun. Jacques Cœur, besides being merchant, shipowner, banker, miner, and coiner, was Chancellor of the Exchequer, Purveyor-General, and Ambassador as well. Lending money—it is said, without interest—to king and nobles alike, he often had to expostulate with Charles VII. for his pusillanimous conduct, to urge him to shake off his unworthy courtiers, and to persuade him to patriotic action. It was Jacques Cœur, indeed, who introduced that system of taxation without permission of the States-General, which—though it may have been necessary and commendable in the desperate condition of France at the time—was fruitful in subsequent misfortune, through the arbitrary power which it vested in the Crown. The *argentier* levied a tax of 20 livres on every one of the million belfries in France, and, limiting the expenses of the royal household to 1,000,000 livres, carefully apportioned the rest to the pay of soldiers, the repair of fortresses, and other services of State. In 1448, when the English were driven from all the rest of France, and the people of Normandy waited only for encouragement in throwing off the foreign tyranny that was hateful to them, Jacques Cœur stirred up the slothful monarch to the work, and lent him 200,000 crowns with which to do it. "Sire," he said at that time, with more loyalty than truth, "to you I am indebted for profit and honour, both at home and in pagan lands ; for it is in honour of you that the Soldan of Egypt has granted me a safe-conduct for my galleys, and that my factors are protected

From all these advantages I have acquired great wealth. Whatever I have is yours."

Charles VII. took him at his word. In 1452 Agnes Sorel, the king's mistress, ate a poisoned apple, and died. Between her and Jacques Cœur there had never been much friendship, the merchant considering that she was partly to blame for the follies and vices of the king ; and ready belief was given, or pretended, to a report, spread abroad by some of his enemies, that the apple had come from him. He was arrested, kept in prison for eleven months, subjected to a sham trial, at which other false charges were brought against him and accepted without proof, tortured, and at length, in May, 1453, condemned as worthy of death. With a hollow show of leniency, the ungrateful monarch spared his life, but confiscated all his property. Others whom he had befriended were not as ungrateful. Sixty or eighty merchants, who owed their wealth to him, are said to have lent him each 1,000 crowns, with which to recover his fortunes ; and this, though heart-broken, he attempted to do. It is said that in 1456 the Pope—to whom in 1448 he had gone as ambassador, in "so great magnificence that such a company was never heard tell of"—appointed him captain-general of an expedition against the infidels, and that, being off Chio with his fleet, he there fell sick, and died in November of the same year. But the story of his life after the disgraceful trial and sentence is uncertain.

By his private trading and his public services alike Jacques Cœur helped mightily to reconstruct the prosperity of France. The first great French merchant, he had many notable successors, but none equal in illustration of the mutual benefits that can be conferred upon one another by commerce and politics, until the time of Jean Baptiste Colbert. Colbert, widely different from Jacques Cœur, both in temperament and in the circumstances of his career, was not a merchant, though the greatest friend of commerce

whose name appears in the annals of France. Of Scotch
descent, and the son of a humble wine-merchant in Rheims.
he was born in 1619, and began life as a woollen-draper's
assistant. A pretty story is told of his having inadvertently
sold some cloth at too high a price to a Paris banker, to
whom he returned the overcharge in spite of his master's
anger, and who, pleased at his unusual honesty, took him
into his employ. He was not long a banker's clerk. In
1649 he entered the service of Cardinal Mazarin, then
Richelieu's well-meaning successor as first minister of France.
His skill soon made him famous, and in 1661 Louis XIV.
made him Comptroller-General of Finance. Holding that
and other offices in succession, he was the good genius of
France during the next two-and-twenty years. Advancing
in the path marked out by Richelieu, who was himself a
pupil of Sully, wiser than his master—these three being the
greatest statesmen of France—he developed a system of
administration, which, if later men had been honest and
shrewd enough to maintain and perfect it, would have saved
their country from two centuries of misery, and averted the
French Revolution. His strictly political work, and his
patronage of art and science, need not here be referred to;
but his services to commerce were sufficient to win for him
high fame. He repaired old roads, and made new ones.
He enabled Riquet to cut the noble canal of Languedoc,
which connects the Atlantic with the Mediterranean. He
built up the French navy and put down piracy. He extended French trade to the East Indies and colonised
Canada, Madagascar, and Cayenne. He founded a Chamber
of Commerce in Paris, and personally aided the merchants
in their deliberations for the furtherance of trade. He
showed how nobles could be merchants without loss of
their nobility; and Nantes, Bordeaux, and St. Malo still bear
fruit from seeds of his planting. He established glass-
works—the first in France—in one part of Paris, and in

another he founded the famous Gobelins tapestry manufactory. Directly and indirectly he did more for the commercial benefit of France than any other statesman has ever done ; and, if much of his good work failed, it failed only through the folly of his successors, blind to the truth that politics and commerce, with liberty for their only law, must be mutually helpful in any nation that is to advance in civilisation.

It is to its growing recognition of this truth that the world owes much of its progress during recent generations. England, especially, has been enriched by it—enabled to crowd its acres with a far greater population than the acres themselves could maintain, and to take, among the larger nations, a place far more influential than, even with its added millions of inhabitants, it could claim on the score of mere population. But the lesson has been learnt with difficulty. There has been plenty of political interference with commerce during the past two centuries, and the doctrines of free trade are even yet but feebly understood. There are still poets and preachers, as well as statesmen, who vaunt the superiority of war over peace, and particularly of that suppressed form of war, known as "armed neutrality," over the mutual trust and sympathy that are most encouraged by international trade.

The history of the bearing upon commerce of the great wars in which England has been engaged is eminently instructive. Sometimes, it must be admitted, war has been a powerful agent in the promoting of commerce, of liberty, and of civilisation. So it was, especially, with the famous struggle waged between England and Spain, in the days of Elizabeth and Philip II., the most necessary and beneficial war in which our country has ever been concerned. Prompted partly by patriotism, which saw the great danger with which the independence of England was threatened by the boundless ambition of the sixteenth century Augustus, partly by

J

religious zeal on behalf of the persecuted Protestants of the
Netherlands, and partly by the commercial activity that
claimed a share in the prosperous traffic with America and
the West Indies, Asia and the East Indian Islands, which
was then engrossed by Spain and Portugal, it was wholly
successful in all its objects.   England's strength as a nation .
was proved by it.   It drove back the advancing tide of
Catholicism, which had seemed likely to overwhelm the
Protestants of the Continent.   It opened up more and easier
ways of traffic and colonisation for English merchants and
adventurers, in both the Western and the Eastern Worlds.
The   British   Empire   in   India   and   the   United   States   of
America   grew   out   of   it,   and   thereby   the   wealth   and
prosperity   of   our   little   island   were   developed   beyond
computation.

No such praise can be accorded either to the causes or to
the effects of England's share in the War of the Spanish
Succession, begun by William III., and completed by Queen
Anne ;   barren   triumphs   were   achieved   by   it,   and   heavy
liabilities were fastened upon posterity.   Its only result was
to lay the seeds of subsequent strife, by which commerce, at
any rate, gained nothing.   The trading privileges and the
trading hindrances that were stated or implied in its treaties
were   alike   pernicious,   and   commercial   enterprise   was
checked, as far as political interference could check it, during
more than a century.

The most commercial of all our wars was that which
ended in the independence of the United States.   Begotten
of the mistaken policy which sought to restrain American
industry, in order that English manufacturers and merchants
might   be   benefited,   and   continued   under   circumstances
wholly discreditable to the mother country, it engendered
hatred and jealousy, which has not yet quite died out.
Perhaps   the   United   States   have   thriven   better   for   their
separation   from   England,   and   the   violent   disruption

of ties that might have hindered the full development
of the ways of self-government and self-advancement, by
which the great republic has progressed with unparalleled
rapidity and completeness ; but it cannot be doubted that,
had it been possible for the severance to take place without
awakening the bad passions then provoked, England,
at any rate, would have gained mightily, and her opponent
would have lost nothing. The only advantage of the struggle
was the lesson taught by it, as to the better method to be
pursued by Great Britain when her other colonies have
reached maturity, and claim their independence.

Yet more melancholy, however, was the long war with
France, which culminated in the Battle of Waterloo and the
Treaty of Vienna. Inexcusable in its origin, one of wanton
interference with the internal politics of France, it was cruelly
disastrous in its consequences. The great exploits of men
like Nelson and Wellington furnish but slender gleams of
light, that light even lurid and ghastly, beside the wretched
waste of life upon the battle-field and the wretchedness
produced in millions of households. Pitt's war crippled
commerce, and brought England to the verge of ruin. " We
have examined," said Brougham, in the House of Commons,
in 1812, "above a hundred witnesses, from more than thirty
of the great manufacturing and mercantile districts ; in all
this mass of evidence there was not a single witness who
denied or doubted the dreadful amount of the present
distress. Take, for example, one of our great staples, the
hardware, and look to Warwickshire, where it used to
flourish. Birmingham and its neighbourhood—a district of
thirteen miles round that centre—was formerly but one village,
I might say, one continued workshop, peopled with about
400,000 of the most industrious and skilful of mankind.
In what state do you now find that once busy hive of men ?
Silent, still, and desolate during half the week ; during the
rest of it miserably toiling, at reduced wages, for a pittance

scarcely sufficient to maintain animal life in the lowest state of comfort; and at all times swarming with unhappy persons, willing, anxious, to work for their lives, but unable to find employment. He must have a stout heart within him who can view such a scene and not shudder." In Yorkshire and the woollen district, as Brougham showed, it was as bad. In Lancashire and its neighbourhood it was worse. " I would draw your attention to the cotton districts, merely to present one incidental circumstance which chanced to transpire respecting the distress of the poor in those parts. The food which now sustains them is of the lowest kind, and of that there is not nearly a sufficient supply; bread, or even potatoes, are now out of the question; the luxuries of animal food, or even milk, they have long ceased to think of. Their looks, as well as their apparel, proclaim the sad change in their situation. One witness tells you it is only necessary to look at their haggard faces to be assured of their sufferings; another says that persons who have recently returned, after an absence of some months from those parts, declared themselves shocked, and unable to recognise the people whom they had left. A gentleman, largely concerned in the cotton trade, whose property in part consists of cottages and little pieces of ground let out to workpeople, told us that lately he went to look after his rents, and when he entered those dwellings, and found them so miserably attired, so stripped of their wonted furniture and other little comforts, when he saw their inhabitants sitting down to a scanty dinner of oatmeal and water, their only meal in the four-and-twenty hours, he could not stand the sight, and came away unable to ask for his rent. Masters came forward to tell us how unhappy it made them to have no more work to give their poor men, because all their money, and in some cases their credit too, was already gone in trying to support them. Some had involved themselves in embarrassments for such pious purposes. One, again, would

describe his misery at turning off people whom his father had
employed for many years. Another would say how he
dreaded the coming round of Saturday, when he had to pay
his hands their reduced wages, how he kept out of their way
on that day, and made his foreman pay them. A third would
say that he was afraid to see his people, because he had no
longer the means of giving them work, and knew that they
would flock round him, and implore to be employed at
the lowest wages, for something wholly insufficient to feed
them."

That dismal picture of the commercial distress caused
by our "great and glorious" war with France, has a counterpart in the misery by which the cotton districts were
afflicted in consequence of the recent civil war in America.
Although in that case England was not responsible for the
misery, the same lesson is taught by it—that war, whatever
else may be said in its praise, is generally and almost wholly
the greatest enemy of commerce. "Although the conflicts
in which this country has during the last hundred and fifty
years involved itself," Richard Cobden said, truly and elo-
quently, "have, in almost every instance, been undertaken
in behalf of our commerce, there is no instance recorded
in which a favourable tariff or a beneficial treaty has been
extorted from an unwilling enemy at the point of the sword.
On the contrary, every restriction that embarrasses the trade
of the whole world, all existing commercial jealousies
between nations, the debts that oppress the countries of
Europe, the incalculable waste owing to the misdirected
labour and capital of communities—these and a thousand
other evils are all the consequences of wars. How shall a
profession which withdraws from productive industry the
ablest of the human race, and teaches them systematically
the best modes of destroying mankind; which awards
honours only in proportion to the number of victims offered
at its sanguinary altar; which overturns cities, ravages farms

and vineyards, uproots forests, burns the ripened harvest; which, in a word, exists but in the absence of law, order, and security—how can such a profession be favourable to commerce, which increases only with the increase of human life, whose parent is agriculture, and which perishes or flies at the approach of lawless rapine? They who propose to influence by force the traffic of the world, forget that affairs of trade, like matters of conscience, change their very nature if touched by the hand of violence; for, as faith, if forced, would no longer be religion, but hypocrisy, so commerce becomes robbery, if covered by warlike armaments."

The name of him who wrote those sentences will live long as a wise benefactor of trade, one of his many great services being the procurement of the commercial treaty of 1860 between Great Britain and France. Notable illustration of the progress of political interference with trade is furnished by the history of commercial treaties. Here, however, it will be sufficient to note the character and some of the effects of two alone, the Methuen Treaty and the Cobden Treaty.

In 1703 John ·Methuen, on behalf of Queen Anne, contracted with the King of Portugal that British woollen cloths should be admitted into Portugal, provided that at all times Portuguese wines were admitted into Great Britain at two-thirds of the duty, whatever that might be, levied upon the wines of France. That treaty, so far as it opened a new market of English manufactures, was wholly beneficial, but its influence upon our wine-drinking was curious. Before 1688, port, or Oporto wine, was a thing unknown in England; whereas during many previous centuries the wine-trade with France had been very great, and the light, wholesome produce of the grapes of Burgundy, Bordeaux, and Champagne had been the favourite drink of all classes of the people, save those with whom beer was the costliest beverage procurable. In William III.'s reign, however, jealousy of France had caused heavy duties to be charged upon it, the increase being from 1s. 4d. to 4s. 10d. a gallon, and with the great advance of price there had been proportionate reduction of the consumption. The Portuguese wine-merchants took advantage of this state of things, but the English taste was not easily educated in favour of port. In a "Farewell to Wine," published in 1693, this dialogue occurs :—

> "' Some claret, boy !'
>   ' Indeed, sir, we have none,—
> Claret, sir? lord ! there's not a drop in town ;
> But we've the best red port.'
>   ' What's that you call
> *Red port?*'
>   ' A wine, sir, comes from Portugal.
> I'll fetch a pint, sir.' . . . . . .
> ' Ah, how it smells ! Methinks a real pain
> Is by its odour thrown upon my brain.
> I've tasted it : 'tis spiritless and flat,
> And has as many different tastes
> As can be found in compound pastes.'"

The Methuen Treaty compelled Englishmen to drink port. They drank it till they liked it ; and, having acquired a bad taste, they passed on to a worse one—even as Dr. Johnson used to say, "Claret for boys, port for men, and brandy for heroes." If that dictum be true, modern adulteration has made heroism easy, by causing bad brandy to be the chief ingredient, after elderberries and water, of popular port-wine, the adulteration being carried on in Portugal as well as in England. During the seven years ending with 1858, the average annual shipment of port from Oporto was 27,000 pipes to the United Kingdom, and 2,000 pipes to all the rest of Europe. By that time claret had become only a luxury of the rich, the cheaper qualities being rendered unmarketable by the heavy duties laid upon them ever since the time of Methuen's convention.

Whether the national taste in wine will be changed back

to its earlier condition remains to be seen, but the Cobden Treaty has already had important results. Nearly every year since 1861 there has been an increase of about an eighth upon the previous year's exportation from France to England.

That treaty, effected by the personal energy of Cobden, who visited France for the purpose in 1860, and subsequently improved upon in some of its details, besides greatly reducing the duty on wine, abolished all imports on French manufactured goods, and secured a large abatement on the duties charged in France on English textile manufactures, iron, coal, and other articles. The time has hardly come for a due estimate of its advantages, but these advantages cannot but be vast. "The old state of things," said Mr. Gladstone in 1862, "in the commercial law between this country and France savoured of the period when it was almost thought a matter of duty to regard Frenchmen as traditional enemies. That opinion does not, I am happy to say, prevail now. The truth is that the union of England and France in the bonds of special amity and harmony is, of all things that can be named, the greatest benefit both to these countries themselves and to the other nations of the world. It is a benefit which we cannot always enjoy, because it is impossible that the views and the policy of governments and of nations should always coincide; but when we can have it we should have it, for there is none other comparable to it in magnitude, there is none other which so completely offers us a guarantee for the general peace and happiness of the world. The policy of governments, as opposed to nations, may sometimes interfere to mar that harmony; therefore it is well that we should not look simply to the policy of governments, but that we should endeavour to unite the two nations in harmonious feelings. And when was there ever at our command any means or instrument so powerful and so valuable for that purpose as the means and instrument employed in the treaty of commerce with France, which increases and multiplies tenfold the quiet, peaceful, unnoticed, and beneficial intercourse between the two countries ? "

Praise of Richard Cobden, the author of that treaty, and the greatest champion of free trade, fitly closes our brief review of the wise and foolish relations that have prevailed between politics and commerce ; and the praise uttered by Lord Palmerston in the House of Commons, on April 3rd, 1865, the day after Cobden's death, was no more than just. "It is many years," he said, "since Adam Smith elaborately and conclusively, as far as argument could go, advocated, as the fundamental principal of the wealth of nations, the freedom of industry and the unrestricted exchange of the objects and results of industry. These doctrines were inculcated by learned men, by Dugald Stewart and others, and were taken up in process of time by leading statesmen, such as Huskisson, and those who agreed with him. But the barriers which long-associated prejudice had raised against these doctrines for a great number of years prevented their coming into use as instruments of progress to the country. To Mr. Cobden it was reserved, by his untiring industry, his indefatigable personal activity, the indomitable energy of his mind, and that forcible Demosthenic eloquence with which he treated all subjects he took in hand—I say it was reserved to Mr. Cobden, by exertions which were never surpassed, to carry into practical application those abstract principles with the truth of which he was so deeply impressed, and which at last gained the practical acceptance of all reasonable men in the country."

CHAPTER VI.

MONOPOLIES.

THE history of monopolies is an important and curious section of the history of political interference with trade. In former times they were often necessary, in certain circumstances they are necessary still; but their gradual removal illustrates the gradual extension of those better principles by which commerce is now for the most part regulated, or left to regulate itself.

In mediæval England, and throughout feudal Christendom, trade itself was almost a monopoly. The privilege of engaging in commerce, whether all the year round, in towns and cities, or on particular occasions, at fairs and markets, was in the gift of the Crown, and was recognised in charters of incorporation as something which could be granted or withheld, and which, if granted, must be paid for. Some evidence has been already furnished of the restrictions put in the way of all traders, and especially of foreigners. It is true that Edward III.—among English kings the greatest friend to commerce before Henry VII.—supplemented many wise measures of a like nature, by enacting, in 1350, that "all persons, as well foreigners as natives, may buy and sell, by wholesale and retail, where, when, and how they please, paying the usual customs and duties, notwithstanding any franchises, grants, or usages to the contrary, seeing that such usages and franchises are to the common prejudice of the king and his people." But the usages and franchises were too strong to be put down, and in this very reign they took effect in ways by which monopolies were greatly increased.

From Anglo-Saxon times, traders of each sort, in each locality, had been in the habit of banding together for mutual protection and assistance. This was a good and necessary arrangement, when war was frequent and piracy and fraud were constant. Single men could have no chance of prospering amid the confusion and danger that prevailed. Their only safety was in common action, and, that the action might be united and controlled by rules conducing to the general welfare, guilds and trading corporations were formed. So important had these guilds become, in London especially, by the middle of the fourteenth century, that Edward III. found it expedient to bring about or to sanction their reorganisation, and, by conferring fresh privileges and appointing more stringent rules, to help them to be, according to their original professions, "for the greater good and profit of the people." Forty-eight London guilds were incorporated by him in the course of his fifty years' reign. The grocers, the mercers, the drapers, the fishmongers, the goldsmiths, the vintners, the tailors, the spinners, the smiths, the brewers, the saddlers, the weavers, the tapestry-makers, the chandlers, the fullers, the girdlers, the stainers, the salters, the masons, the ironmongers, the leather-dressers, the butchers, and six-and-twenty other sorts of traders, had each of them their separate association duly represented in the civic councils, held responsible for the conduct of the members, and bound to look after the general welfare. In

nearly every charter, the malpractices of ignorant or fraudulent intruders are stated as the grounds for assigning special
rights and functions to honest and qualified traders; and, undoubtedly, they not only were meant to be beneficial to commerce and society, but, in many respects, really were so. Their
effect, however, was the solidifying of trade in old ways, in
which improvements were rendered needlessly difficult, and
the shutting out from it of many men who might have
proved very helpful to its progress. The benefits and the
mischiefs of modern trades' unions among working men are
counterparts of the action, good and bad, of the old London
corporations of workmen—who were both masters and servants—and, before long, the guilds of the metropolis were
imitated in every busy town in the kingdom. A few ex-
tracts from the history of one or two will sufficiently illustrate the working of them all.

Not the oldest, but perhaps the most important, was
the Grocers', originally known as the Pepperers' Guild. As
the old name implies, pepper was at first the chief commodity in which its members dealt; and this being obtained from the Italian merchants, who brought the wares
of the East Indies to England, the pepperers soon began
to buy from them, and trade in other spices, as well as
drugs of various sorts; and, before long, they added wholesale to retail trade. The pepperers had formed an irregular but powerful association for some time before 1345,
when twenty-two of their number met together at a dinner
in St. Mary Axe, and resolved to form themselves into a
well-organised company, with two wardens to rule them, a
priest to sing and pray for them, and a room in which they
could meet for social intercourse and consultation upon
business matters. Edward III. granted them, not a charter,
but a license for carrying out their intentions. Rules were
promptly made for strengthening the society, raising contributions for necessary expenses, defining the duties of

apprentices, and, above all, maintaining their "mysteries," or trade secrets. A few years later they changed their name of pepperers to gross-spicers, which, by an intentional or unintentional pun, was shortened to grossers or grocers. In an Act of Edward III.'s reign, passed in 1363, it is complained that "those merchants called grossers have, by covin and by orders made amongst themselves in their guilds, engrossed all sorts of wares, whereby they suddenly raise the prices of them." Before the death of King Edward, the grocers had become the most influential body of native wholesale merchants in England, the London guild being connected with kindred associations in other towns. "The word grocery," says an old historian of the society, "became so extensive that it can now be hardly restrained to certain kinds of merchandises they have formerly dealt in, for they have been the most universal merchants that traded abroad, by which means many and various ways of dealing passed under the denomination of groceries."

The guild grew rapidly in numbers. Starting with twenty-two members in 1345, it had a hundred and twenty-four in 1373, and in 1383 sixteen of its number were aldermen. It was re-organised and endowed with new privileges by Henry VI., in 1429, and additional charters were granted by later sovereigns, so that at length the grocers had a complete monopoly of trade in spices, drugs, confectionaries, sugar, coffee, tea, tobacco, and a hundred other commodities, throughout London, and over three miles of its suburbs. Curious evidence of the extent of their monopoly appears in their indignant protest against the establishment of the College of Physicians, in 1664, on the ground that it was an unlawful interference with their medical control, and "an insupportable inconvenience and prejudice." Till then the apothecaries had perforce been grocers, and the guild had been the chief court of appeal against unskilful and dishonest practitioners. In 1616. for instance, one Michael

Eason, having sold "divers sorts of defective apothecaries' wares, which, on trial, were found to be defective, corrupt, and unwholesome for man's body;" and being proved to be "very unfit in making of compositions and confections, and insufficient and unskilful to deal therein," was, by the guild, committed to the Poultry Compter, "in consideration of the great damage and danger which might happen to the company by permitting such enormities."

A long list of notable merchants might be extracted from the roll-books of the Grocers' Company. Sir John Philpot, the brave merchant who, in 1378, fitted out a fleet at his own expense, with which he put down Scottish piracies in his days, and who, for that and other services, was described by Fuller as "the scourge of the Scots, the fright of the French, the delight of the Commons, the darling of the merchants, and the hatred of some envious lords," illustrates the character and influence of a London grocer in Plantagenet times; while the achievements possible to a grocer under the Stuarts are indicated by the work of Sir Thomas Middleton, one of the principal founders of the East India Company.

Yet more illustrious than the grocers' guild was its chief rival, the Mercers' Company. Merceries, originally, were all sorts of articles sold by pedlars and their like, in fairs and market-places, especially small haberdasheries and toys; and mercers gradually rose from wandering about the country with hand-baskets or trays to the keeping of small shops and stalls, and, eventually, to a more extensive line of trading. As early as 1172 there was a guild of mercers in London, and in 1214 Robert Searle, a mercer, was Mayor of London; but for a long while the drapers were more important in the world of commerce than the mercers and the grocers than either. All through the Middle Ages merceries were, theoretically, at any rate, goods weighed by the little balance, and generally sold in retail, while groceries were weighed by the great balance, and usually sold wholesale; but great merchants, who happened to be members of the mercers' guild, soon broke through the barrier. Whittington enriched himself and his craft by trading operations almost as wonderful as the sale of the cat, whose traditional value still lives in the story-books, and much more, the result of intelligent enterprise and painstaking industry. The mercers' guild in London, joined with a dozen kindred associations in country towns, had for an offshoot the Society of Merchant Adventurers of England, which took the lead in foreign commerce during some two centuries. The London guild outlived that offshoot, and had, in later times. members as rich and influential as Geoffrey Bulleyn, the great-grandfather of Queen Elizabeth, the Greshams, and Sir Baptist Hicks, afterwards Lord Camden, the greatest merchant of James I.'s day.

That monopolies like these, in the main, worked well for the development of commerce cannot be doubted. The great trading-guilds have long since ceased to be anything but associations for energetic feasting and the dispensing of charities that have been entrusted to them by good merchants of former generations; but, while they had an active commercial life, the good-fellowship and unity of work that they secured among their members had great and beneficial results. Admission to them, moreover, was not difficult, and in their best days they were only monopolies in so far as they secured peculiar privileges to those who devoted their lives to the worthy following of their several trades and callings. No one could be admitted to a guild who had not served an apprenticeship to one of its freemen, and given proof of his fitness for the business. Good members were encouraged to train up good members. The Lord Mayor's Court had control over all the guilds, and could inquire into and punish any offence charged by one society against another; and, in like manner, within each guild, the complaints of one member against another, of a master against his apprentice, or of an apprentice against his master, were properly investigated. Each had officers empowered to overlook the operations of its freemen, to see that their weights and measures were correct, that they were guilty of no adulterations, and that they practised no fraud.

These monopolies of the great London guilds, and of the kindred associations in other commercial towns, served rather as necessary and useful schools of the trade than as monopolies in any evil sense. If they inflicted some hardships upon unprivileged traders, the hardships were certainly not greater than all traders would have had to submit to, had there been no privileged societies, during the rough centuries of Plantagenet rule; and the guilds—though they did not die as corporations, having a share in municipal arrangements—for the most part quietly passed out of the way, while commerce made its rapid strides in new paths of enterprise under the Tudors. Some efforts were made to maintain their strength by artificial stimulants, and these efforts were sometimes encouraged by kings and parliaments; but they live only in history as relics of mistaken statecraft.

The efforts were greatest in the case of small towns, whose inhabitants, long accustomed to follow some special callings, had constituted themselves into irregular guilds, and sought to preserve for themselves a monopoly in the pursuit of those callings. Thus, in 1530, one of Henry VIII.'s Parliaments passed an Act in favour of the town of Bridport, in Dorsetshire. "The people of that town," it was said in the preamble, "have out of time that no man's mind is to the contrary used to make most part of the cables, hawsers, ropes, and all other tackling, as well for royal ships as for the most part of all other ships within the realm, by reason whereof the town was right well maintained;" but now "the people of the adjacent parts of the said town have set up rope-making, and make slight goods, whereby the prices are greatly enhanced." The logic of that statement, implying that competition caused increase of price and deterioration of quality, is not very intelligible ; but, for some reason or other, it was found that Bridport was "like to be utterly decayed," and accordingly it was ordered that all the hemp grown within five miles of the town was to be sold in it, and that no one outside the limits of the town was to make any sort of rope. Of course, the law was inoperative, save in helping to ruin both Bridport and its suburbs, and in causing the rope manufacture to be transferred from Dorsetshire to Yorkshire.

Another piece of foolish legislation occurred four years later. In 1534 the inhabitants of Worcester, Evesham, Droitwich, Kidderminster, and Bromsgrove, then the only towns in Worcestershire, represented that their former prosperity was being destroyed, because " divers persons dwelling in the hamlets, thorps, and villages of the county made all manner of cloths, and exercised weaving, fulling, and shearing within their own houses, to the great depopulation of the city and towns." Parliament, therefore, enacted that none but the inhabitants of the petitioning towns should be allowed to carry on the trade, " except solely for their own and their families' wearing ; and the result was another gain to Yorkshire, where Leeds, as a centre of inland manufacture, and Hull, as a great seat of maritime trade, were tolerably exempt from legislative interference.

Yorkshire, however, had a similar grievance. In 1544 · the citizens of York complained that their chief business, the manufacture of coverlets and other bed-coverings, was being taken out of their hands, because " sundry evil-disposed persons, apprentices, had withdrawn themselves out of the city into the county, and divers other persons had intermeddled with the said craft." A law was passed in their favour, but York gained nothing by it.

K

The short-sighted policy often adopted by Henry VIII., when Wolsey's wise counsels were lost to him, was pursued by his son and eldest daughter, or rather by the statesmen who directed their affairs. In 1552, for instance, Edward VI.'s advisers ordered that the making of felt and thrummed hats, of coverlets and diapers, should be limited throughout Norfolk to Norwich and the other market towns of the county ; and in 1554 Queen Mary appointed that linen-drapers, woollen-drapers, haberdashers, grocers, and mercers, who were not free of any corporate city and members of its guilds, should not be allowed to sell their wares therein, "excepting in open fairs, and by wholesale."

That is one of the latest instances of legislative interference on behalf of trading-guilds and the monopolies of chartered towns ; but plenty of protection was in more recent times attempted in the interest of special trades and special traders.

A long list might be made of the foolish measures adopted during half-a-dozen centuries for the fancied benefit of wool-dealers and woollen manufacturers in England. Over and over again the trade was limited to special towns. Often the exportation of the raw article was for-bidden altogether, nearly as often were prohibitions put upon the importation of it in a manufactured state ; and in every case, where the enactments could be enforced, the result was present injury, without future benefit. Every sort of meddlesome and mischievous interference was resorted to ; and when the trade itself had come to have tolerable liberty, measures as short-sighted and obnoxious were introduced for its protection against the trades in other textile goods. Allusion has already been made to the opposition offered to cotton manufacture in the eighteenth century. Similar war was waged during a longer period on behalf of wool against silk and linen. Laws were repeatedly made even to regulate the sort of stuff of which cere-cloths were to be made ; the dead must be buried in woollen, instead of linen, in order that the serge-makers might not lose their profit.

Ireland, nearly always the sport of unwise legislation, furnishes countless instances of pernicious interference with trade. Flax being almost indigenous to its northern counties, the whole history of the island might have been different had free trade in linen been allowed to it. For the sake of English wool, however, Irish flax was long restrained, and every sort of hindrance was put upon its cultivation and manufacture. The Earl of Strafford, Charles I.'s luckless supporter, spent £30,000 of his own money in employing Flemish labourers to teach the Irish how to produce and manufacture linen fibre and stuffs, and in erecting factories ; but that benevolent effort was made one of the grounds of his impeachment. "He had obstructed the industry of the country," said his enemies, "by introducing new and unknown processes into the manufacture of flax." Yet, after centuries of such treatment, the people of Ireland are blamed for disaffection, and for backwardness in the race of prosperity.

With restrictive measures of that sort, and with monopolies assigned to districts, towns, trades, and general branches of industry, no fault was found in times long before our own. But monopolies, strictly so called—peculiar privileges granted to single individuals—have always been condemned by wise thinkers. Pliny says that such monopolies are ever prohibited in well-governed countries, and Bacon wrote to the same effect. "Care must be taken," is his advice, "that monopolies, which are the canker of all trading, be not admitted under specious colours of the public good." Yet in Bacon's day these cankers were grievously abundant and prolific of evil. Queen Elizabeth, more intelligent than her father, brother, and sister in general commercial policy, was the first English sovereign to encourage them in any notable degree.

Her reign furnishes a long array of private monopolies. For many of the earlier ones granted by her there was some justification. Thus, in 1565, she issued a charter to Armigail Wade and William Horle for the sole making of brimstone throughout her dominions during thirty years, as well as for the sole right of extracting from certain herbs, roots, and seeds an oil to be employed in cloth-manufacture, "they having, with great labour and application, and not a little expense, found out these useful secrets." And another document of the same date avers that, licenses having previously been granted to certain Dutch or Germans to dig for alum and copperas, as well as for gold, silver, copper, and quicksilver, she now grants to two of her own subjects, Humphreys and Streete, the exclusive right to search for those metals, as well as for lead and tin, and to refine the same, they having brought over twenty skilled foreign work-men for the purpose. The result of that monopoly was the Company of Mines Royal, incorporated in 1568. These foreigners introduced the process of wire-drawing by machinery, none having been produced before in England, save by the inefficient use of the mere hand.

The monopolies granted by Queen Elizabeth during her later years, however, were very numerous, and quite inex-cusable. To recompense her courtiers, or to enrich herself by a share of the profits, she assigned to them exclusive powers of trading in special articles, and these powers being let out to merchants at high rates, vastly increased the price to the public. Parliament protested against these proceed-ings in 1597, and had for an unsatisfactory answer a message from the Queen that, "with regard to these patents, she hoped her dutiful and loving subjects would not take away her prerogative, which was the chief flower in her garden, and the principal head-mark of her crown and diadem, but that they would leave these matters to her disposal." The monopolies increasing, the Parliament of 1601 refused to leave matters at the Queen's disposal. Lawrence Hyde introduced a bill "for the explanation of the common law in certain cases of letters patent," and an angry discussion followed. Bacon, in spite of his objection to monopolies, which has been cited, adopted a courtly tone. "The Queen, as she is our sovereign, hath both an enlarging and a restraining power. By her prerogative she may set at liberty things restrained by statute law or otherwise ; and by her prerogative she may restrain things which be at liberty. With regard to monopolies and such-like, the case hath ever been to humble ourselves unto her Majesty, and by petition desire to have our grievances remedied. I say, and say it again, we ought not to deal, to judge, or to meddle with her Majesty's prerogative." Other speakers took a different tone. The monopolies then in force were enumerated, with vehement protestations of disapproval. Among them were the exclusive right to deal in currants, salt, iron, steel, powder, cards, calf-skins, ox-bones, oil, vinegar, coal, saltpetre, glass, paper, starch, tin, sulphur, dried pilchards, beer, horn, leather, Spanish wool, and Irish yarn. When the list was read out, a member exclaimed, " Is not bread in the number? Yea, I assure you, if affairs go on at this rate, we shall have bread reduced to a monopoly before next Parliament." The evil of these monopolies may be gathered from the fact that salt had been raised in value from sixteen pence to fourteen shillings a bushel. " I know the Queen's prerogative is a thing curiously to be dealt withal," said one speaker ; "yet all grievances are not comparable. I cannot utter with my tongue or conceive with my heart the great grievances that the town and country for which I serve suffereth by some of these monopolies. It bringeth the general profit into a private hand, and the end of all this is beggary and bondage to the subjects. We have a law for the true and faithful currying of leather. There is a patent sets all at liberty, notwithstanding that statute ; but to what purpose is it to do anything by Act of Parliament, when the Queen will undo the same by her prerogative? There is no act of hers that hath been or is more derogatory to her own majesty. more odious to the subject, more dangerous to the commonwealth, than the granting of these monopolies." "I do speak for a town that grieves and pines," exclaimed another member, "for a country that groaneth and languishes under the burden of monstrous and unconscionable monopolies of starch, tin, fish, oil, cloth, vinegar, salt, and I know not what—nay, what not? The principalest commodities, both of my town and country, are engrossed into the hands of these bloodsuckers of the commonwealth. The traffic is taken away, the inward and private commodities are taken away, and dare not be used without the license of these monopolitans. If these bloodsuckers be still let alone, to suck up the best commodities which the earth there hath given us, what will become of us, from whom the fruits of our own soil and the commodities of our own labour, for which, with the sweat of our brows, even up to the knees in mire and dirt, we have laboured, shall be taken by warrant of supreme authority, which the poor subject dare not gainsay?"

Queen Elizabeth's answer to these angry complaints would have been a model of royal yielding to popular rebuke, had it been quite honest and completely acted upon. "Gentlemen," she said, "I owe you hearty thanks and commendations for your singular goodwill towards me, not only in your hearts and thoughts, but which you have openly expressed and declared, whereby you have recalled me from an error proceeding from my ignorance, not my will. These things had undoubtedly turned to my disgrace—to whom nothing is more dear than the safety alone of my people—had not such harpies and horse-leeches as these been made known and discovered to me by you. I had rather my heart and hand should perish, than that either my heart or hand should

allow such privileges to monopolists as may be prejudicial
to my people."

Only some of the obnoxious monopolies, however, were
withdrawn, and therewith the Commons had to be content
during the brief remainder of Elizabeth's reign. Others were
annulled, on his accession, by James I., who in his opening
speech to Parliament made virtuous show of toleration in
commercial as well as other matters : but plenty of fresh
monopolies were soon granted by him, and others followed
all through the course of his reign. They formed, indeed,
an important section of the constitutional battle-ground on
which he and his son were met again and again, and ever
with growing force on the side of the people, by the
champions of national liberty. The struggle, familiar to
readers of political history, need not here be detailed. Its
two great victories were in 1624 and 1640. In the former
year Parliament declared, and James I. was forced to agree,
that no patents of monopoly were legal except those granted,
"for fourteen years and no more, for new-invented manufactures and arts, never practised before and not mischievous
to the State." That limitation—which was the beginning of
the present patent law, considered by most statesmen to afford
only reasonable recompense to inventors for their achievements—was crippled, however, by a load of exceptions. All
charters already granted, or to be granted, to towns and
public companies were held to be exempt from it. Printing
was still recognised as a monopoly of the Crown, and, with a
little less injustice, the right of making arms, gunpowder,
and other munitions of war, seeing that these were especially
under the control of the State. Particular exceptions were
also made in favour of two important patents—one granted to
Sir Robert Mansell for the manufacture of glass, and another
granted to Edward, Lord Digby, for smelting iron with coal.
To these legalised monopolies a crowd of illegal ones were
added by James I., and yet more by Charles I. At length in

1639 the grievance became so great that Parliament protested with more than usual vehemence. In that year Charles I. was compelled to cancel twenty-seven monopolies, which were reckoned to yield him an annual revenue of £200,000. In 1640 the Long Parliament, as one of its first acts, abolished all the rest, and from that time monopolies of this sort came to an end in England.

A few of the most noteworthy privileges granted by James I. and Charles I. to private traders may here be enumerated. They illustrate, not only one phase of royal interference with trade, but also the directions that were being taken by commercial activity.

In 1608, the manufacture of alum in England having been for the first time successfully practised under the patronage of Lord Sheffield, Sir John Bourcher, and other gentlemen of Yorkshire, a patent was accorded to them, and all importation of alum from foreign countries was prohibited. On the strength of that monopoly, Sir Paul Pinder, who succeeded to it, was able, in 1625, to lend to Charles I. a sum of £130,000—all which he lost through the civil wars.

In 1618 we find a patent granted to Sir John Gilbert "for the sole making and vending of an instrument, which he calls a water-plough, for the taking-up of sand and gravel out of the river Thames and other rivers and havens, and of an engine, also invented by him, for the raising of water in greater quantity than is heretofore known, to be moved and drawn either by some stream of water, or, for want of that, by strength of horses." And in the same year David Ramsay and Thomas Wildgate obtained charters for "the sole use and benefit of certain inventions and discoveries made by them ; first, for ploughing land without horses or oxen ; second, for improving of barren grounds ; third, for raising of water from any low place to the houses of noblemen and gentlemen, and to cities and towns ; and, fourth, to make boats for the carriage of burthens and passengers, to run upon the water, as swift in calms and more swift in storms than boats full-sailed in great winds." That last seems to have been a rude anticipation, doubtless unsuccessful, of the steam-engine.

Many of the monopolies granted by Charles I. were for worthless or sham inventions, which could only have been profitable to their producers in so far as they were able to dupe those to whom they sold them. Thus, in 1625, we find William Beale, a London goldsmith, agreeing to pay forty shillings a year to the King, for " the sole making and practice of certain compound stuffs, extracted out of certain minerals, called by the name of cement, or dressing, for ships, to prevent them from burning in fights at sea, and also from the sea-worm or barnacle." In 1632, again, a physician obtained a string of useless patents, one being for "a movable hydraulic, like a cabinet, which, being placed in a room or by a bedside, causeth sweet sleep to those, who, by hot fevers or otherwise, cannot take rest; and it alters the dry, hot air into a moistening and cooling temper, either with musical sounds or without."

Other monopolies were the beginnings of great manufacturing improvements; instance that granted in 1627 to Lord Dacre and two others, "for the sole making of steel, according to the invention of Thomas Letsome." Another patent of the same year was assigned to Thomas Rouse and Abraham Cullen, " for the sole making of stone pots, jugs, and bottles." A third was issued to Sir John Hachet and Octavius Strada, "for rendering sea-coal and pit-coal as useful as charcoal for burning in houses without offence by the smell."

Two other and very different patents concerning coal were granted by Charles I. The old prejudice against its use as a substitute for wood-fuel—which, in Edward I.'s reign, had caused a man to be hanged for burning it in

London—had been overcome, and by this time trade in it was becoming important. Serious injury, therefore, threatened to result from Charles's assignment to Sir Thomas Tempest and his partners of the exclusive right of selling all the coal exported from Newcastle-on-Tyne during twenty-one years from 1637, and yet more from his incorporation, in 1638, of a company of coal-monopolisers, empowered to buy all the produce of Newcastle, Sunderland, and Berwick, and to sell it in London for any price not exceeding the very high rate of seventeen shillings a chaldron in summer-time and nineteen shillings in winter—one shilling a chaldron being the King's share of the profit. But the Long Parliament put an end to that grievance, along with a thousand others; although coal still illustrates the vice of monopolies, by reason of the unnecessarily high price put upon it in order that the Corporation of London may be enriched by the duties it is empowered to levy on every ton brought into the Thames.

Another illustration is furnished by the printing-monopoly, happily now obsolete, which was reserved to the Crown by the Parliament of 1624, and which was long maintained, having begun long before. William Caxton, who abandoned his trade as a mercer to set up, in 1477, the first printing-press in England, did so under the patronage of the abbot of Westminster, and bore the title of *Regius Impressor* to Richard III. During forty years his craft, and that of his successors, was encouraged by Church and State, and, instead of any efforts to interfere with liberty of printing, praiseworthy attempts were made to increase the number of books produced in England, or brought from abroad for English reading.

The Reformation disturbed this arrangement, but it could not break down the theory that had fastened itself in people's minds, that printing was a business specially subject to the King's control and to priestly regulation.

Bold books began to be printed in Henry VIII.'s reign, and immediately all the weight of authority was brought to bear against the publication of everything obnoxious to the men in power. Cardinal Wolsey shrewdly warned his clergy in convocation that, if they did not put down printing, they would themselves be put down by it; and the prophecy was partly fulfilled, in his own case, at any rate. His downfall must be in some measure ascribed to the popularity of a fierce pamphlet, "The Supplication of Beggars," which he vainly attempted to suppress. The censorship of the press was a direct outcome of Papal influence, but was not abrogated in England when the authority of the Pope was repudiated. In 1526 Henry VIII. condemned anti-Popery books, and all who traded in them, as heretical; and in 1535 all books favouring Popery were denounced by him in like terms. Many lost their lives during his reign for printing or importing works favouring Lutheran doctrines, or any opinions of which he did not approve, and his successors perfected the tyranny in literature which he initiated.

The Stationers' Company was incorporated by Queen Mary, as the sole agency for the printing and publication of books, and with full inquisitorial powers for maintaining its prerogatives. The Company was authorised to search the house of every printer, bookseller, and bookbinder, whenever it thought fit, and to seize or destroy any book which it there found, either obnoxious to the State or prejudicial to its own interest. It was made custodian of the national mind, and every one was ordered to aid it in its functions. "Whosoever finds books of heresy, sedition, and treason," runs what Strype calls "a short but terrible proclamation" of Queen Mary's, "and does not forthwith burn the same, without showing or reading them to any other person, shall be executed for a rebel." The national standard of "heresy, sedition, and treason" changed greatly when Elizabeth succeeded to Mary. There was not quite so much severity shown towards Catholic books as had just before been shown towards Protestant publications; but the functions and powers of the Stationers' Company were quite as great. It was held responsible for "any unruly printer who might endanger the Church and State," and was to search everywhere for "unlawful and heretical books." And every book was declared to be unlawful which had not, before printing, been "licensed by her Majesty by express words in writing, or by six of her Privy Council."

In that way began the thraldrom of the press, which lasted through all the period of Stuart misrule, and weighed heavily on England during the times of its greatest intellectual activity—the times of Shakespeare, Bacon, and Milton. A decree of the Star Chamber, in 1586, further limited the number of printing-presses; it provided that none should be set up out of London, save at the two Universities, and that all of those sanctioned should be lodged in convenient places, where they could always be readily inspected by the agents of the Stationers' Company. Later enactments, and more or less illegal injunctions, sought constantly to stem and guide the current of literature that poured forth, in spite of all restraints. The only lessening of the monopoly of the Stationers' Company came from the granting of special monopolies to particular individuals. One establishment had the exclusive right of printing Bibles, another had all the law-books, another all the "almanacs and prognostications." One private gentleman procured a monopoly of grammars and other school-books, and none could be published without fees to him, whereby the price was greatly increased. So it was in a hundred cases. The errors of Elizabeth's reign were exaggerated in those of James I. and Charles I., and they were not abolished by the Long Parliament, notwithstanding Milton's famous exposition, in his "Areopagitica," of their futility and injustice.

Restrictions on printing, and efforts to convert the press

into a mere instrument of political and religious partisanship, were yet greater after the Restoration. In 1662 was passed an Act of Parliament "for preventing abuses in printing seditious, treasonable, and unlicensed books and pamphlets, and for regulating printing and printing-presses," which confirmed all the old privileges of the Stationers' Company, limited the number of master printers to twenty, and assigned the filling up of any vacancies in that number to the Archbishop of Canterbury and the Bishop of London; and this Act was several times renewed by Charles II., and left undisturbed by William III. during six years. It was abolished, and freedom of the press began, in 1694, though its complete attainment is only very modern. The special provisions made for preventing seditious and blasphemous publications have subjected printers and publishers to a supervision which has often served as a handle for the persecution of persons obnoxious to the men in power. It can easily be understood why this vestige of tyranny has survived, chiefly in connection with newspapers and political periodicals.

The Stationers' Company, made influential mainly by its employment as a sort of literary police agency to the Crown, quickly lost most of its importance after the withdrawal of the printing-monopoly. Some special privileges remained with it, however, and of these the exclusive privilege of publishing almanacks, shared by it with Oxford and Cambridge Universities, illustrates the mischief of monopolies. For a long time *Moore's Almanac* and *Poor Richard's Almanac*, issued with the imprimatur of the Arch bishop of Canterbury, were the best publications of this sort produced in England. "It would be difficult to find," it has been truly said, "in so small a compass such a quantity of ignorance, profligacy, and imposture as was condensed in these publications." A hundred years ago a bookseller named Carnan issued an almanack which the Stationers' Company failed to suppress, and a legal decision in 1775 theoretically abolished the monopoly. But it was practically maintained through the wealth of the Company, whereby it was enabled to buy up, if it could not crush, all rival publications, till 1828, when the Society for the Diffusion of Useful Knowledge started the *British Almanac*, and it opened the gates for free trade in almanacks of all sorts.

Another monopoly, still theoretically vested in the Crown, concerns the publication of the Authorised Version of the Bible. That the head of the Church should take especial care of the sacred volume, and see that the copies of it supplied to his subjects were complete and trustworthy, is not to be wondered at. But if this was ever thought of as a justification for the Bible monopoly, its results were as unsatisfactory as those of all other monopolies. The privilege of printing Bibles has always been reserved to the King's Printer and Oxford University; but the privilege was very soon abused, and two hundred years ago English Protestantism seemed likely, by help of it, to be deprived of its main source of strength. The University Press was idle, and the office of King's Printer being retained in one careless family, the Bibles issued were so faulty that they were hardly legible, and when legible could not be relied upon. One important text was, in the edition of 1653, printed, " Know ye not that the unrighteous" (instead of "righteous") "shall inherit the kingdom of God?"   "Fie! for shame!" exclaimed old Fuller, with good reason.   "Considering with myself the causes of the growth and increase of impiety and profaneness in our land, amongst others this seemeth to me not the least, the late many false and erroneous impressions of the Bible. Now know, what is but carelessness in other books is impiety in setting forth of the Bible." The books, moreover, were, in consequence of the monopoly, so expensive that ordinary persons could not afford to buy them. It was reserved for Thomas Guy, the eccentric bookseller who left his wealth to found the hospital in Southwark that bears his name, to bring about a better state of things. As a good Christian and a shrewd tradesman, he resolved to provide better and cheaper Bibles for his countrymen. He employed an agent in Holland, who bought for him good paper and fine types, and entrusted them to competent Dutch printers, who had not yet lost the skill in printing which Caxton had learnt from their forefathers, and introduced into England two centuries before. In this way correct Bibles were produced, and, being smuggled over to England, Guy was able to sell great numbers of them at a low price, and yet with good profit to himself. Other booksellers took up the trade, and made money by it, before the monopolists began to protect their vested rights. "This trade," says the old historian, "proving not only very detrimental to the public revenue, but likewise to the King's Printer, all ways and means were devised to quash the same, which being vigorously put in execution, the booksellers, by frequent seizures and prosecutions, became so great sufferers, that they judged a further pursuit thereof inconsistent with their interest." Thomas Guy, shrewder than the rest, did not so judge ; but he bethought him of a better way of carrying on his well-meant enterprise. After much persuasion, he induced the University of Oxford to farm its monopoly to him ; and then, bringing over Dutch types and Dutch workmen, he started a busy little printing-office in his shop at the corner of Lombard Street. There he began to make his fortune, and to do good service to religion and literature, by issuing a large supply of cheap Bibles, in the name of the Oxford University. The monopoly being thus evaded, Bibles continued to be good, cheap, and plentiful; and in later times it has been held in abeyance.

Other monopolies, of much greater commercial importance, have also been suppressed. Contemporary with the crowd of personal licenses of exclusive trade granted by Queen Elizabeth and the early Stuarts, were the monopolies assigned

to the great trading-companies which grew out of the enterprise of sixteenth and seventeenth century merchants and
adventurers. The greatest of all, the East India Company,
started in 1600—has been already referred to. Several like
associations had been founded earlier, the chief being the
Turkey or Levant Company, dating from 1581, and others
—notably those which led the way to the colonisation of the
United States—followed in quick succession. Each had
special privileges of trade with special districts, and the
monopolies assigned to them were necessary and, at first.
wholly beneficial. In the presence of hostile fleets, it would
have been impossible for single traders, unprotected by the
State, to carry on the extensive occupations upon which these
companies entered; and, under the political arrangements
that then prevailed, State protection was not to be expected
without payment being made for it. Therefore these new
monopolies were founded, and the result has been the steady
growth of our vast colonial empire, and an increase, proportionately vast, of the commercial enterprise of England.

The history of these various companies forms an important section of the history of English progress during the past
three centuries. Not always successful, not rarely dishonour-
able, their main issues have been wonderfully advantageous,
and their careers have generally been marked by fewer
blemishes than might have been expected. If in any case it
can be considered that bad means are justified by good ends,
the misdeeds of the East India Company, especially, have
been fully excused. With indomitable energy, it overcame
the resistance of foreign rivals—Portuguese, Dutch, and
French—and the hardly less formidable opposition of enemies
at home, and, at last, in 1858, surrendered to the English
Crown those charters which had enabled it to secure a
dominion far greater and more important than any other
corporation of traders has ever succeeded in obtaining.

Most of the old rivals of the East India Company died

long before it. The story of the only one that outlived it furnishes a singular contrast to its progress. It was by futile efforts to discover a north-west passage to India that the northern parts of America were first made known ; and the greatest, after the Cabots and Frobisher, of the explorers whose accidental work was so advantageous was Henry Hudson. By him, before his death, in 1611, were discovered Hudson's Straits and Hudson's Bay, and the vast coast of that great sea Others followed in his track, and in 1668 Prince Rupert fitted out a vessel designed to put to use the extensive territories that had hitherto been only nominally subject to the English Crown. The expedition succeeded, and in 1670 the Hudson's Bay Company, with Prince Rupert at its head, was formed, for appropriation of the Hudson's Bay Territory, or Prince Rupert's Land, as it was then called. The charter issued by Charles II. granted to the Company " the sole trade and commerce of all those seas, straits, bays, rivers, lakes, creeks, and sounds, in whatsoever latitude they shall be, that lie within the entrance of the straits com- monly called Hudson's Straits, together with all the lands, countries, and territories upon the coasts and confines of the seas, straits, bays, lakes, rivers, creeks, and sounds aforesaid, which are not now actually possessed by any of our subjects, or by the subjects of any other Christian prince or state." A monopoly of trade to all regions reached, across land or water, by passing through this territory, as well as lordship over all, was also assigned to the Hudson's Bay Company, which thus had ownership, for nearly two centuries, of more than 3,000,000 square miles of land, an area thrice as large as that of India.

The use made by the Company of its monopoly has been strangely disproportionate to the vastness of the territory assigned to it. Much of this territory, it is true, was too near to the arctic regions, barren and frozen, to be of value, and a large section was quickly claimed by the

L

French settlers in Canada as their property, by virtue of an older charter; and with that which remained it was impossible for a great trade to be rapidly developed, as was the case with the East India Company's operations. But much more might have been done than was ever attempted by the Hudson's Bay Company. All the vice of monopoly granting appeared in its working. A settlement was soon formed at Rupert River, near the southern corner of Hudson's Bay, and stations and factories were founded in its neighbourhood, for carrying on a trade in furs with the Indian tribes there resident; and this trade proved so lucrative, yielding sometimes as much as fifty per cent. profit in a year, that the shareholders preferred to keep it all in their own hands, rather than admit fresh capitalists, and so found another great English colony. That they managed their affairs successfully, as far as their own interests were concerned, cannot be doubted. Their gains continued, in spite of long warfare with the French Canadians, who repeatedly attacked and sometimes destroyed their forts during twenty years previous to the Peace of Ryswick, and their position was only made strong by the Treaty of Utrecht in 1713. Through the eighteenth century the Company had a lazy course of money-making, generally sending three ships every year from London to Rupert River, which exchanged guns, gunpowder, brandy, and coarse clothing, for furs, feathers, and like native produce. Little enterprise was needed to induce the neighbouring Indian tribes to collect these articles and bring them to the factories, to be bartered for the powder and shot with which they could kill their enemies, and the spirits with which they found pleasure in killing themselves. In 1742 four-pennyworth of brandy could purchase a beaver-skin valued at about nine shillings, or the same article might be procured with a pound of shot, or four ounces of powder.

The immorality of this trade was not found fault with;

but repeated complaints were made that it was not opened up to others who wished to join in it. " The Company's four factories," it was said, in 1749, by one of its agents, "contain only one hundred and thirty servants, and two small houses with only eight men in each. There are incontestable evidences of rich copper and lead mines ; yet the Company gives no encouragement for working them, nor for their servants going into the inland countries. If the least evidence had been suffered to transpire that the climate is very habitable, the soil rich and fruitful, fit both for corn and for cattle, rich in mines, and the fisheries capable of great improvements, the Legislature would have taken the matter into its own hands, and would have settled the country, and laid the trade open for the benefit of Britain. The Company, therefore, have contented themselves with dividing a large profit upon a small capital amongst only about one hundred persons, and have not only endeavoured to keep the true state of the trade and country an impenetrable secret, but have also industriously propagated the worst impressions of them."

That policy prevailed till early in the present century, when the exclusive claims of the Hudson's Bay Company were boldly attacked. A North-west Company was founded, with powers to carry on its trade in the unused portions of Prince Rupert's Land ; and a Quebec Fur Company, claiming to be older than even the Hudson's Bay Company, but which had long confined its operations to trade with the Indians bordering upon Canada, now became more active. The rivalship of the three companies, sometimes issuing in bloodshed, and often involving great loss of property, had very beneficial results. Their agents pressed on into the far West. Exploring parties were formed, and fertile districts were discovered, until the whole vast belt of North America was traversed, and the wealth of British Columbia and Vancouver's Island began to be opened up. The feuds died out, but not the enterprise, in 1821, when the North-west Company was merged into the Hudson's Bay Company. The venerable monopolists had been forced to discern the importance of their possessions, and more adequate use was made of them. In 1837 the Hudson's Bay Company, with a capital of £400,000, and in the hands of two hundred and thirty-nine proprietors, had a hundred and thirty-six separate establishments, extending east and west from Labrador and the Atlantic Ocean to British Columbia and the Pacific, and north and south from the boundaries of Canada and the United States to Baffin's Bay and the Arctic Ocean. Its factors, clerks, and servants, stationed at these settlements, then numbered some fourteen hundred, and their business was to trade with the native population scattered over the vast area, and estimated at about ninety thousand. That was a wonderful advance upon the earlier activity; but it was patent to all the world that the advance was due solely to violations of the Company's monopoly, and the abolition of that monopoly came to be regarded as a necessary step in the development of British North America. British Columbia and Vancouver's Island were wrested from it, and established as separate and flourishing colonies in 1857, and in 1868 an Act was passed by the English Parliament sanctioning the transfer of all its remaining territory and trading privileges to the new Dominion of Canada.

Almost the only monopolies now tolerated by Englishmen are those granted for a limited period to inventors, and those guardedly assigned to railway companies, gas companies, and the like, which need capital and enterprise impossible to private traders, and hardly to be risked without special protection by the State, but which receive that protection under conditions designed to render the monopolies harmless, and to cause their withdrawal whenever they cease to be beneficial to the community.

CHAPTER VII.

SCIENCE IN TRADE.

THE relations of politics to trade show a varied course of benefits and injuries, the injuries being generally wrought by local prejudice, class tyranny, and other outcomes of political temper at variance with all true principles of political economy, the benefits, unless accidental, being the result of wise use of experience in overturning the follies of the past. The relations of science to trade, on the other hand, show an even course of progress. "Founders of states, generals, great lawgivers," as Lord Bacon said, "were, with much noise, honoured as demigods, such as were Hercules, Theseus, Minos, Romulus; but inventors and discoverers of new arts to benefit man's life were ever consecrated as gods themselves, as Ceres, Mercury, Apollo. One was mixed with strife and perturbation, confined to one nation or age; but the latter hath the true character of Divine presence, coming *in aurâ leni*, without noise or agitation."

So noiselessly came most of the inventions and dis-coveries of the old world that their authors and even the time of their commencement are unknown. Ceres, Mercury, and Apollo live only in mythology as heavenly patrons of the agriculture, trade, and physic of the ancients. For thousands of years man has been gradually advancing in scientific skill, and by it commerce has gradually been made easier and more extensive. All the principles of scientific research and application were long ago, in a rude way, at any rate, laid down, and their benefits appeared in the modes pursued for cultivating and fertilising the ground, for sowing crops and gathering them in, for building houses and making apparel, for weaving and dyeing, for carrying goods across land and sea, and the like. But the wonderful growth of science that has taken place in recent genera-tions has necessarily had a wonderful effect on commercial activity; and the achievements of science as a promoter of trade have, during these generations, been very much more notable than in former times. Science awoke from a long slumber in Francis Bacon's day, and, partly at his call; and concurrent with its progress in abstract speculations has been the development of commerce through wise use of those speculations.

This development is in England very intimately con-nected with the history of the Royal Society, in whose charter of incorporation, issued in 1662, Charles II. is made to utter sentiments altogether absurd as an expression of his own temper, but quaintly indicative of the way in which science and commerce were to go hand-in-hand. "Out of paternal care of our people," it was there written, "we re-solve, together with those laws which tend to the well adminis-tration of government and the people's allegiance to us,

inseparably to join the supreme law of *Salus Populi*, that
obedience may be manifestly, not only the public, but the
private felicity of every subject, and the great concern of his
satisfactions and enjoyments in this life. The way to so
happy a government we are sensible is in no manner more
facilitated than by promoting of useful arts and sciences,
which, upon mature inspection, are found to be the basis of
civil communities and free governments, and which gather
multitudes by an Orphean charm into cities and connect
them in companies ; that so, by laying in a stock, as it were,
of several arts and methods of industry, the whole body may
be supplied by a mutual commerce of each other's peculiar
faculties, and, consequently, that the various miseries and
toils of this frail life may be, by as many various expedients
ready at hand, remedied or alleviated, and wealth and plenty
diffused in just proportion to every one's industry—that is,
to every one's deserts."

The annals of the Royal Society abound in evidence of
the ways, great and little, direct and indirect, in which it
helped on the growth of commerce. Thus we find it, in
January, 1663, recommending the adoption of measures " to
extend the growth of apple and pear trees, for making cider
all over England ;" and in the following March urging its
supporters " to plant potatoes, and to persuade their friends
to do the same, in order to alleviate the distress which would
accompany a scarcity of food." It was to the Royal Society
that, in 1687, Denis Papin, then its curator, propounded his
discovery of the motive power of steam, the simplest and
the most valuable discovery by which the world has ever
been enriched, but one that had to be made over and over
again, before and after Papin's day, before its value was appre-
ciated. Papin's idea of a steam-pump was crude enough,
but it contained the principle upon which all subsequent
extensions of the use of steam are based. In 1708 Papin
himself so far extended it as to be able to inform the Society

of a newly-invented boat, to be rowed by oars moved with heat; and, though this boat seems never to have been actually made, Newton not only approved of the theory, but hinted at its employment in many other ways in which the steam-engine is now used.

The establishment of the Society of Arts and other off-shoots of the Royal Society, more distinctly aiming at the employment of science in the service of commerce, has rendered it unnecessary for the parent institution now to turn aside from its abstract studies and give advice about cider-making and potato-growing. But every page in its two centuries' history shows how even the most abstract studies have a distinctly practical bearing. " You owe to experimental philosophy some of the most important and peculiar of your advantages," said Sir Humphry Davy, whose own safety-lamp and other inventions aptly illustrate the value of science to commerce. " It is not by foreign conquests that you are become great, but by a conquest of Nature in your own country. It is not so much by colonisation that you have attained your pre-eminence or wealth, but by the cultivation of the riches of your own soil. Why are you able to supply the world with a thousand articles of iron and steel necessary for the purposes of life? It is by arts derived from chemistry and mechanics, and founded purely upon experiments. Why is the steam-engine now carrying on operations which formerly employed in painful and humiliating labour thousands of our robust peasantry, who are now more nobly or more usefully serving their country? It is in consequence of experiments upon the nature of heat and pure physical investigations. In every part of the world manufactures made from the mere clay and pebbles of your soil may be found ; and to what is this owing? To chemical arts and experiments. You have excelled all other people in the products of industry, but why? Because you have assisted industry by science."

Some of the most important applications of science to trade, however, began by accident, and were initiated by men whose only science was common sense, aided by a quick eye and a ready hand. There are a hundred stories like that told of Samuel Astbury, the Staffordshire potter, who, going to London in 1720, halted for the night either at Banbury or at Dunstable. There something was found to be wrong with one of his horse's eyes, and, as a rude remedy, the ostler thrust a flint into the fire, and, as soon as it was red-hot, flung it into a basin of water, whereby it was easily reduced to a fine white powder, some of which was applied to the injured eye. Astbury watched the process, and at once shrewdly guessed that here was the solution to a riddle that had long perplexed him. Strong and well-shapen pottery he could produce, but its beauty was spoilt by its dirty colour. Astbury sent home a cartload of flint stones, and, after his return, had them fired and pulverised. He mixed the powder with pipeclay and water, washed his dirty ware with it, and was delighted, after final baking, to find it come out white and shining. He afterwards improved upon his invention by introducing the calcined flint into the body of the ware, and his expedient soon came to be universally adopted.

The value of science to commerce is well illustrated, in one way at any rate, by the progress of the pottery trade in England. Babylonians, Egyptians, and Etruscans excelled in the manufacture of earthenware, and it was more or less rudely practised by all nations as soon as they emerged from their primitive barbarism. In Britain it began in times unknown, and by the very favourable soil of the Staffordshire district the ingenious workmen of the Celtic, Roman, Saxon, and Plantagenet periods were tempted there especially to cultivate the art. In the towns and villages some eight or ten labourers would club together, and make such coarse articles as they had skill for, and as their neighbours cared

to buy. " In the wilder districts of the moorlands," says the
biographer of Wedgwood, the prince of potters, "a pot-work
would be carried on by the joint exertions of a single man
and his son, or a labourer.   The one dug the necessary clay,
the other fashioned and lined the ware, whilst the mother or
daughter, when the goods were ready, loaded the panniered
asses, and took her way to distant town and hamlet, till her
merchandise was sold.   She then returned with shop-goods
to the solitary pot-work.   In places of this kind were only
produced the very coarsest descriptions of ware, such as
crocks, pitchers, slab-like baking-dishes and porringers, all
of which were partially glazed with lead ore.   Their owners
were a rude and lawless set, half-poachers, half-gipsies, who
met at fairs and markets, and occasionally held drunken
revels in the wilder parts of their own districts."   Under the
Tudors and the Stuarts this state of things was gradually
improved upon.   From common labourers, the ablest workmen rose to be master potters, and they often sent their
sons to study in the potteries of Holland, and so bring home
experience to be used in improving the English art.   There
was rude science in that long first period of pot-making ; but
in England no great scientific advance was made till less
than two centuries ago.

Long before that it had begun on the Continent.   The
Dutch were the first great potters for Europe, and Delft-
ware, the name of which shows its origin, was for a long
time the best that could be procured.   Vast improvement
grew out of the enterprise of the early traders to the far
East, who brought home the delicate porcelain of China and
Japan, which native traders quickly sought to imitate.   Bernard Palissy, the great Frenchman, spent sixteen years in
conquering the secret of the white enamel, hitherto peculiar
to the china of China ; and out of his enterprise, well imitated by others, grew the famous factories of Sèvres and
Dresden.

Improved pottery came to England with the Dutch and Huguenot immigrants of the sixteenth and seventeenth centuries. Two brothers, named Elers, in particular, arrived from Germany, and set up a manufactory near Burslem, employing the most stupid persons they could find to do the drudgery, and keeping the finer parts for their own manipulation in secret. They managed to produce pottery far superior to any before known in Staffordshire, and their very efforts at concealment naturally aroused the jealous curiosity of the English workmen round about. One especially, Samuel Astbury, resolved to discover their secret. Disguising himself, and pretending to be half an idiot, he obtained employment from them, and affected such utter ignorance and incompetence that he was by degrees allowed to watch all their movements, and make himself master of their plans for imitating the red unglazed ware of Japan, and for producing the black ware since known as Egyptian—two varieties in which earlier Englishmen had been quite unskilled. That done, Astbury threw off his disguise, left his masters, and set up a rival establishment of his own. Therein he throve famously, partly by the discovery of the use of calcined flint, which has been described. Others followed in his lead, made further improvements, and occasioned a wonderful growth of the Staffordshire potteries.

Of these younger men by far the most notable was Astbury's nephew by marriage, Josiah Wedgwood. Born at Burslem in 1730, he began his trade in a humble pot-work that had belonged to his family during several generations. That business, however, descended to his brothers, and in 1751 or 1752 he became manager for another potter, in whose service he began to make considerable improvements in the shape, colour, and consistency of the snuff-boxes, pickle-dishes, tea, coffee, and chocolate pots, and candlesticks, that were the staples of his employer's trade. The more artistic work on which his heart was set he was not

allowed to engage in. Therefore, as soon as he had saved
money enough, in 1759, he started in business on his own
account. He made tea-services, vases, white tiles for fire-
places, and other articles, ornamenting them with raised
figures of animals and the like, composed of coloured clay;
and these were so well received that in little more than a
year he was able to double his business, and to make bolder
efforts at the advancement of his art. " He had for a considerable period," says Miss Meteyard, his biographer,
"turned his attention to the improvement of the ordinary
cream-coloured ware; he now concentrated all his energies
in this one direction. Every essential of the body, glaze,
form, and ornament was alike the object of his care. But
through the various necessary processes his patience was
often sorely tried, and his repeated failures were most dis-
heartening. One kiln after another was pulled down, in
order to correct some defect, or effect some necessary improvement. His losses from this source alone were, at this
period, very heavy, and the ware itself was often destroyed
before he could bring his firing processes to the requisite
degree of perfection. His chemical combinations often
baffled him, and his experiments, both in body and in glaze,
would, after the greatest pains, turn out entire failures. He
had to invent, and, if not that, to improve, every tool, instrument, and apparatus, and to seek for smiths and mechanics
to work under his guidance. He often passed the whole
day at the bench beside his men, and in many cases instructed them individually. Unwearied and indomitable in
spirit, he persevered, and success came." By the end of
1761 his main object was gained. He had found the way
of making cream-ware lighter, brighter, and in every way
much more perfect than any that had been produced before.

There was a ready market for it in England, but a large
quantity found its way to America, by way of Liverpool,
where Wedgwood's chief agent in disposing of it was

Thomas Bentley, a young and noble-hearted merchant. A firm friendship grew up between the maker and the dealer, and the result was their joining in partnership, as managers of the new and famous works set up by them at Etruria, near Burslem, in 1767. "If you think you could really fall in love with and make a mistress of this new business, as I have done," wrote Wedgwood to Bentley, in a characteristic letter, proposing the partnership, "I should have little or no doubt of your success; for, if we consider the great variety of colours in our raw materials, the infinite ductility of clay, and that we have universal beauty to copy, we have certainly the fairest prospect of enlarging this branch of manufacture to our wishes; and, as genius will not be wanting, I am firmly persuaded that our profits will be in proportion to our application. I am as confident that it would be, beyond comparison, more congenial and delightful to every particle of matter, sense, and spirit in your composition to be the creator, as it were, of beauty, rather than merely the vehicle or medium to convey it from one hand to another." That letter shows with what high and worthy views Wedgwood pursued his calling. Bentley was a fit partner for him. Under their guidance Etruria throve wonderfully. Bentley soon settled in London, to carry on, through the London market, a busy trade with all the world. That trade had become very great before Bentley's early death in 1780. It continued to thrive, and to have ever fresh impetus from Wedgwood's continued improvements in his art, during the ensuing fifteen years. Dying in 1795, he had brought the manufacture of earthenware to so excellent a state that there has been little for his successors to do besides following in his steps. The scientific methods that he brought to bear upon English pot-making have converted a rude craft into a noble art, and, besides gratifying the refinements of life among rich and luxurious persons at home, have added another staple to British trade with foreign countries, and by many times multiplied the prosperity of the Staffordshire district in which the manufacture is chiefly carried on.

Other great English manufactures, however, show yet more strikingly the trade-value of science, and its marvellous development in modern times. All our principal manufactures have been revolutionised by scientific improvements in machinery, and the improved construction of machinery has been made possible by the discovery of scientific processes in the extraction and use of coal.

Coal was dug up and employed in manufactures, as well as in domestic ways, by the Roman civilisers of Britain. Coal-cinders were found in the buried city of Uriconium, now Wroxeter, which was discovered a few years ago ; and a huge cinder-heap, supposed to be a relic of Roman times, used to exist at Aston, a suburb of Birmingham, while in Wednesbury Old Field, another of its suburbs, have been found numerous ancient coal-pits, "which," says the local historian, "the curious antiquarian would deem as long in sinking as the mountain of cinders in rising." Coal seems to have been also employed by the Anglo-Saxons and their successors in their rude workmanship ; and early in the Middle Ages Newcastle began to be famous for its supply of the fuel which, in spite of prejudice, expressed in Acts of Parliament as well as in popular outcries, was gradually coming into fashion as a substitute for wood, already growing scarce. But till very recent times the coal was only shovelled up from those fields in which it was most easy of access ; and the lack of better means of obtaining it was a hindrance to its extensive application in manufacturing ways. Those hindrances were overcome by the same scientific energy to which the direct development of the manufactures was due.

The first great difficulty experienced by the coal-workers, as soon as they had picked all the outermost portions of their mineral store, was the flooding of the remainder with

water, which for a long time they had no better means of
removing than the old-fashioned air-pump, quite unequal to
such extensive work. Several attempts were made during
the seventeenth century to provide a more suitable instrument; but the first of any practical value, and that only a
suggestion which others had to perfect, was Thomas Savery's
"fire-engine," made in 1698, and based on an independent
discovery of the motive-power of steam, Papin's discovery
having occurred some ten years before. In this engine, a
cylindrical vessel filled with steam was plunged into the
water, which by its coldness at once condensed the steam,
and rushed through a valve to fill the vacuum, where, its
egress being prevented by a clack, it was forced out through
a stand-pipe by a fresh blast of steam, and so fitted for re-
immersion in the water, while that previously sucked up was
being drained away. The ingenious machine enabled a boy
to do easily as much pumping as had previously given
laborious occupation to twenty or thirty men; but it was
quickly superseded through Newcomen's invention, in 1705,
of his "atmospheric engine," in which the steam was made
to work a piston, and the work of pumping was greatly
facilitated. Newcomen's machine was also soon improved
upon, and other improvements followed, until they culminated in Watt's steam-engine, invented in 1765, but vainly
advocated by him until 1774, when he entered into partnership with Matthew Boulton of Birmingham, and Boulton
and Watt's engines at once began to effect an entire change,
not only in the mode of pumping water from coal-mines,
but in every branch of manufacture dependent upon coal.
Steam-power, employed in clearing the mines of water, was
quickly employed also in sinking shafts, in lifting the coal
itself, and in other processes connected with this dangerous
and important industry. A main inducement with Watt in
prosecuting his great invention was the economising of coal,
which, by Newcomen's engine, was used very wastefully in

the process of pumping. The result of that invention is that, while the economy per ton is very great, the use of coal in manufacturing ways has been increased more than a hundredfold.

Next to coal-working, the great promoter of all other workmanship is iron-working. Ever since the time of the Romans, there have been iron-works in England, although, in the Middle Ages, iron brought from the coast of Biscay was preferred to that of native produce. Our superiority over other nations dates from the time when coal took the place of wood as fuel. Until then, indeed, no great effort was made to extend the trade. In 1354 the exportation of iron was forbidden, on account of the scarcity of timber; and in 1581 the erection of iron-works within certain distances from London and the Thames was prohibited, "for the preservation of the woods." Forty years later, in 1621, Lord Dudley obtained a monopoly of "the mystery and art of melting iron-ore, and of making the same into cast works or bars, with sea-coals or pit-coals, in furnaces, with bellows," which had been introduced by his famous son, Dud Dudley. Dudley suffered much from the opposition of rival iron-workers; "but," he said, "I went on with my inventions cheerfully, and made annually great store of iron, good and merchantable, and sold it unto divers men at £12 per ton. I also made all sorts of cast-iron wares, as brewing-cisterns, pots, mortars, and the like, better and cheaper than any yet made in their nations with charcoal." After persevering efforts, Dudley succeeded in producing seven tons of iron a week, "the greatest quantity of pit-coal iron ever yet made in Great Britain," as he said; and in his efforts to advance the trade he had an able coadjutor in Andrew Yarranton. In 1677, too, a Dr. Frederick de Blewstane obtained a patent for "a new and effectual way of melting down, forging, extracting, and reducing of all metals with pit-coal and sea-coal, as well and effectually as ever hath yet been done by charcoal, and with much less charge," though we are not informed as to the nature and results of his method. Before the close of the seventeenth century, it was reckoned that 180,000 tons of iron were produced in England in the course of a year; and in 1719 iron was considered to be third in the rank of English manufactures, and to give employment to 200,000 persons.

Then and for long afterwards, however, notwithstanding the inventions of Dud Dudley and others, and mainly because of their exclusive patents for the use of coal, the ore was chiefly smelted, and in rude ways, by help of wood and charcoal. The consequent waste of timber frightened short-sighted politicians, who, instead of attempting to encourage the use of coal, sought only to check the production of iron by other means. "The waste and destruction of the woods in the counties of Warwick, Stafford, Hereford, Monmouth, Gloucester, and Salop, by these iron-works," it was said in the House of Commons, "is not to be imagined. If some care be not taken to preserve our timber from these consuming furnaces, there will not be oak enough left to supply the Royal Navy and our mercantile shipping." Exportation of iron was accordingly discouraged; and, at the same time, as a false favour to the iron-masters, in the hope that their prices might be increased, cruel restrictions were put by Parliament upon the preparation of iron in the American colonies, where both ore and timber were abundant. It was enacted in 1719 that "none in the plantations should manufacture iron wares of any kind whatever, out of any sows, pigs, or bars whatever." That law could not be enforced. But the colonies, eager to develop their resources, were hindered by heavy restrictions upon the sending of their metal to the English market; and when, in 1750, a somewhat better policy prevailed, and a law was passed "to encourage the importation of pig and bar iron from his Majesty's colonies in America," it was coupled

M

with a cruel clause, "to prevent the erection of any mill or other engine for slitting or rolling of iron, or any plating-forge to work with a tilt-hammer, or any furnace for the making of steel, in the said colonies;" that is, only the roughest work was permitted, and all the fine manipulation was reserved for England, to which the pig-iron was to be shipped. It was by unmotherly legislation of that sort that the mother country was parted from her first and fairest offspring, and the United States were forced to win their independence by war and hatred.

England, also, of course, suffered by the foolish legislation. In the course of half a century the iron-trade was reduced to a tenth of its former proportions. In 1740 only 17,350 tons were produced; yet in the meanwhile the scientific manufacture had been greatly developed. Dud Dudley's plan of using coal instead of charcoal was only partially successful, the old-fashioned furnaces being unfit for the new kind of fuel. Coal and coke burning slowly, and with feeble chemical affinities for the iron-ore, it required to be subjected to a much more powerful blast than could be obtained in the shallow furnaces then in use. The secret of this blast was discovered by Abraham Darby, whose father had purchased the Coalbrook-dale Iron-works in 1709. "Young Abraham Darby entered upon the management about 1730," says Mrs. Darby. "As the supply of charcoal was fast failing, he attempted to smelt with a mixture of raw coal and charcoal, but did not succeed. Between 1730 and 1735 he determined to treat pit-coal as his charcoal-burners treated wood. He built a fire-proof hearth in the open air, piled upon it a circular mound of coal, and covered it with clay and cinders, leaving access to just sufficient air to maintain slow combustion. Having thus made a good stock of coke, he proceeded to experiment upon it as a substitute for charcoal. He himself watched the filling of his furnace during six days and nights, having no regular sleep, and taking his meals at the furnace-top. On the sixth evening, after many disappointments, the experiment succeeded, and the iron ran out well. He then, in the bridge-house at the top of his old-fashioned furnace, fell asleep so soundly that his men could not wake him, and carried him, sleeping, to his house, a quarter of a mile distant. From that time his success was rapid. To increase the power of his water-wheels of twenty-four feet diameter, he set up a 'fire-engine' to raise water from under the lower and send it to the upper pond, which supplied water to the works, and put in motion the largest bellows that had been made. He obtained additional leases, and erected seven furnaces, with five fire-engines. In 1754 the first furnace at Horsehay was blown in. In December, 1756, ' Horsehay's work' was declared to be ' at a top pinnacle of prosperity, twenty and twenty-two tons per week, and sold off as fast as made, at profit enough.'"

Darby's great improvement, however, was quickly improved upon. In 1760, at the Carron Ironworks, near Falkirk, Smeaton substituted a new blowing-apparatus, consisting of large cylinders, with closely-fitting pistons, for the old clumsy bellows. In 1766 the Cranages introduced a reverberatory or air furnace, by which, without any bellows, the pig-iron was made malleable and rendered fit for the forge hammer; and in 1783 Peter Onions, of Merthyr-Tydvil, started the idea of a puddling-furnace, wherein, with help of a current of air from beneath, the fire was left to act upon the metal until it was brought, as he said, "into a kind of froth, which the workmen, by opening the door, must turn and stir with a bar or other iron instrument, and then close the aperture again, applying the blast and fire until there was a ferment in the metal," and the dross could be cleared away. In the same year, Henry Cort, of Gosport, made independent discovery of that process, and, by working it out successfully, brought iron manufacture very

near to perfection. In 1783 he patented a method of fagot-
ing the bars, and then passing them through rollers which
pressed out the earthy particles, and rendered the iron tough
and fibrous. In 1784, with a second patent, "he introduced
a reverberatory furnace heated by coal, and with a concave
bottom, into which the fluid metal is run from the smelting-
furnace, and he showed how, by a process of puddling, which
exposed it to the oxidising current of flame and air, the cast
metal could be rendered malleable." These inventions of
puddling and rolling, now aided by the application of Watt's
steam-engine, proved of immense value. In 1860 upwards of
eight thousand of Cort's furnaces were in operation in Great
Britain alone, each one producing more iron in a week than
could often with the old appliances be obtained in a year.
But Cort himself, after spending more than £20,000 in perfecting his inventions, was robbed of all reward, and left to
die almost in beggary.

Among later improvements in the manufacture of iron,
the most important is the hot-blast process, invented by
Mr. Neilson, of Glasgow, in 1824. Hitherto all furnaces and
forges, requiring the use of the bellows or any other blowing-
apparatus, had been fed with cold blasts, which absorbed
much of the heat before they could act on the metal.
Mr. Neilson suggested the simple plan of heating the air
at a separate fire before applying it to the iron, and the
method has been found to give so much fresh power over
refractory ores that from three to four times the old quantity
of iron can be worked, at the cost of only one-third more
fuel, and that, generally, without the coal needing to be
coked, or the ore to be calcined. The result of this and
all other inventions connected with iron-manufacture is that
now more than 4,000,000 tons of iron are annually extracted
from some 12,000,000 tons of ore, at a market value of
about £12,000,000.

It is not necessary here to set forth the stages, for the

most part somewhat similar to those of iron, by which other metals have advanced in manufacture; and many volumes would be needed to detail all the applications of science by which manufactures in metal have kept pace with the manufacture of metals. From railways and steamships down to gold watches and silver spoons, steel pens and brass pins, each has a separate history, illustrating the gradual and always serviceable application of science to trade.

The most important metal wares, of course, are those by which the staple textile manufactures have been revolutionised. By them the cotton trade has been almost created, while the progress of the older woollen, linen, and silk manufactures has been hardly less wonderful.

Spinning and weaving have been practised in the world for at any rate forty centuries, and the importance to England, in past times, of its wool trade, greatly increased by the immigration of skilled workmen from Flanders and other parts, has been already referred to. Its value cannot be overstated, and its growth was steady. But the workmen of a century and a half ago used nearly the same sort of tools and followed nearly the same ways as had been in fashion for a thousand years before, or as still prevail in India, the birthplace of textile workmanship. Most of the manufacture, true to the original meaning of the word, was done by hand in private houses, and the largest factories rarely comprised more than twenty or thirty workmen, hand-work being then supplemented by mill-power derived from the streams at the side of which the humble buildings were erected.

The old process of manufacture may be briefly described. The wool or cotton to be converted into cloth, having been first cleaned, was carded—that is, its filaments were opened up by a minute sort of fork, and spread out in parallel lines, so as to form a loose ribbon of eight or more fibres, according to the thickness of the yarn required. A band of leather, supplied with iron bristles and coiled round a cylinder, was

the card; and this preliminary stage has only been improved
upon by scientific appliances for making the tufts perfectly
regular, and working the card by machinery instead of by
hand. The fibrous ribbon was next coiled round the spindle
and subjected to the spinning-wheel, which till a century
ago differed little from the rude instrument now in use in
India. The spinner, or spinster, having adjusted one end of
the ribbon to a large wheel, which she turned with one hand,
fed it with the other, giving the fibre a slight twist as she
did so, in order that the roving, as it was called, which was
worked off from the wheel upon the bobbin, though still frail
and porous, might have a little of the strength and cohesion
of thread; the roving had to be again worked round the
wheel, with slower feeding and a more rapid twist, to convert
it into yarn fit for the weaver to work up. This yarn was
made of two sorts—the warp-yarn had to be very firmly
twisted, so as to form the longitudinal substance of the
web; the weft-yarn, to form the transverse substance or woof,
though of equal thickness with the other, was looser and
lighter. The yarns having been thus prepared by the spinner,
were handed over to the weaver, who adjusted them to his
old-fashioned and clumsy loom. In this loom the warp was
wound round a beam, and thence drawn through two heddles
consisting of twines looped in the middle, one half being
through the front heddle, the other half through the back
heddle, and the two being so arranged that they could be
alternately lifted and depressed by a treadle, which the
weaver worked with his foot, while, as the threads rose and
fell, he threw backwards and forwards between them the
shuttle, from which the weft uncoiled as it passed. The cloth
thus produced was generally rolled on a beam opposite to
that covered by the warp-yarn, and was then ready for the
market. The workmanship alone of a pound of coarse cloth,
half cotton and half linen, as was then common, cost about
4s. 6d. in 1741; now good cotton fabric can be obtained

for about 2d. per lb., including both the cost of the raw material and the expense of manufacture.

A series of notable inventions have effected this change, and rendered the textile manufactures of England nearly a hundred times as extensive as they were a hundred years ago. Started mainly in the interests of the new trade in cotton, they have been extended, with easy modifications, to wool and linen, and in a lesser degree to silk. The first important step in the way of scientific improvement was made by John Kay, a native of Bury, but then working as a loom-maker at Colchester, who, in 1733, invented the fly-shuttle, which, as its name implies, moved much more swiftly and easily than the older shuttle, and enabled the weaver to do his work in half or a third of the time previously required. His invention, however, brought him nothing but trouble. The men whom he thought to benefit, and whose descendants he did benefit immensely, rejected his machine, and, after long and sullen opposition, mobbed his house, in 1753, and nearly killed him. " I have a great many more inventions than what I have given in," he wrote, with a pathos not lessened by the clumsy phrasing that certainly betrayed his lack of education, in 1764, a few years before he died, an unknown pauper, in France, "and the reason that I have not put them forward is the bad treatment that I had from woollen and cotton factories, in different parts of England, twenty years ago ; and then I applied to Parliament, and they would not assist me in my affairs, which obliged me to go abroad, to get money to pay my debts and support my family."

There can be no excuse for the ill-usage that Kay received; but it is partly explained by the fact that his fly-shuttle and his other inventions had to do with weaving only, and, there-fore, while lessening the weaver's toil in making each yard of cloth, reduced the wages which he received for it, without enabling him to fill up his leisure, and add to his wages, by making a greater quantity than he had produced before. The weaver was dependent on the spinner for his yarn, and, until improvements were made in spinning, Kay's improvements in weaving were only of partial benefit. That hindrance, however, was soon removed, although it lasted for a generation longer than it need have done.

John Wyatt is one of the neglected heroes of commerce. Born about the beginning of the eighteenth century, he was residing in a village near Lichfield, and in some way connected with the cotton manufacture, then in its infancy, and suffering much from the competition of wool and flax, when, in 1730, he thought of a plan by which the spinning of all fibres might be greatly facilitated. In lieu of passing the carded fibre twice round the hand-worked one-thread spinning-wheel, he proposed to draw it between a pair of revolving cylinders, one plain and the other fluted, whereby it was converted into roving, and then to pass it at once between another pair of rollers, revolving three, four, or any number of times more quickly than the first pair, according to the fineness to which the yarn was to be brought, and thus to convert it at once into warp or weft, not only in very much less time than was required by hand-spinning, but also with very much more exactness. He spent some three years in developing the idea. "In 1733," says his son, "by a model of about two feet square, in a small building near Sutton Coldfield, without a single witness to the performance, was spun the first thread of cotton ever produced without the intervention of human fingers, we, to use his own words, 'being all the time in a pleasing but trembling suspense.'"

Suspense that was not pleasing followed. Having no money of his own with which to bring his great invention before the world, Wyatt went to Birmingham, and there he made the acquaintance of Lewis Paul, an ingenious man, who made many important suggestions for improving textile machinery, but whose treatment of Wyatt seems to have

been somewhat unfair. By offers and bargains which he
never fulfilled, he persuaded Wyatt to transfer to him the
invention, and, after adding to it some other details, he obtained a patent for it, in his own name, in 1738. A bookseller named Warren advanced £1,000, and in 1741 or
1742 a small mill, "turned by two asses walking round an
axis," while ten girls attended to the details, was set up in
the Upper Priory, at Birmingham. "This establishment,"
we are told by Wyatt's son, "unsupported by sufficient property, languished a short time, and then expired. The
resources were exhausted, and the inventor much injured by
the experiment, but his confidence in the scheme was un-
impaired. It was tried again, and on a larger scale, a few
years later, at Nottingham, the money being provided by or
through Edward Cave, the famous editor of the *Gentleman's
Magazine*, and Dr. Johnson's friend. Here the mill was
turned by water, and fifty pair of hands worked two hundred
and fifty spindles; but this, too, failed. Leaving Paul to
superintend the work, Wyatt visited London for some time,
on other business; and when he returned to Nottingham
he found that, although 3,300 lbs. of cotton had been spun
by the new process, the machinery had fallen out of order,
and everything was in hopeless confusion. Dissatisfied with
his partners, and perhaps disheartened as to the value of his
invention, he went back to Birmingham, and gave his attention to other matters. He died in 1766, surviving by seven
years Lewis Paul, who had also occupied himself with fresh
inventions, among the rest with one for a new method of
carding wool and cotton; and the spinning-machine was
forgotten until its idea was revived and made successful by
Sir Richard Arkwright.

Arkwright's history is well known, and only too much
praise has been accorded to him for his share in the good
work by which he, unlike most inventors—being unlike most
inventors in shrewd self-seeking and steady business habits—

profited as much as the world. Prospering in a humble
way as a cheap barber at Bolton, and as a travelling
dealer in false hair and hair-dye, he appears, about the
time of Wyatt's death, to have obtained the details of his
invention. Soon after that, being in Warrington, he there
luckily fell in with a watchmaker who had just before
assisted a Thomas Highs in constructing a spinning-machine,
which was either based on knowledge of Wyatt's invention,
or a kindred and half-developed invention of his own.
Arkwright employed the watchmaker to help him in making
another machine, which was in the main a copy of Wyatt's,
and by showing this to influential friends, to whom he represented that the device was his own, he easily obtained
money enough to bring it into notice. More than all, he
obtained ·the co-operation of Jedediah Strutt, the great
mechanician and stocking-manufacturer of Derby, and of
Strutt's partner, Samuel Need. In 1769 he procured a
patent " for the making of yarn from cotton, flax, or wool,"
in which Wyatt's principle was adopted, but greatly improved
upon. In 1771 he established a mill at Cromford-on-the-
Derwent, which worked successfully. In 1775 he obtained
his second great patent, " for carding, drawing, and roving
machines, in preparing silk, cotton, flax, and wool for spinning," which was subsequently withdrawn, on the ground
that its specialities had already been anticipated.

But though Arkwright's claims as an inventor are open
to dispute, there can be no question as to his services to
manufacturing enterprise. With marvellous powers of application, fertility of resource, and administrative ability, he
was the pioneer in a famous race of progress. Resolved to
succeed, he persevered against the opposition of both friends
and enemies, and, after many years of pecuniary loss, of
battling against difficulties in the management of machinery,
and of yet greater difficulties in overcoming prejudice, he
triumphed himself, and showed others how to triumph.

Before Arkwright's spinning-machine, or water-frame, as it was called, from being worked by a water-mill, found favour, another great improvement had been quietly initiated. James Hargreaves, an illiterate weaver of Stand-hill, near Blackburn, was waiting one day for the weft which his wife was producing, when her one-thread wheel fell on its side, and the spindle was thus thrown from a horizontal into an upright position. Both wheel and spindle continued to revolve, and it occurred to Hargreaves that, by widening the wheel, and placing a number of upright spindles side by side, he might be able to spin several threads at once. He accordingly contrived a frame with spindles, and machinery for feeding them. This machine, though rudely made, worked well. His wife being named Jenny, he called it the spinning-jenny, and used it for a year or two in his own house, producing eight times as much yarn as before, until the neighbours, at first only astonished at the rapidity of his work, became jealous, broke into the house, and destroyed the jenny. That was in 1768. Hargreaves was forced to leave Blackburn, but settling in Nottingham, he there found a partner with intelligence and money, and set up a small mill. His invention, in which the number of spindles was increased from eight to sixteen, was patented in 1770, and soon came into general use, the number of spindles being augmented till they amounted to a hundred and twenty, or sometimes even more. The Lancashire manufacturers, preferring it to Arkwright's more novel and complicated machinery, paid him £4,000 for permission to adopt it, and, in spite of serious riots, which, in 1779, drove old Robert Peel and other masters from Blackburn, the spinning-jenny held its ground, until both it and Arkwright's machine were in part superseded by another great invention.

Samuel Crompton, born in 1753, was the son of a farmer settled near Bolton, but, left an orphan when he was very young, had to support himself by spinning. He was sixteen

when he began to use Hargreaves' spinning-jenny, and soon
afterwards he heard of Arkwright's drawing-machine. When
he was about one-and-twenty, he bethought him that his
work might be done more easily if he could construct a
machine combining the principles of both the others, and,
after five years of experimenting, in 1779 his project was
successful. With the poor tools and out of the poor materials at his disposal, he fashioned what, with the simplicity
and modesty natural to him, he called a mule, as being the
offspring of two different kinds of instruments. It drew out
the roving by help of an adaptation of the water-frame, and
then passed it on to be finished and twisted into yarn by an
adaptation of the spinning-jenny. Nothing could be simpler,
nothing more efficacious. Twelve hundred spindles are now
often worked by it at once, and by one spinner, with a few
boys or girls to assist him in seeing that no knots or flaws
are allowed to spoil any of the twelve hundred threads; and
the threads produced by this wonderful economy of labour
are finer, firmer, and more uniform than any that the earlier
inventions were able to draw out.

Crompton, a plain, honest, working man, did not himself perceive the whole value of his machine. Having
roughly made it for his own use, he fixed it in his garret,
and was only annoyed at the curiosity of his neighbours,
who marvelled at the great quantity of yarn, and better than
they could spin, which he produced each day. They used
to climb up and try to peep in at the window. He built a
screen to impede their view ; but, at length, when he was
tired of keeping his troublesome secret, he told them that,
if fifty of them would subscribe a guinea a-piece, he would
show them his instrument, and teach them how to make
others like it for themselves. The money was soon found,
and thus it was published to the world. It was quickly
copied by thousands, and improved upon by Crompton
himself. At the close of 1811 more than four and a half

million spindles worked by mules were in use in various parts of England, spinning about forty million pounds of cotton in a year, and giving occupation to seventy thousand workpeople, besides a hundred and fifty thousand more who were employed in weaving the yarn thus spun. By that success, however, Crompton was only a sufferer. Brought out of the seclusion in which he would have preferred to live, and thus forced to spend more money than he could earn, he received nothing for his invention, save the first sum of fifty guineas, till 1812, when Parliament voted him a grant of £5,000. He died in poverty in 1827.

There was one great difficulty, however, yet to be overcome. Spinning being now so much easier than it had hitherto been, there was, instead of the lack of yarn for weaving which had at first resulted from Kay's invention, more yarn to be worked up than the weavers could handle. Dr. Cartwright, a Kentish clergyman, when conversing with some manufacturers, suggested that the next thing necessary was a machine for weaving. They all declared that this was impracticable. "They adduced arguments," he said, "which I certainly was incompetent to answer, or even to comprehend, being totally ignorant of the subject, having never at that time seen a person weave. I controverted, however, the impracticability of the thing, by remarking that there had lately been exhibited in London an automaton figure which played at chess. 'Now, you will not assert, gentlemen,' I said, 'that it is more difficult to construct a machine that shall weave than one which shall make all the variety of moves that are required in that complicated game.' Some little time afterwards I employed a carpenter and smith to carry my ideas into effect. As soon as the machine was finished, I got a weaver to put in the warp, which was of such materials as sail-cloth is usually made of. To my great delight, a piece of cloth, such as it was, was the produce. As I had never before turned my thoughts to anything mechanical, either in theory or practice, nor had ever seen a loom at work, or knew anything of its construction, you will readily suppose that my first loom was a most rude piece of machinery." But the principle was there, and though Cartwright's power-loom, patented in 1785, was of but very little value, more expert mechanicians easily adapted its idea, and the result was the establishment of power-looms, in lieu of the old hand-looms. They were perfected by Horrocks, of Stockport, in 1813.

Thus was completed the great series of inventions, started especially for the benefit of the cotton manufacture, but by which the spinning and weaving of wool and linen as well were revolutionised. Inventions in aid of carding, and other auxiliary processes, were made before Crompton's mule, and a hundred minor improvements were made afterwards, but it is not necessary here to detail them. All these, however, would have been very much less advantageous than they have proved to be, had not Watt's steam-engine come to their aid. That engine, patented in 1769, which is also the date of Arkwright's memorable patent, had quickly found favour as an auxiliary to mining operations; but its first application to textile manufacture, in improvement of the old water-mills, was in 1785, when a Nottinghamshire cotton-spinner had one set up in his works. In 1787 three others were started in Nottingham and one in Warrington, and from that time they began to be rapidly employed, so rapidly that Boulton and Watt were hardly able to execute the orders sent to them. The immeasurable advantages of steam-power over water-power were at once apparent. Moreover, the necessity of erecting all mills, in which any other than hand-work was to be done, by the side of running streams being removed, manufacturers were at liberty to choose sites convenient in other ways, and a much wider field of factory enterprise was open to them. Of this they made prompt use.

All the improvements in textile manufacture that have been referred to were the outcome of mechanical science; but the services of the sciences, and especially of chemistry, have been hardly less important. Even woollen fabric, as it comes from the weaver's loom, is not fit for the uses to which it has to be put; and this is still more the case with linen, cotton, and, above all, silk. They need to be dyed, bleached, and otherwise treated by chemical processes, before they can satisfy the tastes of those who are to wear them.

The art of dyeing fabrics, practised by Flemings and Englishmen from very early times, is older than Flemings and Englishmen. The great skill in colouring, now displayed by the natives of India, was practised by their ancestors in times far remote, and taught by them to other nations. "Garments are painted in Egypt in a wonderful manner," said Pliny, "the white clothes being first smeared, not with colours, but with drugs which absorb colour. These applications do not appear upon the cloths; but when the cloths are immersed in a caldron of hot dyeing liquor, they are taken out painted the moment after. It is wonderful that, although the dyeing liquor is only of one colour, the garment is dyed by it of several colours, according to the different properties of the drugs which have been applied to the different parts; nor can this dye be washed out. Thus the vat, which would doubtless have confused all the colours if the cloth had been immersed in a painted state, produces a diversity of colours out of one, and, at the same time, fixes them immovably." That process shows, not only considerable knowledge of chemical arts, but also considerable skill in applying them to manufacturing purposes. As great proficiency was not displayed in England till the eighteenth century, coarse dyeing with woad, logwood, and a few other substances being the best that could be done; but since then marvellous advances have been made.

The first dyeing in Europe was effected upon the yarn
before it was woven, a plan that, for certain fabrics, can
only be improved upon by improving the quality and variety
of the dye, and which therefore still prevails. By it, of
course, only one colour could be given to the cloth, which,
if the proposed garment was to be of many colours—like
Joseph's coat—had to be joined together by patchwork ;
but thus a goodly number of colours were long ago produced. An English Act of Parliament, passed in 1552,
limited the variety to "scarlet, red, crimson, murray, pink,
brown, blue, black, green, yellow, orange, tawny, russet,
marble-grey, sadnew colour, azure, watchett, sheep's colour,
motley, and iron-grey." And, by a law of William III.'s,
"violet, azure, friar's grey, crane, purple, and old medley,"
were added to the list. Wiser legislation of later times has
allowed free trade in colours, and chemists and manufacturers have made good use of the license.

The simplicity of workmanship two centuries ago is
illustrated by the exploits of William Flakefield, son of a
Glasgow trader, who, having been bred as a weaver, abandoned his calling to enlist in the Cameronians, and afterwards joined the famous regiment of Scots guards in France.
He lived some years abroad, till, having met with a blue
and white check handkerchief, woven in Germany, a great
novelty in those days, it occurred to him that he would try
and make others like it. He accordingly returned to
Glasgow in 1700, and set about the work. "A few spindles
of yarn fit for his purpose," said the old local historian, in
1793, "was all at that time that William Flakefield could
collect, the which was but ill-bleached, and the blue was
not very dark. They were, however, the best that could be
found in Glasgow. About two dozen of pocket-handker-
chiefs composed the first web. When the half was woven,
he cut out the cloth, and took it to the merchants. They
were pleased with the novelty of the blue and white stripes,

and especially with the delicate texture of the cloth, which
was thin-set in comparison with the hollands that they
generally dealt in. The new adventurer asked no more for
his web than the net price of the materials and the ordinary
wages for his work. All he asked was readily paid him, and
he went home rejoicing that his attempts were not unsuccessful. This dozen of handkerchiefs, the first of the kind
ever made in Britain, was disposed of in a few days."
Others were disposed of in abundance, as quickly as they
could be made. Weavers from all parts came to learn the
trick, and many of them settled down in Glasgow to practise
it with success, and to eclipse the humble enterprise ot
Flakefield, who died, poor and forgotten, as a town drum-
mer. " The number of looms," it is added, " daily increased, so that Glasgow became famous for that branch of
the linen trade. The checks were followed by the blanks,
or linen cloth for printing ; and to these is now added the
muslin trade."

The delicate figured muslins out of which ladies' dresses
are now often made, as well as the stout and many-coloured
carpets whereon they tread, illustrate the perfection to
which fabric-dyeing and other intricacies of manufacturing
art have been brought in modern times. In carpets various
yarns are variously dyed in sections, and the several colours
are brought to the surface at the proper times, with marvellous exactness. In muslins the colours are successively
impressed upon the material after it is woven, the old-
fashioned wooden blocks, used by hand, having been
replaced by much more rapid and much more exact printing-
presses, worked by steam. To the same sort of improvements are due the advances that have been made in calico-
printing, and in the production of coloured silks, art here
especially being the handmaid of science.

The progress of silk-manufacture, like its process, differs
in some important respects from that of the other textile

N

articles. Rudely practised in England at an early date, and greatly encouraged by the settlement of Huguenot refugees, the silk-working establishment of the Lombes at Derby, which has been already described, furnishes an instance of the extensive application of machinery to its development in times when mechanical improvements were little thought of with reference to other fabrics. But the Lombes' manufactory was only a prodigy, wondered at, but not imitated. The trade, chiefly carried on by French workmen in Spitalfields, and by French-taught workmen in Coventry, had no extensive footing in this country, and being practised almost entirely for the benefit of the rich, who often took pride in paying high prices for their goods, there was no national movement for reducing the cost of production, and bringing it, like wool and linen, into direct competition with cotton. In France there was, until recently, hardly any cotton, woollen, or linen manufacture for it to compete with, and so long as the workmen found a ready market for their wares, they had no mind to abandon the old mode of labour. The special character of the fibre, moreover, needing much less toil and ingenuity than those of shorter staple in reducing it to yarn, lessened the demand for improved spinning arrangements, in order that the weaver might have material to work upon. Therefore the old-fashioned processes, to a large extent continued to this day, were not interfered with till long after the other trades had been revolutionised.

The first and almost the only great change effected was due to Joseph Marie Jacquard, born at Lyons in 1752, a humble silk-weaver by inheritance, but also at different times a bookbinder, type founder and cutter. In 1802 he saw in an English newspaper that our Society of Arts had offered a prize to any one who should invent a plan for weaving nets by machinery. He set his wits to work, and, for his own amusement, soon produced a loom adapted to the purpose; but he made no attempt to obtain the reward, and, after showing his invention to a friend, put it aside, and for some time it was forgotten by him. To his surprise, he was one day sent for by the prefect of the department, who inquired about the machine, and requested him to make another, the original having been lost or destroyed. That he did, and a few weeks later he was summoned to Paris and introduced to Bonaparte. "Are you the man," asked Carnot, the minister, "who pretends to do what God Almighty cannot do, tie a knot in a stretched string?" Jacquard answered that he could do, not what God could not do, but what God had taught him to do. He explained his device to the Emperor, who rewarded him with a pension of a thousand crowns, gave him employment in the Conservatoire des Arts, and, while thus enabling him to exercise his ingenuity in other ways, encouraged the adoption of the excellent Jacquard loom. That, however, was almost more than imperial patronage could effect. The loom was publicly destroyed by the Conseil des Prud'-hommes, the official conservators of the trade of Lyons, and Jacquard was denounced as a man worthy only of hatred and ignominy. Many years passed before the means which it afforded for vast improvement in the manufacture of figured silks were recognised, and Jacquard, dying in 1834, hardly lived long enough to see the good fruits of his invention.

It was first generally adopted, indeed, in St. Étienne, the chief rival of Lyons in France; and in England it was soon used extensively in other manufactures besides that of silk. The first Jacquard loom was set up in Coventry in 1820. In 1838 that town and its adjoining villages had 2,228, and the number continued to increase till 1858, when they began to be speedily replaced by the superior *a-la-bar* looms, invented by two brothers weaving at St. Étienne. A great cause of the change was the change of fashion by which

plain silks, now for the first time able to be made of clear
and smooth colour and texture throughout, in great measure
superseded the more gorgeous figured silks. Mechanical
appliances have never found much favour with the weavers
of France ; but they more than compensate for their folly
in this respect by their laudable zeal in cultivating artistic
tastes, and thus rendering their wares more attractive than
any that can be produced in other countries.

None of the thousand inventions by which all other
branches of manufacturing skill have been aided nearly as
much as those concerned in the production of textile fabrics
—old trades being renovated and new ones created—need
be here detailed ; and it is hardly necessary to call attention
to the marvellous effect upon commerce produced by the
mechanical exploits, growing directly out of Watt's steam-
engine, and kindred achievements of science, which have
opened up railways upon land and ploughed the sea with
steam-ships. These have been described often enough. It
is the fortunate blending of science with trade in England,
whereby its rich stores of coal and iron have been utilised,
that has made possible its unparalleled development during
the past three generations. The story of that development,
leading to political and social results of the very highest
import, is, more notably than any other, a romance of trade.

CHAPTER VIII.

FASHION IN TRADE.

The Services of Fashion to Commerce—The Introduction of Forks—
Porcelain and China-ware—Wedgwood as a Caterer to Fashion—
Fashion in Dress—Gloves—Shoes and Stockings—William Lee and
the Stocking-frame—The Results of his Invention - Other Fashions
and their Value—The " Isabella" Colour—Fashions in Travelling—
Coaches—Bianconi and his Cars.

OF the effects of fashion upon trade there is no lack of
curious instances. Nearly every stage, indeed, of man's
progress from his first rude barbarism to his present civilisation, and of the consequent increase of commerce, called
upon to satisfy his growing needs and artificial requirements,
may be said to have been in part built up by fashion.
Thousands of commodities, now looked upon as absolute
necessaries of life, or only proper luxuries, have been
brought into use by novelty-hunters, whose whim or wisdom
has been imitated by others, until each new-fangled fashion
has given birth to an important trade.

So it is with articles of food, as we have already to
some extent seen ; so yet more with food-utensils of every
sort. Forks, for example, now indispensable at every
dinner-table, and furnishing employment to half-a-dozen
different trades, have hardly been in common use in England
for two hundred years. " I observed," said an old traveller,
Thomas Coryate, in his " Crudities," published in 1611, " a
custom in all those Italian cities and towns through the which
I have passed that is not used in any other country that I
saw in my travels ; neither do I think that any other nation
of Christendom doth use it, but only Italy. The Italians do
always at their meals use a little fork when they cut their

meat. For while with the knife, which they hold in one
hand, they cut the meat out of the dish, they fasten the
fork, which they hold in their other hand, upon the same
dish ; so that one who should unadvisedly touch the dish of
meat with his fingers, from which all the table do cut, will
give occasion of offence unto the company, insomuch that
for his error he shall be at the least browbeaten, if not
reprehended in words. This form of feeding is generally
used in all places of Italy; their forks being, for the most
part, made of iron, steel, and some of silver, but those are
used only by gentlemen. The reason of this their curiosity
is because the Italian cannot by any means endure to have
his dish touched with fingers, seeing that all men's fingers
are not alike clean. Hereupon I myself thought good to
imitate the Italian fashion by this forked-cutting of meat,
not only while I was in Italy, but also in Germany, and
oftentimes in England, since I came home." Forks seem
to have been employed in Italy—by some, at any rate—since
the eleventh century ; and though Coryate may be correct
in his boast of having first brought them into use in England, they were known in this country before his time. To
Queen Elizabeth were presented, at different times, " a fork
of crystal, garnished with gold slightly, and sparks of
garnets ;" " a fork of coral, slightly garnished with gold ;"
and " a fork of gold, garnished with two little rubies, two
little pearls pendant, and a little coral." But the dainty
Queen preferred the old habit of fingering her meat, and
forks were for a long time regarded as a worthless, foppish
institution. One divine, in James I.'s reign, preached a
sermon against forks, declaring it to be "an insult on Pro-
vidence not to touch one's meat with one's fingers ;" and
Fynes Morison, in his "Itinerary," published in 1617,
advised all young travellers, "returning home, to lay aside
the spoon and fork of Italy, the affected gestures of France,
and all strange apparel." *Mercraft*, in Ben Jonson's

" Devil is an Ass," makes fun of forks, when speaking of his
" pains at Court" to obtain for himself a monopoly in
favour of

> " The laudable use of forks,
> Brought into custom here, as they are in Italy,
> To the sparing of napkins,"

which would have resulted in his making of gold and silver
forks " for the better personages," and of steel ones " for the
commoner sort." In one of Beaumont and Fletcher's plays,
" your fork-carving traveller " is spoken of as an object
of contempt. Even in 1652, Heylin, speaking of the ivory
sticks used for eating in China, said " the use of silver forks
came from hence into Italy, and with us, taken up of late
by some of our spruce gallants, from thence into England."
Forks were then, and for some time after, looked upon as
the absurd affectations of coxcombs; they only came into
general use late in the seventeenth century.

Hardly older is the common employment of earthenware
plates and dishes instead of wooden platters; but the effects
of fashion upon trade have been shown more notably in
the case of the finer sorts of pottery. It was the demand for
antique Etruscan wares that first gave an impetus to improvement in the rude earthenware manufacture of old times; and
fresh encouragement came with the introduction in Europe
of the delicate workmanship of China and Japan. The
Dresden factory owes its greatness to this cause, and it was
to rival Dresden that porcelain-manufacture was started at
Sèvres, where the business threatened to die out before
Madame de Pompadour's passion for china induced Louis
XIV. to buy up the establishment, and put it in a fair way
of success. Josiah Wedgwood, our own great potter, also
owes half his renown to his skill in catering for purely
fashionable requirements, and Queen Caroline greatly
helped to make his fortune when she made him " royal
potter." " The demand for the cream-colour, *alias* queen's

ware, *alias* ivory," he wrote to his friend and partner
Thomas Bentley, "still increases. It is really amazing how
rapidly the use has spread almost over the whole globe, and
how universally it is liked. How much of this general use
and estimation is owing to the mode of its introduction, and
how much to its real utility and beauty, are questions in
which we may be a good deal interested for the government
of our future conduct; for, if a royal or noble introduction
be as necessary as beauty to the sale of an article of luxury,
then the manufacturer, if he consults his own interest, will
bestow as much pains in gaining the favour of these advantages as he would in bestowing the latter." Wedgwood, at
any rate, profited by the pains which, with this end, he took.
For many years, from 1770, his showroom in St. Martin's
Lane was one of the sights of London, a fashionable resort
for idlers about Court, as well as an object of attraction to
foreigners and country visitors. By it his fame was spread
abroad, and commissions came to him from every part of
Europe. One memorable commission was from the Empress
of Russia, for an immense cream-ware service, of which each
piece was to have a separate English landscape painted on
it. " I am just returned," wrote Mrs. Delaney, in June, 1774,
"from viewing the Wedgwood-ware that is to be sent to the
Empress of Russia. It consists, I believe, of as many pieces
as there are days in the year. There are three rooms below
and two above filled with it, laid out on tables." The
price paid for this service was £3,000, and it became a
splendid advertisement of Wedgwood throughout the whole
of Europe. There has been no diminution in later times in
the production of costly earthenware and kindred articles to
meet the requirements of fashion.

But it is in articles of dress and their materials that the
influence of fashion upon trade is most of all apparent.
Wedgwood's friend, Matthew Boulton, of Birmingham,
Watt's partner in the introduction of the steam-engine,

began his famous career by making better buttons and shoe-buckles than had hitherto been known, and thousands of localities have been enriched by their manufacture of articles of dress less useful than buttons and buckles.

Gloves may serve as one illustration. Worn in England from Anglo-Saxon times, they were, all through the Middle Ages and long after, reserved as ornaments for the rich and noble ; although, made only of coarse leather and laden with heavy accessories, it is not easy to see how they can have been ornamental. Better gloves came into fashion in the sixteenth century. Queen Elizabeth's Earl of Oxford is reported to have been the first Englishman who brought perfumed gloves from Italy ; and in 1578 a pair which cost sixty shillings, perfumed and garnished with embroidery and goldsmith's work, was presented to the Queen by the University of Cambridge. " Her Majesty, beholding the beauty of the said gloves," says the old chronicler, "as in great admiration, and in token of her thankful acceptation of the same, held up one of her hands, and, smelling into them, put them half-way upon her hands." Italian gloves soon became fashionable in England, until special skill in their manufacture passed from Italy to France. Fifty thousand or more persons are now employed in glove-making in England, and, in addition to all their produce, some nine or ten million pairs, worth nearly £1,000,000, are annually brought over from France.

Coverings for the feet are more necessary than coverings for the hands, and we find that shoes and stockings were of more ancient use than gloves ; but here also fashion has wrought great changes. The early Britons wore coarse bags of hide, made all of one piece, and tied round the ankle, but the Romans introduced daintier foot-gear, and from them the Anglo-Saxons learnt to make both boots and shoes of leather, both being generally of one piece, laced from the toes all the way up with strings, and sometimes protected at

the sole with a sort of wooden clog. A pair of shoes worn
by Bernard, King of Italy, and grandson of Charlemagne,
were recently found in his tomb. "The soles were of wood
and the upper parts of red leather," says an Italian writer.
"They were so closely fitted to the feet that the order of
the toes, terminating in a point at the great toe, might easily
be discovered." Finer, neater, and greater ornamentation
came to be employed in later times. Some one with a
deformed foot is said to have first had shoes pinched at the
toe, and the innovation was so much admired that, in spite
of the denunciations of monks and priests, it was widely
followed by courtiers and gallants of the Middle Ages. There
were scorpion-tail shoes and ram's-horn shoes ; the long curly
points being stuffed with tow as well at toe. Shoe-toes
became more natural, but high heels, then called chopines,
were introduced in Elizabeth's reign. "By'r lady," *Hamlet*
says to one of the lady actors, in his play before the King of
Denmark, "your ladyship is nearer heaven than when I saw
you last, by the altitude of a chopine !" This fashion also
came from Italy, and Coryate reports that in his time the
chopine was so common that no one could go without it.
"It is a thing made of wood," he says, "and covered with
leather of sundry colours, some white, some red, some
yellow. Many of them are curiously painted, some also of
them I have seen fairly gilt. There are many of these
chopines of a great height, even half a yard high ; and by
how much the nobler a woman is, by so much the higher
are her chopines. All their gentlewomen, and most of their
wives and widows that are of any wealth, are assisted and
supported either by men or women when they walk abroad,
to the end they may not fall." Chopines as absurd as that
were not common in England, but pantofles, or high-heeled
slippers, worn to protect the daintily-embroidered shoes of
courtly folk, found favour, and these pantofles even came to
be extravagantly ornamented with silver and gold buckles,

costly rosettes, and the like. The heels were not more than two or three inches high. The changes of fashion in shoes and boots during the last two or three centuries may be traced in familiar paintings, such as Hogarth's.

Stockings have necessarily varied less in shape and style, though the alterations in their material and mode of production have had greater influence upon trade. They were made of coarse cloth, and, in fact, were little other than tight-fitting trouser-legs or gaiters with feet, till early in the sixteenth century when the art of spinning them out of worsted, silk, and other materials was discovered in Scotland, improved upon in France and Spain, and soon adopted in England. Stubbes, in his "Anatomy of Abuses," in 1596, complains loudly of the innovation. "They have nether-stocks," he says of the spendthrifts of his day, " not of cloth, though never so fine, for that is thought too base, but of worsted, silk, thread, and such-like, or else, at the least, of the finest yarn that can be got, and so curiously knit, with open seam down the leg, with quirks and clocks about the ankles, and sometimes haply interlaced about the ankles with gold or silver threads, as is wonderful to behold. And to such impudent insolency and shameful outrage is it now grown that every one almost, though otherwise very poor, having scarce forty shillings wages by the year, will not stick to have two or three pair of these silk nether-stocks or else of the finest yarn that may be got, though the price of them be twenty shillings or more, as commonly it is. The time hath been when one might have clothed all his body well, from top to toe, for less than a pair of these nether-stocks will cost."

The "nether stocks" were at first produced by the same process of hand-work which is followed by good housewives and country people at the present day ; but, to meet the demands of the fashion for knitted stockings, something else was needed. It was supplied by William Lee, a native of

Woodborough, in Nottinghamshire, who, after graduating
at St. John's College, Cambridge, settled down as curate
of Calverton, very near to his birthplace, about the year
1586. Two pretty stories are told concerning him. The
one represents that, while still a student, he courted a pretty
country lass, whose trade was stocking-knitting, and that,
finding she was always, when he went to visit her, too busy
about her work to pay to his love-making all the attention
he desired, he set his wits to work at finding some expedient
by which her stockings might be made more quickly, and
she might have more time to talk and walk with him. The
other story is to the effect that after leaving college he forfeited his fellowship, that he might marry the maiden, and
only found when the deed was done that his curacy did not
provide money enough to maintain himself, his wife, and the
children who began to come ; that, consequently, the young
wife had to bring out her knitting-needles again and do her
share of the bread-winning ; and that it was Lee's distress
at seeing her toiling over her work from early morning till
late at night that led to the invention of his stocking-frame.
Both stories are doubtful, but both may be true. Perhaps
the invention may have been begun while he was a dreamy
lover, but have been left unfinished until he had to fulfil the
duties of a practical husband. It is only certain, however,
that in 1589 Lee produced his stocking-frame, in which a
row of knitting-needles, kept going by a treadle, did the
work very much more quickly and easily than it had before
been done by hand ; and out of his machine, the principle
being the same, but the details very much more complicated,
have grown all the devices now in force for the manufacture
of stockings, and of every other sort of knitted hosiery as
well.

The romance does not end with Lee's mechanical triumphs
in 1589. During two years or so he spent, in perfecting
his invention, more money than he made. That done, he

threw up his curacy, and brought the machine to London, hoping that fashionable people would aid him in developing his plan for helping the world of fashion. He gained access to Lord Hunsdon, who informed Queen Elizabeth that there was a poor parson lodging in Bunhill Fields who had a wonderful machine for making stockings, which he wanted her Majesty to see. Her Majesty went to see it, but, while admiring its ingenuity, expressed her disgust that it was adapted only for coarse worsted stockings, and not for the finer workmanship in silk. When Lord Hunsdon urged her to grant a patent for the invention, she refused. " My lord," she said, " I have too much love for my poor people who obtain their bread by the employment of knitting to give my money to forward an invention that will tend to their ruin, by depriving them of employment, and thus make them beggars. Had Mr. Lee made a machine that would have made *silk* stockings, I should, I think, have been somewhat justified in granting him a patent for that monopoly, which would have affected only a small number of my subjects ; but to enjoy the exclusive privilege of making stockings for the whole of my subjects is too important to be granted to any individual." If Lee really coveted the exclusive right of stocking-making, Queen Elizabeth had good reason for her refusal, although that reason did not weigh in the case of other monopolies granted by her ; but it is likely that he asked, and she certainly might have given it, only some protection in the use of his machine, and in sending out its produce to compete with hand-knit hose.

Lord Hunsdon, however, seems to have rendered the inventor some assistance, and he showed his appreciation of the invention in a very notable way, by apprenticing his son, Sir William Carey, to the new trade begun by him. For seven or eight years Lee worked on in Bunhill Fields, making stockings and improving his machine, bearing always in mind the Queen's hint that she might help him if he could make a frame delicate enough for silk-work. That was really a second invention, and he completed it about the year 1598. The first pair of silk stockings made by him he carried to Court. Queen Elizabeth praised their elasticity and beauty, but she gave him nothing but praise. Parliament had just begun to quarrel with her about her monopoly-granting, and, while she could not venture upon aiding him thus, she had no money to spare in other sort of aid; therefore, he was left to toil on as best he could. He had nine machines at work, and made plenty of stockings; but popular prejudice hindered their sale, and the debts he had incurred in developing his plans made him very poor indeed. Lord Hunsdon, his patron, and Sir William Carey, his aristocratic apprentice, moreover, both died, and thereby he lost his only friends at Court. On James I.'s accession, he is reported to have made another attempt to secure royal favour; but, if so, he was disappointed, and he is said to have been, during some time, in such utter dejection that he hardly cared to carry on his work.

Brighter but false prospects came to him in 1605, when, by Henry IV.'s invitation, he went to France with a few workmen, and set up his machinery at Rouen. Here the royal patronage helped him to prosper for a short time; but Henry's assassination by Ravaillac proved his ruin. Persecuted, both as a Protestant and as an Englishman, he wandered miserably from place to place, and, at length, in 1610, died, broken-hearted and starving, in Paris, just as his invention was beginning to give ease and comfort to thousands.

Two of his workmen remained in France, and there kept alive his secret. The other seven returned to Nottingham, and entered the service of Aston, a former apprentice of Lee's, who had, in the interval, effected some improvements in the machine, and under whose management the stocking manufacture was developed in England. So extensive was this trade in Cromwell's time that its London members sought to be incorporated in a guild. Cromwell refused, but Charles II. assented, and the Stocking-weavers' Corporation dates from 1663. It lasted till 1753. It was in Nottinghamshire, however, the place of its birth, and in the adjoining counties of Leicester and Derby, that the trade fared best, great advances having been made in recent times, through the improved machinery of Jedediah Strutt and others, and through the use of cotton as a cheaper if not better material than silk or worsted. In 1670 there were 700 stocking-frames in England; in 1753 the number had risen to 14,000. In 1845 it was reckoned that 73,000 persons were engaged in making 3,510,000 dozen pairs of stockings, and the trade has increased greatly during the last five-and-twenty years. Great Britain now makes nearly four-fifths of the stockings worn all over the world; and all this useful trade has grown out of Lee's kindly effort to lessen the toil of his wife in catering for a fashion that grew up in Queen Elizabeth's reign.

Other fashions have had yet greater results. "The advantages of the East India Company," said one, writing in 1690, "is chiefly in their muslins and Indian silks, and these are becoming the general wear in England. Fashion is truly termed a witch—the dearer and scarcer the commodity, the more the mode. Thirty shillings a yard for muslins, and only the shadow of a commodity when procured!" Our trades in silk, linen, wool, and cotton owe much, if not most, of their encouragement to the demand for better and handsomer clothing and for showy and luxurious accessories that has grown up in recent centuries, and been especially brought over by English fashion-mongers from France. As the old satirist exclaimed—

> "O France, whose edicts govern dress and meat,
> Thy victor, Britain, bends beneath thy feet.
> Strange, that pert grasshoppers should lions lead,
> And teach to hop and chirp across the mead.

Of fleets and laurel'd chiefs let others boast,
Thy honours are to bow, dance, boil, and roast ;
'Tis thine thy slaves to teach the shantiest cuts,
Give empty coxcombs more important struts,
Prescribe new rules for knots, hoops, mantuas, wigs,
Shoes, soups, complexions, coaches, farces, jigs."

Even the most foolish fashions, however, have generally
been of benefit to trade, in helping to promote the industry
and enterprise of the country, and to transfer money from
the empty-headed rich to the empty-handed poor.   Hoops,
furbelows, hair-dyes, and face-powders have not been altogether useless, and many fancy tastes, like those in lace and
embroidery; have had a very perceptible eflect upon national
refinement.

Many fashions have a strange origin, but few stranger
than that attributed to the once fashionable dye called
"Isabella."   "When Ostend was besieged by the Spaniards,
under the command of the famous Spinola," we are told,
the Infanta Isabella of Spain, animated with a most heroic
zeal for her country, made a solemn vow not to change her
linen till the town should be taken.   The besieged held out
till time, which sullies everything, brought her royal highness's linen to a colour which wanted a name.   In a person
of that rank it could not be dirty, it was therefore called
' Isabella.'   It became the fashionable loyal colour, was worn
with honour by all, and with great convenience by many."

If fashion has been most influential upon trade in articles
of dress and dyes, and other articles accessory thereto, its
influence has also been very great in other ways, notably
in matters of house-furniture and the like.   Its share in the
construction of railways, and of the other great machinery
of transit, has been only indirect ; but upon some notable
modes of conveyance its effect has been great and immediate.

Till a few centuries ago, foot-journeying satisfied all
the requirements of travellers over short distances, while
longer journeys were taken on horseback by men and

women ; and carriages were only clumsy carts and wagons, thought fit to hold nothing but baggage and lumber. Light cars were used by numerous ladies on the Continent, and especially in Italy, from the thirteenth century ; but they were long regarded as disgracefully effeminate, hardly tolerable for women, and quite unsuitable for men. Gradually they came to be looked upon with more favour, and, after foreign princes as well as princesses had begun to use coaches upon state occasions, they were introduced into England. The first English coach is said to have been made in 1535, for the Earl of Rutland, by Walter Rippon ; and in 1564 the same man built a cumbersome and gaudy vehicle for Queen Elizabeth. " The first coach," says John Taylor, the water-poet, " was a strange monster in those days, and the sight of it put both horse and man into amazement ; some said it was a great crab-shell brought out of China, and some imagined it to be one of the pagan temples in which the cannibals adored the devil." The coaches of those days were not adapted to make rapid progress, but the fashion for using them ran apace. Stow records how, soon after the building of the Queen's coach, "divers great ladies, with great jealousy of the Queen's displeasure, made them coaches, and rid in them up and down the country, to the great admiration of all the beholders ; and then, by little and little, they grew usual among the nobility." By James I.'s reign gentlefolk had learnt to follow the nobility ; coaches became necessary adjuncts of fashionable life, and that in spite of the mockery and denunciations of satirists. " I think," said John Taylor, in 1623, "since Phaeton brake his neck, never land hath endured more trouble and molestation than this hath, by the continual rumbling of these upstart four-wheeled tortoises. Whence comes leather so dear, but by reason, or, as I should say, against reason, of the multitude of coaches and carriages, who consume and take up the best hides that can be gotten in the kingdom? by which

o

means many honest shoemakers are either undone or undoing, and infinite numbers of poor Christians are enforced
to go barefooted in the cold winters.   They have been the
universal decay of almost all the best ash-trees in the kingdom ; for a young plant can no sooner peep up to any perfection, but presently it is fitted for the coach; nor a young
horse bred of any beauty or goodness, but he is ordained
from his foaling to the service of the coach.   And if it be
considered in the right cue, a coach or carriage are mere
engines of pride, which no one can deny to be one of the
seven deadly sins ; for two leash of oyster-women hired a
coach, on a Thursday after Whitsuntide, to take them to the
green-goose fair at Stratford-the-Bow, and, as they were
hurried between Aldgate and Mile End, they were so be-
madame'd, be-mistress'd, and ladyfied by the beggars, that
the foolish women began to swell with a proud supposition
of imaginary greatness, and gave all their money to the
mendicanting canters, insomuch that they were fain to pawn
their gowns and smocks the next day to buy oysters.   The
superfluous use of coaches hath been the occasions of many
vile and odious crimes, as murder, theft, cheatings, hangings,
whippings, pillories, stocks, and cages; for housekeeping
never decayed till coaches came into England."

Honest Taylor lost his head in his abuse of coaches.
Though some blame might fairly be laid upon them, as
causes of extravagance and effeminacy, they were useful in
many ways, and the use was greatest when the fashion
passed out of aristocratic circles, and hackney-coaches and
the like came to be common among common folk.   That
was in 1625.   Some ten years later, a new and worse fashion
was introduced by the Duke of Buckingham, who brought
sedan-chairs from Spain.   They were necessities of life to
the hooped and powdered ladies of the Restoration days
and after, but, in turn, gave place to the newer sorts of
carriage that came into use one after another.

Stage-coaches and omnibuses were a direct outgrowth of the fashionable want begotten of the old carriages of Queen Elizabeth's and James I.'s times; and stage-coaches, almost entirely, and omnibuses, in part, have been replaced by railways and tramways. A new life has been developed by the facilities of travel that modern ingenuity has produced; and everywhere a test of the prosperity of any district is to be found in the opportunities of access to it, and of interchange of its local products with those of other districts.

Of the good that may be so done, and of the benefits that may result from one man's wise guidance of fashion, a curious instance may be given. About the year 1800, Carlo Bianconi, a native of Milan, settled in Dublin as a humble picture-dealer and frame-maker. Prospering therein, he went, some ten years afterwards, to start a larger business at Clonmel, but found that the town, with excellent natural facilities for trade, suffered greatly by its isolation from other towns. In 1815 he started a cheap car, shaped somewhat like the ordinary "jaunting-car," but as large as a London omnibus, which went every day to Cahir and back, and conveyed passengers for about twopence a mile. That experiment succeeding, he extended the distance to Tipperary and Limerick, and sent other cars to Cashel and Thurles, to Carrick and Waterford, and new cars and routes were added every year. In 1857 he had sixty-seven conveyances, worked by nine hundred horses, running to and from all the towns and most of the villages in the south and west of Ireland. "The advantages which these cars have afforded to the country," says Mr. S. C. Hall, "are immense. In the interior of the country, from which farmers come to the little villages, they have only a few facilities for obtaining their commodities, and that at an enormous rate. But since the introduction of these cars, people in business, who hitherto were obliged to go to market at a very heavy

expense, which prevented their doing so frequently, now
find their way to the larger towns, and have been enabled
to secure supplies at once from the first-cost market ; and,
from the cheapness of bringing the articles home, they were
enabled to reduce their prices considerably, and in those
districts the consumption has, in consequence, wonderfully
augmented.   Shops and fresh sources of competition continually increase, thereby enabling parties to use articles
hitherto inaccessible to them.   A great saving of time is
also effected.   For example, it took a man a whole day to
walk from Thurles to Clonmel, the second day to do his
business, and the third to walk back ; now, for seven shillings, he purchases two clear days, saves himself the trouble
of walking sixty English miles, and has four or five hours
to transact his business."

CHAPTER IX.

GREAT FACTORIES.

The Rise of Great Factories—The Transitions from Single-handed to Co-operative Labour—The Growth of Manchester—Its Early Manufactures and the Habits of its Manufacturers—The Peels' Cotton-works at Bury—John Rylands and his Enterprises in Manchester, Wigan, and Ainsworth—The Wealth of the Manchester District—The Glasgow Cotton District—David Dale and Robert Owen's Factory at New Lanark—James Monteith's Factory at Blantyre—Woollen Manufacture —The Progress of Halifax and Leeds—Benjamin Gott—Bradford and its Worsted Manufacture—Linen Manufactures—Belfast and its Linen Factories—Dundee—The Baxters' Factories—Leeds—John Marshall's Mills—Metal Factories—The Carron Iron-works—The Manufacturing History of Birmingham—John Taylor—Matthew Boulton—Soho and its Manufacture of Steam-engines—Boulton's other Good Works —The Extent of English Factories—French Factories—The Silk Trade and Lyons—St. Étienne—Cotton Factories at Rouen and Mulhouse— American Factories—New York—Philadelphia—Pittsburg—The New England Factories—Lowell.

THE migrations and developments of manufacturing and trading energy, in successive ages, and in various portions of the world, form a curious and instructive study; and equally noteworthy, though within a narrower area, are the similar migrations and developments that have occurred in our own land, and in comparatively modern times. To these a few allusions have been made in earlier pages; some further illustrations may here be given. Commerce is, in its own way, as true an index of human progress and national health as politics or religion, literature or art; and the index is aptly reflected in the past and present condition of great marts and great factories.

There were great marts but, apparently, no great factories in the ancient world. Then men dealt chiefly in the easy

produce of the soil, and in manufactures which were chiefly
handiwork, and which were prepared for the market by
single labourers, or little groups of toilers, who toiled whenever they chose, without being crowded together by mechanical appliances like those of modern times, which make it
easier for work to be done, under one roof or in close
proximity, by hundreds, or thousands, or tens of thousands
of workers, subject to one rule, and guided by one master-
mind.   Ghent and other cities of the Middle Ages were in
the place of great factories, but it was only because independent producers found it more for their own convenience
to band together in guilds, or live, as mere neighbours,
within easy reach of the merchants who periodically collected
their wares, and conveyed them to Bruges and other great
marts, for distribution far and near.   Thus in England, even
after it had become an important manufacturing country,
while we find many towns serving as centres of production,
there was among the dwellers in them, notwithstanding the
influence of close corporations and monopolies of all sorts,
much less cohesion than is found now; and, in spite of the
jealousy of towns and townsmen, manufacturing energy was
much more loosely spread over the whole country, and discharged by separate labourers in towns and hamlets.

So it was with that simplest form of manufacture by
which the commercial strength of the kingdom was in
great measure begun, the shearing and skinning of sheep,
and packing up the wool and hides, for conveyance to the
fairs and markets at which they were to be sold or bartered;
and so, when England began to make its own clothing, for
a long time it continued.   In every village there were small
manufacturers, who set their wives and daughters to spin,
and, with help of their sons, and, perhaps, a few labourers,
wove the yarn into coarse cloth, some of which they sold
to their neighbours, while the rest found its way to the
fairs, and markets, and other centres of trade.   The Spital-

fields silk-weavers furnish an illustration of the way in which, with a certain show of independence, but under great pecuniary disadvantage, the old arrangement prevails in the case of manufactures that are now best carried on by aggregation of labour ; and illustrations of the way in which other trades are still mainly and wisely carried on in old ways, are furnished by bootmakers and tailors—although even bootmaking and tailoring are beginning to be taken out of the hands of men who are their own masters and their own workmen, and to be concentrated in special localities and in huge establishments.

As regards the staple trades, of course, a certain amount of concentration in special localities has always occurred ; and this has resulted both from natural and from artificial causes. Woollen manufacture, for example, was necessarily most abundant in districts where sheep were most plentiful, and within those districts preference was given to sites easy of access to suitable marts and ports, and, as soon as the business had made sufficient progress for mill-work to be used as a substitute for or supplement to hand-work, on the banks of a rapid stream. Where a few enterprising men settle down and prosper, moreover, others are sure to follow, and of this striking instances occur in the history of the wool trade. While it was a trade, but not a manufacture, or, at any rate, one of very little note, Winchester, through favour of the Romans, was its centre ; and St. Giles's Fair caused Winchester to prosper long after the manufacture had been chiefly developed in other parts. The planting of Flemish colonists in Gloucester and elsewhere, on the banks of the Severn, by Henry II., made Bristol a great centre of manufacture, as well as of trade, during the Middle Ages ; and no sooner did Hull become the great rival of Bristol as a trading-town, chiefly by reason of its convenient nearness to Flanders, than Leeds and other well-placed towns in Yorkshire attained importance as col-

lecting-places for wool, the importance being retained when
trade in wool gave place to trade in cloth. The later settlement of wool-working Netherlanders in Norfolk, again,
made Norwich a great manufacturing resort in Elizabeth's
time and after. Woollen manufacture, however, was plentiful all through those early centuries in all the midland
counties, from Berkshire up to Derbyshire. The first
great English clothier on record was John Winchcombe,
better known as Jack of Newbury, and perhaps his was
the first great woollen factory in England. A hundred
looms, it is said, always worked in his house, and he was
rich enough to put a hundred of his journeymen in armour,
and send them to Flodden Field. His kerseys were famous
all over Europe.

The progress of Manchester, the greatest manufacturing
town in the world, and the capital of a great manufacturing commonwealth, may help to show how, in modern
times, great factories have arisen. It had existed as a
little town or village from Roman times, but first became
important in the fourteenth century, like Halifax, Bradford,
Leeds, and other northern towns, as a seat of woollen
manufacture. There some Flemings settled, and began
to develop their craft, in 1331, and they had shrewd followers. Martin Byrom was its great clothier in Henry
VIII.'s reign, and, according to an old writer, "kept a
great number of servants at work—carders, spinners,
weavers, fullers, dyers, shearmen, &c." Linen manufacture was also extensively carried on in it. "The town
of Manchester," it was stated in an Act of Parliament,
passed in 1542, "is, and hath of long time been well
inhabited, and the inhabitants have obtained, gotten, and
come unto riches and wealthy livings, and have kept and
set many artificers and poor folks to work within the said
town; and, by reason of the great occupying, good order,
and straight and true dealing of the inhabitants, many

strangers, as well of Ireland as of other places within this realm, have resorted to it with linen yarn, wool, and necessary wares for making of cloths, and have used to trust the poor inhabitants which had not ready money to pay in hand for the said yarns, wools, and wares, until, with their industry, labour, and pains, they might make cloths of the said wools, yarns, and other wares, and sell the same to content and pay their creditors; wherein hath consisted much of the common wealth of the said town, and many poor folks have living, and children and servants, all these virtuously brought up, in honest and true labour, out of all idleness." Manchester cottons, or coatings, were then and afterwards a coarse kind of woollen cloth, much esteemed for its warmth and durability; but, as soon as the fibre we now know as cotton was brought to England, Manchester had a share in its manufacture, which also spread rapidly to Bolton, Blackburn, Bury, and other neighbouring towns, that had begun, in like manner, as seats of trade in wool and linen.

Manchester, though famous at the beginning of the eighteenth century, was still in its infancy, and its greatest men lived and worked in a way that their successors of the present times have far surpassed. "An eminent manufacturer of that age," says Dr. Aikin, "used to be in his warehouse before six in the morning, accompanied by his children and apprentices. At seven, they all came in to breakfast, which consisted of one large dish of water-pottage, made of oatmeal, water, and a little salt, boiled thick and poured into a dish. At the side was a pan or basin of milk, and the master and apprentices, each with a wooden spoon in his hand, without loss of time, dipped into the same dish, and thence into a milk-pan; and, as soon as it was finished, they all returned to their work." More luxurious ways gradually crept in, but, for a long time, kitchens, garrets, sheds, and poor outhouses were large enough and good enough for the most extensive manufacturing operations that were carried on.

Old Robert Peel, the founder of the great manufacturing house that bears his name, and the grandfather of the statesman, began his career at Blackburn, in that humble way ; and was as humble when, in 1779, he was driven out by the operatives, enraged at his use of Hargreaves' spinning-jenny, and forced to carry on his business at Burton-on-Trent. His partners, Haworth and Yates, developed a large business at Bury, but that establishment was re-shaped and made the first princely manufactory by his son, the elder Sir Robert Peel, the first princely cotton-manufacturer of England. " The principal of these works," said Dr. Aikin, in 1795, " are situated on the side of the Irwell, from which they have large reservoirs of water. The articles here made and printed are chiefly the finest kinds of the cotton manufacture, and they are in high request both at Manchester and London. The printing is performed both by wooden blocks and by copper rollers, and the execution and colours are some of the very best of the Lancashire fabric. The premises occupy a large portion of ground, and cottages have been built for the accommodation of the workmen, which form streets, and give the appearance of a village. Ingenious artists are employed in drawing patterns and cutting and engraving them on wood and copper ; and many women and children in mixing the colours, and so forth. The company has several other extensive factories in the neighbourhood, as well on the Irwell as on the Rock. Some of them are confined to the carding, stubbing, and spinning of cotton ; others to washing the cottons with water-wheels, which go round with great velocity, but can be stopped in an instant, for taking out and putting in the goods. Boiling and bleaching the goods are performed at other works. In short, the extensiveness of the whole concern is such as to find constant employment for most of the inhabitants of Bury and its neighbourhood, of both sexes, and all ages ; and, notwithstanding their great number, they have never wanted work in the most unfavourable times. The peculiar healthiness of the people may be imputed partly to the judicious and humane regulations put in force by Mr. Peel." The whole town of Bury became a sort of appendage to Peel's factories, and, in consequence of his great success, its population steadily advanced, from being about 2,000, in 1773, to upwards of 15,000, in 1831. His own operatives in 1803 numbered about 15,000, though more than half of them were at Tamworth and in other parts of England, in which also he established factories.

Peel's busy factory still thrives, under the management of his successors, but other establishments have in later times arisen to vie with it in greatness ; and, just as the Peels began early to combine into one great trade the trades, formerly separated, of cotton-spinning, cotton-weaving, and calico-printing, so the more enterprising of the younger firms have found it best to make their business yet more composite. They not only, besides selling their own goods, buy the produce of some of their neighbours' mills, for disposal in the public market, and so have become merchants, as well as manufacturers ; they have also become iron-workers, in order that they may most cheaply construct their own tools ; and even colliers, in order that they may most advantageously procure their own fuel, both for making and for using the machinery. The way in which this composite development of the factory system has grown up will be best illustrated by a glance at the progress of one of the younger and more enterprising of the Lancashire houses.

Joseph Rylands, born at Parr, near St. Helens, in 1761, was the son of a hand-loom weaver in a small way of business, for whom he worked, in company with a few other labourers, and, as the business was well managed, and only the best calicoes were produced, it had grown considerably by 1787, when young Rylands became master, and it continued to grow under his shrewd direction. In 1810 he opened a draper's shop at St. Helens, where other goods were sold besides the outcome of his own mill. His three sons were taught to fight their own way in the world. John, the youngest son, born in 1803, was the ablest scholar of the three. When he was about fourteen, he spent his pocket-money in buying a parcel of trinkets put up at an auctioneer's sale, and, having sold these at a good profit, he found himself with an unusually large sum of money in his· pocket. He told his good fortune to an old nurse of the family, who, with her husband, had been trained in hand-loom weaving. "Why don't you buy a little warp and weft with the money you've got," she said, "and let us weave them?" John liked the suggestion, bought some material for the old lady to work up, and, the speculation proving profitable, continued to employ her, and thus became both merchant and manufacturer in a very small way, while he was still only a schoolboy. Promoted to serve in the draper's shop, he carried on the trade, and spent his leisure hours in weaving himself, whereby he was able to increase his stock-in-trade.

If there was no great romance in that beginning of life, there was promise of future success. The eldest brother, Joseph, had gone to Wigan, there to start a small mill of his own, and there he prospered so well that in 1821 he asked John, then eighteen, to join him as partner, and to undertake the travelling part of the business. That was agreed to, and for a short time John Rylands followed the old fashion, going on horseback to the various towns of Lancashire, Yorkshire, Cheshire, and North Wales, with his pack-saddle full of patterns, there to solicit orders for the calicoes, ginghams, and other cotton goods which his brother prepared at home. The business was so successful that old Joseph Rylands offered to become a partner, and put into it more capital than his sons could command, and the result was the establishment of the since famous firm of Rylands and Sons, with weaving-mills at Wigan and St. Helens, and a large draper's shop in the latter place. The draper's shop was given up in 1824, but before that a larger establishment had been started at Manchester. At first the Rylands sent most of their goods to Chester, at that time, relatively to Manchester, a very much more important trading-place than now. "I tell you what," said John to Joseph, in 1822, "instead of sending goods to Chester fair, let us send them to Manchester fair, and open a warehouse in that town." The suggestion was promptly acted upon. Before the close of the year, a house had been taken in High Street, and stocked with cotton wares, which John Rylands, living on the spot, made the centre of his trading operations. Cotton goods being then, even more than now, mixed with linen, the firm had early developed a trade with the flax-growers and spinners of the north of Ireland, and as it had also added dyeing and printing to its other operations, it had already made a good beginning to its many-sided trade.

Accident helped its further extension. In 1824 the firm bought two large estates near Wigan, on one of which dyeing and bleaching works were already erected, while on the other they set up a spinning-mill, for producing both cotton and linen yarns. This mill was a monster establishment when they built it, but, though increased in the interval, was of pigmy proportions, as compared with its rivals, when they gave it up in 1854. In that year it was four storeys high, was worked by engines of sixty-six horse-power, contained 20,000 throstles, and gave employment to about 350 hands. The chief value of the new purchase, however, was in the fact—unknown at the time—that under the adjoining land there were veins of excellent coal, both for domestic and manufacturing purposes. The Rylands established a colliery, which now gives employment to nearly a hundred colliers, besides clerks and other agents, and, while selling the house-coal to others, employed the coarser quality in their own works. Thereby all the coal-dealer's profit, and the cost of transit from a distance, were saved, and the firm was able to work on and increase its operations with very great advantage.

In 1839 Joseph Rylands the younger retired from the business, and proceeded to establish and be chief partner in a huge concern in Hull, known as the Hull Flax and Cotton Mills. In the same year, John Rylands and his father, who lived on till 1847, bought the Ainsworth Cotton Mill, between Bolton and Bury, where now, by about 600 operatives, some fifteen tons of cotton are weekly spun, and woven into some 30,000 lbs. of cotton fabric, for sale at the great warehouse in High Street, Manchester, which, by successive additions, has been converted into a vast establishment about a hundred yards long. In it, besides its own cottons and linens, the firm sold woollen and silk goods of every sort, and a thousand articles of haberdashery and millinery—from umbrellas and bonnets to stays and stockings.

This mercantile business, however, was always subordinate to the manufacturing business. In 1864 Rylands and Sons, now represented by only one of the sons, bought some extensive cotton-mills at Gorton, which they furnished with new machinery, and converted into one of the largest factories in England. They cover 16,000 square yards of land. There is a mechanics' shop, for producing all the necessary tools. The spinning-shed contains 32,000 throstles and 31,000 mule spindles, able to produce 75,000 lbs. of yarn every week. In the weaving-shed there are 1,500 power-looms. The whole machinery is turned by six high-pressure engines, with an aggregate of 300 horse-power; and on the estate there are 150 cottages for the use of some of the 1,500 hands employed. But this factory is surpassed by another, set up a year later by the same firm, near Wigan, and known as the Gidlow Works. "This magnificent mill," we are told, "is three storeys high, and the whole of it is fireproof. The top room of the north end is for receiving cotton, brought from the railway over a viaduct of 292 feet in length, crossing a reservoir, whose area is 7,306 square yards, and holding above 8,000,000 gallons of water for condensing purposes. The second floor contains the machinery for cleaning, opening, and making ready for the card-room. The bottom room is for boilers, mechanics' shop, &c. The second or middle division contains four horizontal steam-engines, of 200 horse-power, and the chief gearing for driving the mill. The south end has three storeys, each 273 feet by 108 feet. The bottom and top rooms are for throstles and mules, and contain 60,000 spindles, producing about 70,000 lbs. of yarn weekly. The middle room is for carding and preparing for these spindles. The weaving-shed, 540 feet long, 196 feet wide, and 20 feet high, is calculated to hold 2,940 looms, driven by two horizontal engines, of 100 horse-power." Of the whole establishment, the present Earl of Derby said, while it was being built, "I saw the other day, near Wigan, a new mill of vast extent rising, which is not, as usual, an eyesore, but a pleasure to the eye to rest on, so well has architectural effect been studied in its construction." The three mills at Gidlow, Gorton, and Ainsworth give employ to more than 4,500 operatives.

These three mills, like most of their great rivals or compeers, are situated at some distance from Manchester. Manchester, indeed, with its population of 358,000, is now chiefly the mart and centre of a busy trading province of workshops, stretching into Yorkshire, Derbyshire, and Cheshire, as well as Lancashire, giving employment to more than two million persons, directly and indirectly, in the

manufacture of cotton.   "In 1860," says Mr. Bazley, "the
number of spindles employed was about 32,000,000, the
number of looms about 340,000.   The production in the
machine-making trade had doubled within ten years.   Bleach-
works, print-works, and dye-works had been largely extended
during the same period.   The first investments, including
the value of land and rights to water, amounted to not less
than £60,000,000, to which must be added a working
capital of £20,000,000 ; add to these again the value of
merchants' and tradesmen's stock at home and abroad, the
value of raw cotton and subsidiary materials, and of bankers'
capital, and the grand total of capital employed in the trade
will not be less than £200,000,000."

All that wealth of trade, however, is not promoted by
Manchester and its far-reaching suburbs alone.   While, in
1861, there were 2,639 factories in the Manchester district,
in which 397,462 operatives worked 28,000,551 spindles
and 364,323 power-looms, the Glasgow district, and chiefly
Lanark and Renfrewshire, had 138 factories, in which 41,237
operatives worked 1,915,398 spindles and 30,110 power-
looms.

The first, or almost the first, cotton-mill established in
the northern counties, was begun at Rothesay, by an English
company, in 1778.   It was bought, in 1783, by David Dale,
a great Glasgow merchant and eccentric philanthropist, and,
in making it the nucleus of a vast enterprise, he was largely
helped by his famous son-in-law, Robert Owen, no less
eccentric, and no less philanthropical.   For the first fifteen
or sixteen years, Dale managed the concern alone.   He
greatly enlarged the new Lanark Mills, as they came to be
called, built numerous cottages for the use of his labourers,
procured Highlanders and Irishmen to do the factory work
that the Lowland Scots had no taste for, and brought from
the poorhouses of the great towns hundreds of orphans and
pauper children, whom he trained to become good work-

people. " His little kingdom," said one who visited the
establishment, in 1797, "consists of neat, well-built houses,
forming broad, regular, and cleanly streets. Near the middle
of the town stand the mills, and opposite to them the chief
mansion of the place, the residence of the superintendent
of the works. The town contains 2,000 inhabitants, mostly
Highlanders, all of whom that are capable of labour are
employed by Mr. Dale in his service, either in working
at the cotton manufactory, or in repairing and keeping the
mills in order. Five hundred children are entirely fed,
clothed, and instructed at the expense of the venerable
philanthropist. The rest of the children live with their
parents, in comfortable and neat habitations in the town,
and receive weekly wages for their labour. The health and
happiness depicted in the countenances of these children
show that the proprietor of the Lanark Mills has remembered
mercy in the midst of his gain. The regulations adopted
here for the preservation of health, both of mind and body,
are such as do honour to the goodness and discernment of
Mr. Dale, and present a striking contrast to the generality
of large manufactories in this kingdom. · It is a truth that
should be engraven in letters of gold, to the eternal honour
of the founders of New Lanark, that, out of nearly three
thousand children working in these mills, during a period of
twelve years, from 1785 to 1797, only fourteen have died,
and not one hath suffered criminal punishment. The lesser
children, that are not yet old enough to work, are instructed
in the daytime ; the elder children learn in the evening,
when the daily labour is concluded. Proper masters and
mistresses are employed, to teach both the boys and the
girls. The boys learn to read and write, and cast accounts ;
the girls, in addition to these, are taught to work at the
needle."

In 1799 David Dale, having more than his old age permitted him to do in attending to his other businesses, sold

P

the cotton-mills to a company, of which Robert Owen was
partner and acting manager; and by him, during more than
twenty-five years, the concern was superintended, and, while
being greatly extended as a commercial enterprise, was
diligently used in developing his socialist ideas, not then
as far advanced as they were in later years.   Both experiments succeeded, and the New Lanark Mills won the admiration of men as different as Jeremy Bentham and William
Allen, the Quaker.   But Owen's partners disapproved of his
communism, and, after long disputing about the religious
and social questions mixed up with the trading concern,
he parted from them in 1825.   New Lanark passed into
other hands, and, following the fashion of other factories, has
continued to share their prosperity.

In 1785 David Dale had established another cotton-
factory at Blantyre.   He sold it, in 1792, to James Monteith,
the great promoter of linen manufacture in Glasgow, and its
neighbourhood.   Wisely administered during nearly eight
years, it has grown into another famous manufacturing out-
post of Glasgow, excelling in the dyeing and weaving that
it has added to the spinning with which it began.   " The
buildings," it was said in 1860, "in which the cotton-spinning
was carried on in the year 1805 have remained very much
as they were, but, by the introduction of improved machinery,
the work is now efficiently carried on by two hundred and
sixty workers, of whom two hundred and one are females,
and fifty nine males."   These labourers now do twenty times
as much work as in 1805 was done by thrice as many hands;
and the whole number employed in the factory, rather more
than a thousand, maintain one of the most efficient and
comprehensive cotton-factories to be found in Scotland.

With woollen manufacture Glasgow has not much to do;
but it gives occupation to multitudes in various parts of
Scotland, as well as in nearly every county of England.   Of
most of the trade, however, Leeds is the centre, and it

abounds most in the districts adjoining it; the woollen province extending through northern Yorkshire, till it touches the cotton province, with Manchester for its capital.

Leeds, though a very ancient town, has only lately become considerable. Under the Plantagenets and Tudors, it was surpassed by Halifax. "The parish of Halifax and other places thereunto," we read in an Act of Parliament of Queen Mary's reign, "being planted in great wastes and moors, where the fertility of the soil is not apt to bring forth common good grass, but in rare places, and by exceeding great industry of the inhabitants, the inhabitants do altogether live by cloth-making; and the greater part of them neither groweth corn, nor is able to keep a horse to carry wool, nor yet to buy much wool at once, but hath ever used only to repair to the town of Halifax, and some other nigh thereunto, and there to buy of the wool-dealer, some a stone, some two, and some three or four, according to their ability, and to carry the same to their houses, some three, four, five, or six miles off, upon their heads or backs, and to make and convert the same into either yarn or cloth, and to sell the same, and so buy more wool of the wool-dealer; by means of which industry the barren grounds in these parts are much inhabited, and above five hundred households there newly increased within these forty years past." That paper shows in what humble ways all our great woollen towns rose to importance. Wakefield was for a long time the chief rival of Halifax, and Leeds only began to surpass them about the middle of the eighteenth century. Even then, however, it was much more a mart than a manufacturing town. To its weekly cloth-market came the small manufacturers of the surrounding districts, to sell their wares to the traders of Hull and Boston, and the traffic increased so rapidly that, a great Mixed Cloth Hall having been erected in 1758, another wool-exchange, known as the White Cloth Hall, had to be set up in 1775. In that year

r 2

Leeds contained 17,117 inhabitants. By 1865 the number had risen to 224,025, and, while the trade in wool had grown rapidly in the course of those ninety years, the town and its suburbs had been crowded with great manufactories, in which all the famous improvements introduced in the spinning, weaving, dyeing, and finishing of cotton fabric had been adapted to the working of woollen fibres. In 1858 Leeds had 128 factories, giving employment to more than 10,000 operatives. The whole woollen and worsted manufacture of Yorkshire is nearly eight times as extensive, and Yorkshire enjoys about a fourth of the woollen manufacture of Great Britain, in which more than 300,000,000 lbs. of fibre are worked up by about 300,000 operatives.

The foremost woollen manufacturer of Leeds, and the man who helped most to form the character of the improved woollen trade of modern times, was Benjamin Gott. Born in 1762, and the son of a working man, who rose to some distinction as a civil engineer, he began work in a small factory, though one of the largest then existing in Leeds. Therein, from being a humble clerk, he rose to be a partner, and, at length, he succeeded to the entire management of the concern, which grew mightily under his hands. At the time of his death in 1840, about eleven hundred workpeople, aided by the most improved machinery, were employed in dyeing, spinning, weaving, fulling, and dressing cloth, made of the best Saxony wool, the whole arrangement of the factory being a model of wise and successful management. One of Gott's great merits was the scrupulous regard always shown by him for the men in his employ, and the class to which they belonged. Beginning his enterprise just when the old ways of private work were being in great part superseded by factory labour, he strove hard to perpetuate the spirit of manly independence which had been begotten by the older institutions ; and from first to last he encouraged the private workers to bring him their wares, and use him as their agent in disposing of them. Much of the woollen trade of York-shire, as of other parts, is still of that sort, and it prevails especially in the wide-spread area of Scotland, which has for it staple work the production of woollen goods.

Woollen manufacture embraces two distinct trades. In the one close, firm yarn is prepared, and converted into cloth; the other produces the loose yarn known as worsted, which is converted into a great variety of articles, from winter stockings and mats for drawing-room tables, to carpets and tapestry of all sorts. While Leeds is the centre of the cloth trade, the neighbouring town of Bradford is the chief place of worsted manufacture.

In Tudor times Bradford vied with Leeds as a seat of cloth-making, though both were inferior to Wakefield. It fell behind in the race of progress during the seventeenth and eighteenth centuries, but has in later times done much to retrieve its position. Worsted-making had been one of its special crafts, and in this it was for a long time surpassed by Norwich, fortunate in the immigration of great numbers of Flemish artisans in Queen Elizabeth's reign. But the Norwich workmen, it is said, proud of their supremacy, began early in the eighteenth century to claim higher wages than the masters could afford, and on that account the trade was in great measure carried back to the cheaper labour-field of Yorkshire. The change, however, was not made without opposition, even from the inhabitants whom it was to enrich. In 1793 an enterprising Bradford manufacturer, named Buckley, proposed to start a mill, to be worked by steam-power; but was deterred by a threat from his neighbours that, in the event of his doing so, he would be prosecuted for causing a nuisance. The first spinning-machine of Cromp-ton's make was set up in 1794, by James Garnett, founder of one of the largest factories in England. " I remember spinning-machines being used in the Paper Hall by Mr. James Garnett," said an old workman, "who employed in the work ten or a dozen hands. There were three men regularly at work, the rest being women. The machines were turned by hand." Within ten years of that time, Bradford had several mills and thousands of spinning-machines; and, the first mechanical apparatus being once introduced, the progress of the town was steady and rapid, save in the year or two following a great strike of combers and weavers in 1825. In 1815 there were 10 mills, with an aggregate of 250 horse-power. In 1825 the numbers and power had severally risen to 26 and 706; in 1835 to 73 and 1,647; and in 1850 to 194 and 4,185. In 1856 there were in the United Kingdom 525 worsted factories, giving employment to 87,794 persons, and of these factories Bradford and its suburbs claimed 186, employing 30,517 labourers.

Of both cotton and woollen manufacture England has the chief share, and nearly all the rest is carried on in Scotland, hardly any being in Ireland. Ireland, however, is largely concerned in flax-spinning and linen manufacture, though Scotland has slightly surpassed it, and England engrosses about a sixth of the trade. Belfast, Dundee, and Leeds are the centres in the three countries.

Belfast owes its greatness chiefly to English and Scottish enterprise. Given, in 1604, to Sir Arthur Chichester, it was by him converted into a flourishing town, a good example of industry being afforded to the Irish residents by the Devonshire workpeople whom he transplanted. Later immigrants came from Scotland, and by them especially, having Louis Crommelin, the Huguenot refugee, for an instructor, the cultivation of flax and the preparation of linen cloth were developed. "No women are apter to spin linen thread well than the Irish," said Sir William Temple in 1681, "who, labouring little in any kind with their hands, have their fingers more supple and soft than women of the poor condition amongst us. And this may certainly be advanced and improved into a great manufacture of linen, for the soil and climate are proper for whitening, both by the frequent brooks, and also by the winds of that country." Though much less has been done than was possible, the progress of its linen trade has been the main source of the improved condition of Ireland in recent times, and both social prosperity and wealth have been most abundant in Belfast and its outlying districts. In 1758 Belfast had a population of 8,549, and exported to Liverpool more than 14,000,000 yards of linen. In 1861 the population had increased to 121,602, and the linen exportation of 1865 was nearly 100,000,000 yards. The value of the linen trade to Belfast and its suburbs is reckoned at £10,000,000 a year.

The trade might have been greater, however, had the Belfast manufacturers made prompt and full use of the mechanical inventions by which, during the eighteenth century, textile workmanship was improved. Flax-growing was increased, and its preliminary manipulation was extended ; but tardiness in adopting the best ways of weaving allowed that part of the trade to be transferred in great measure to Dundee and Leeds. It has since been considerably reclaimed, and Belfast now contains the best power-looms, as well as the best spinning-machines that can be obtained. In and near Belfast there were, in 1862, a hundred great factories, in which 592,981 spindles and 4,666 power-looms were worked by 33,525 operatives.

Dundee had linen manufacture for one of its trades as early as Belfast; but during many generations the work was spread over nearly the whole of Scotland, and Dundee was no more conspicuous for it than a dozen other towns. In 1742 its linens were described as "the poorest and meanest" of any produced in Scotland, and long after that date its chief manufacture was very coarse cloth, sent undressed and unbleached to Sweden and Germany. Its superiority dates only from about the commencement of the present century, and was caused solely by the energy of a few wise manufacturers, who made good use of the machines already adopted in the making up of cotton goods. Even then the enterprise was chiefly shown in spinning, and but little attention was paid to improvements in weaving. As late as 1833 it was said that in Dundee power-looms had not been employed with any advantage, and that those set up were nearly abandoned. The change that has been effected in later years is especially due to William Baxter and his sons, whose achievements illustrate Scottish enterprise in linen manufacture at its best.

In 1822 William and Edward Baxter erected a small spinning-mill, worked by a steam-engine of fifteen horse-power, on the Dens Burn, in the north-eastern part of Dundee, which succeeded so well that, three years later, another engine of thirty horse-power was added, and these were replaced in 1833 by one large engine of ninety horse-power, the firm then altering its name to Baxter Brothers and Company. In 1836 it set up the first successful power-loom factory known in Dundee, therein alone employing 300 workpeople. Other additions followed in later years, and now more than ten acres of land are covered by mills, factories, warehouses, and other premises necessary to the conversion, in a year, of more than 77,000 tons of flax into about 20,000,000 yards of cloth, by between 4,000 and 4,500 operatives, the whole forming by far the largest linen-factory in the world. In it there are twenty-two steam-engines, with an aggregate power of 750 horses, and thirty-two steam-boilers, which consume about fifty tons of coal every day. The whole process of manufacture is here carried on. The flax arrives in bales, whence it is taken out in bunches, and subjected to the pickling-machines, which vary according to the quality of the raw fibre and the quality of the finished fabric to be made from it ; after that it is bleached, roved, and spun into suitable yarn. It is then, by 1,200 power-looms, woven into cloth of every kind, from fine cambrics and lawns to rough sheetings, towellings, and osnaburgs.

Jute manufacture, conjointly with or apart from linen, forms an important addition to the staple trade of Dundee. In 1867 the town and its suburbs contained 72 factories, employing in all 35,310 operatives. There were in all Forfarshire 108 factories, and 51 in Fifeshire, the whole linen manufacture of Scotland being represented by 197 factories, containing 487,579 spindles and 19,917 power-looms, and giving work to 77,195 men and women.

Leeds has kept pace with Dundee in this department of labour, and here also its progress is mainly due to the enterprise of one famous family. John Marshall, born in 1765, was a shop-boy when, flax-spinning having been carried on in a humble way throughout Yorkshire and Lancashire during many previous generations, he began to devise improvements on the best spinning-machinery then in use. In 1788, with the help of two partners, who found the money, he started a small mill at Meanwood, near Leeds; and in 1791 he transferred his operations to Leeds itself, setting up in Water Lane the modest mill which, during the half-century prior to his death in 1845, was mightily increased, and, by its own work and the example it has set to others, has added another great trade to Leeds. In 1821 there were nineteen mills in Leeds, of which four belonged to John Marshall, these four being as extensive as all the spinning-machinery then in Dundee. In 1856 there were 37 linen-factories in Leeds, with an aggregate steam-power of 1,831 horses, and in which 198,076 spindles and 140 power-looms were worked by 9,458 hands.

The largest of John Marshall's three great mills is one of the wonders of the world. It forms one vast room, seven times as large as Exeter Hall in London. "It is 132 yards long, 72 yards wide, and 20 feet high," it was said in 1867. "The roof consists of 72 brick arches, supported on as many iron pillars, and secured together by strong iron-work. The brick roof has a thick coating of composition, to prevent the water from coming through, and it is covered with earth, from which has sprung up a beautiful grass sward. There are 66 glass domes in the roof, each 48 feet round, and 11½ feet high, containing 10 tons of glass in iron window-frames. The total weight of the roof is 4,000 tons. There are four steam-engines of 100 horse-power, and two of 80 horse-power; and one engine of 7 horse-power which does nothing but blow hot or cold air into the room. The building covers more than two acres of ground, and it is supposed that 80,000 persons might stand in the room. This hall is occupied for spinning and weaving by power, and the whole processes incidental to the trade, subsequent to pickling, are performed in it, the flax going in in bundles, and the linen out in bales. To non-practical people it is one of the most interesting sights that can be witnessed, as regards both the beautiful machinery, with its many and curious motions, and the immense number of active and apparently happy male and female workers, who guide its operations, and turn out the beautiful yarns and linens, the production of which has rendered the Marshalls so famous. To those practically acquainted with the trade, this sight is worth seeing, as even the most advanced would learn much, as to both the construction of the machinery and its arrangement." Here, as in most of the other factories of Leeds, the more delicate kinds of linen—damasks and the like—are chiefly made.

Metal-factories, of course, differ essentially from clothing-factories, although some of the most important of them have grown famous by producing the tools and engines needed for textile manufacture. Manchester, Leeds, Glasgow, and every other cloth-making town, has many great establishments of this sort, one of the oldest and most notable being the Carron Iron-Works, near Glasgow, founded in 1760, and which Burns was once not allowed to inspect, the porter supposing that he wished to discover the secrets of the concern. Burns consoled himself by scratching these lines on the window-pane of the inn at Carron :—

> " We cam' na here to view your warks,
>   In hopes to be mair wise,
> But only, lest we gang to hell,
>   It may be nae surprise :
> But when we tirlèd at your door,
>   Your porter dought na hear us ;
> Sae may, should we to hell's yetts come,
>   Your billie Satan sair us ! "

The Carron Iron-works are specially memorable, in that at them James Watt, for a brief time the partner of their founder, Dr. Roebuck, constructed his first steam-engine. All his others were made at Soho, in Birmingham, where he found a more congenial partner in Matthew Boulton ; and, if only on that account, Soho would be the most important factory, as it has been directly and indirectly the most beneficial, in the world.

Birmingham, however, was a great centre of metal manufacture long before the time of Boulton and Watt. "The beauty of Birmingham, a good market-town, in the extreme parts of Warwickshire," said Leland, in Henry VIII.'s reign, "is one street, going almost from the left bank of the brook up a mean hill, by the length of a quarter of a mile. There be many smiths in the town, that use to make knives and all manner of cutting tools ; and many lorimers, that make bits ; and a great many nailers ; so that a great part of the town is maintained by smiths, who have their iron and sea-coal out of Staffordshire." These trades continued, and others were added to them. Iron, steel, and brass workers abounded in the town throughout the eighteenth century, and Birmingham wares then, as now, included a hundred different sorts of articles—swords, guns, knives, tools, pots, pans, pins, needles, buckles, and buttons, in especial ; the manufacture of buttons alone, in glass, horn, bone, pearl, steel, and other substances, being so extensive that it was divided into nearly sixty separate branches.

A representative manufacturer of Birmingham, in the eighteenth century, was John Taylor, who was born in 1714, and died in 1775. Beginning life as a common labourer, he made buttons, buckles, snuff-boxes, and other fancy articles, with so much taste and tact, that he soon became master of a large establishment. His shop-sweepings, consisting of quicksilver, brass-scrapings, and the like, he sold for £1,000 a year. A nobleman, who visited Birmingham, and made several expensive purchases in Taylor's shop, is reported to have said that " he plainly saw he could not live in Birmingham for less than £200 a day." From being a great button-maker, Taylor became a great banker, and he died worth £200,000.

His contemporary, and a much greater man, was Matthew Boulton, born in 1725, who made much wealth by trade akin to Taylor's before 1762, when he bought a small mill that had been set up eight years before at Soho, then a dreary Staffordshire heath, about two miles distant from the town, which at that time contained, within narrow limits, about 40,000 inhabitants, about an eighth of the present population. " I founded my manufactory," he said in 1790, " upon one of the most barren commons in England, where there existed but a few miserable huts, filled with idle, beggarly people, who, by help of the common land and a little thieving, made shift to live without working. The scene is now entirely changed. I have employed a thousand men, women, and children in my manufactory for nearly thirty years past. The lord of the manor hath exterminated those very poor cottages, and hundreds of clean, comfortable, cheerful houses are found erected in their place."

The history of the progress at Soho during these thirty years and the years that followed is very instructive. Boulton began his enterprise as a mere extension of his old "toy"-making trade, using his larger establishment for the honest and artistic manufacture of the various minor articles on account of which Birmingham was styled by Burke "the toy-shop of Europe." "The building," it was said in 1774, "consists of four squares, with shops, warehouses, &c., for a thousand workmen, who, in a great variety of branches, excel in their several departments, not only in the fabrication of buttons, buckles, boxes, trinkets, &c., in gold, silver, and a variety of compositions, but in many other arts, long predominant in France, which ·lose their reputation on a comparison with the products of this place; and it is by the natives hereof, or of the parts adjacent, whose emulation and taste the proprietors have spared no care or expense to excite and improve, that it is brought to its present flourishing state. The number of ingenious mechanical contrivances they avail themselves of, by the means of water-mills, much facilitates their work, and saves a great portion of time and labour. The plated work has an appearance of solid silver, more especially compared with that of any other manufactory. Their excellent ornamental pieces in ormulu have been admired by the nobility and gentry, not only of this kingdom, but of all Europe, and are allowed to surpass anything of that kind made abroad; and some articles lately executed in silver-plate show that taste and elegance of design prevail here in a superior degree, and are with mechanism and chemistry happily united." A large and profitable trade with foreign countries, as well as in England, resulted from Boulton's praiseworthy devotion to his business. "If, in the course of your future travelling," he wrote, in 1767, to an agent in Italy, "you can pick up for me any metallic ores or fossil substances, or any other curious natural productions, I should be much obliged to you, as I am fond of all those things that have a tendency to improve my knowledge in mechanical arts, in which my manufactory will every year become more and more general, and therefore wish to know the taste, the fashions, the toys, both useful and ornamental, the implements, vessels, &c., that prevail in all the different parts of Europe, as I should be glad to work for all Europe, in all things that they may have occasion for—gold, silver, copper, plated, gilt, pinchbeck, steel, platina, tortoise-shell, or anything else that may become an article of general demand."

In 1770 Boulton truly described Soho as "the largest hardware manufactory in the world." "I have almost every machine," he added, "that is applicable to these arts. I have two water-mills, employed in rolling, polishing, grinding, and turning various sorts of lathes. I have trained up many and am training up more plain country lads into good workmen, and wherever I find indications of skill and ability I encourage them." That zeal in the education of good workmen and constant care of his subordinates was a notable trait in his character. "I have built and furnished," he said to an applicant, who came prepared to pay a premium of several hundred pounds for admission to Soho as an apprentice, "a house for one kind of apprentices—fatherless children and hospital boys—and gentlemen's sons would probably find themselves out of place in such companionship." Boswell visited Soho in 1776, and observed a pleasant instance of Boulton's treatment of his men. "One of them came to him complaining grievously of his landlord, for having distrained his goods, 'Your landlord is in the right, Smith,' said Boulton ; 'but I'll tell you what—find a friend who will lay down one half of your rent, and I will lay down the other, and you shall have your goods again.'" "I shall never forget Mr. Boulton's expression to me, when surveying the works," adds Boswell : "'I sell here, sir, what all the world requires to have—Power.' I contemplated him as an iron chieftain, and he seemed to be the father of his tribe."

A year before that, in 1775, Boulton had begun to be, much more than previously, an iron chieftain. He then, after much earlier negotiation, entered into partnership with James Watt, who, during the ten years preceding, had been vainly trying to bring his steam-engine into public favour. Boulton's practical energy, supplementing Watt's scientific enterprise, succeeded in overcoming popular prejudice ; but the difficulties of the work during the first five years absorbed all the profits that had been made at Soho from the time of its commencement, and necessitated an outlay of £11,000 besides. Boulton had to borrow money from all his friends— Thomas Day, the eccentric author of "Sandford and Merton," being one of them—and was for some time hardly able to save himself from bankruptcy. He and Watt and the steam-engine, however, triumphed in the end. Watt, in despair, over and over again proposed to abandon the business as hopeless. "Almost the whole county is against us," he wrote to his partner, in 1782, from Cornwall, when he was superintending the first application of the steam-engine to mining operations, "and look upon us as oppressors and tyrants, from whose power they believe the horned imps of Satan are to relieve them." "The care and attention which our business requires," he complained, in another letter, "make me at present dread a fresh order with as much horror as other people with joy receive one. What signifies it to a man, though he gain the whole world, if he lose his health and his life? The first of those losses has already befallen me, and the second will probably be the consequence of it, without some favourable circumstances, which at present I cannot foresee, should prevent it." But Boulton was never faint-hearted.

The hardware-works at Soho were not abandoned, but they were rendered insignificant by the setting up, in the same establishment, of the engine-factory, in 1775. In 1785 that factory began to pay its working expenses; thenceforward it prospered. The steam-engine, at first only used for mining, was found equally helpful to manufacturing purposes. Once used, its use soon became general, in Manchester, Leeds, Glasgow, and all other factory-towns. In 1795 Boulton and Watt's extensive business necessitated the establishment of a separate establishment for making engines, and the Soho Foundry was started. Watt's patent expired in 1799, and then similar institutions were set up in various parts of the country; but the fame of Soho, well maintained by the ability with which it was managed by the first proprietors and their successors, made it, for a long time, the chief seat of engine manufacture. During the seven years prior to 1866, the Soho Foundry, now covering an area of ten acres, produced 1,878 steam-engines, with an aggregate of 70,958 horse-power. Of these, 319 were pumping-engines, 1,090 were rotative engines, for manufacturing purposes, and 469 were marine engines, the largest of these latter being the works for the *Great Eastern*, with 1,700 horse-power.

Boulton's energy was shown in many other ways, and he was the author and producer of many other famous inventions and improvements, by which Birmingham and all the world have been greatly aided. The common copying-press was introduced by him. He was the first silver-plater in his native town, now so famous for its work in that way. To him are due the great improvements in coining which, · after trial at his own Soho Mint, were introduced by him in the London Mint on Tower Hill, and also in the mints of Russia, Spain, Denmark, Calcutta, and Bombay. "Had Mr. Boulton done nothing more in the world than he has accomplished in improving the coinage," said Watt, "his name would deserve to be immortalised; and if it be considered that this was done in the midst of various other important avocations, and at enormous expense, for which, at the time, he could have no certainty of an adequate return, we shall be at a loss whether most to admire his ingenuity, his perseverance, or his munificence. He has conducted the whole more like a sovereign than a private manufacturer, and the love of fame has always been to him a greater stimulus than the love of gain."

Boulton died in 1809, Watt in 1819. In 1800 they had handed over the management of the Soho Foundry to their sons, Matthew Robinson Boulton and James Watt the younger. In 1848 the good old name of Boulton and Watt was abandoned, and the firm began to be known as James Watt and Company. The older Soho hardware manufactory has long since been discontinued.

Other hardware factories, however, abound in Birmingham, and the trade, like the town, has grown mightily, in consequence, to a great extent, of Matthew Boulton's example, and of the assistance afforded by his introduction of the steam-engine. Many Birmingham factories, like those in which the Elkingtons produce electro-plated goods, the Gillotts pens and the Edelstons pins, have attained worldwide notoriety; and hundreds of others, large and small, contribute to the wealth of the town and the prosperity of its inhabitants. Birmingham's chief rival, in old times as in the present, Sheffield, has shared its progress, and kindred factories have arisen in abundance in all parts of the country. Much of the work done in Sheffield is in steel, and Birmingham has brass for one of its specialities; but brass and steel, as well as other metals and other wares, are worked up in a hundred other districts, and the result of all is a vast increase of English enterprise, giving wealth to thousands and maintenance to hundreds of thousands. By help of its countless factories, England is able to carry on a commerce of unparalleled greatness with all the world, and to feed a population more than thrice as large as the agri-

Q

cultural resources of the country, unaided by the fruits of other nations, bought with the profits of its factory labour, could possibly support.

No other nation has factories as large or manufacturing establishments as various as those of England; but every nation has learnt something of England's skill, and many, either as learners or as pioneers, have acquired special excellence in special departments. This has been shown by recent international exhibitions, better and more pleasantly than could be done by any mere description, however lengthy, and it is needless here to attempt to show it in a few short paragraphs. Nor is it necessary to heap up old statistics concerning the extent and operations of foreign factories in textile goods, in metal wares, and in other articles. It will suffice to furnish very brief illustrations of the manufacturing condition of the two chief manufacturing countries after England—France and the United States.

France, excelling England in many minor branches of manufacture, excels her notably in one great staple article of trade. Henry IV. and our James I. sought with equal zeal to naturalise the silkworm in their respective dominions. The experiment failed in England, but succeeded in France, and to that natural advantage must be in part attributed the superiority of France in silk-working.

The history of the French silk trade is noteworthy. A slight manufacture was carried on at Marseilles, Avignon, and other places as early as the fourteenth century, just about the same time that London had its silk-women, both countries being supplied with their raw material from Spain, Italy, and the Levant. But the craft made but little progress for three centuries. Henry IV., growing mulberry-trees in the garden of the Tuileries, and breeding silkworms in his own palace, was not able to advance it much; and its first great development was due to the violent energy of Colbert, who caused mulberry-trees to be planted along all the high roads of the south, and offered a premium of twenty-four sous for every tree that was three years old. The bribe succeeded, and before long the south-eastern provinces abounded in food for the worms that became plentiful as soon as there was suitable sustenance for them. Great increase of silk-spinning and silk-weaving quickly resulted, the Protestants of Languedoc being the chief workers.

Then religious fanaticism nearly stifled the trade. The revocation of the Edict of Nantes, in 1685, reduced the number of looms from 9,000 to 3,000, and a large proportion of their owners, settling in Spitalfields, helped to develop in England so much of the trade as it has since acquired. Many years elapsed before it revived in France. In 1788, however, the first year concerning which we have authentic details, it was found that 1,600 tons of raw and thrown silk were annually wrought in the country, two-thirds being of native growth, and one-third imported ; and that the value of the fabric produced amounted to about £5,000,000, nearly a fifth being converted into stockings and a fourth into ribbons and braid. Only £1,000,000 worth was exported, the rest being used chiefly by the Court ladies, gallants, and superior clergy in attendance on Louis XVI.

The French Revolution brought another violent reverse. At the siege of Lyons, the Royalists, for whom almost exclusively the silk had been made, destroyed the factories. In the adjoining districts, the mulberry-trees were rooted up, and the worms died out. The aristocrats being exiled, moreover, as the local historian says, "the only remaining use of silk was to make the victorious standards of the army of France." In 1812 only a third as much silk was produced and a third as much imported as in 1788, and of this a larger proportion, when made into tissue, was exported. The rise of wages and other circumstances, however, caused this smaller quantity to be of nearly equal value to the supply of 1788, and the augmented price has been since maintained. Jacquard's loom facilitated the manufacture. But the increasing intelligence of the workpeople, ever on the watch for artistic improvements, and the growing requirements of fashion, stimulated the demand for their produce, both at home and abroad. In 1812 the number of looms at work were 27,410, yielding fabric worth £4,300,000. In 1853 the looms numbered 220,000, the manufacture was valued at £21,000,000. In the ensuing sixteen years both have been doubled, if not more. In 1865 the exports alone amounted in value to £17,000,000. In recent times, however, the internal trade has been greatly altered. In 1853 the total yield of native cocoons was 26,000 tons ; but in that year a disease appeared among the silkworms, by which the supply has been rapidly reduced. In 1865 the yield was only 5,500 tons. The deficiency, as well as the increased demands of commerce, have had to be met by importation of raw silk from other parts, and this, in 1864, amounted to upwards of £10,000,000, showing a great gain to foreign trade, but a serious loss to the farmers and peasants in the silk-producing districts. The value of the yield in the department of the Drôme, which has suffered most of all, sank from about £600,000 in 1853 to about £100,000 in 1864.

One effect of this change has been to concentrate the enterprise, more than ever, in Lyons and its neighbourhood. Here, at present, about two-thirds of the silk-manufacture of France is carried on, while the other towns in which it prevails make considerable use of Lyons as their market.

Lyons, advantageously placed at the junction of the Rhône and the Saône, which provided easy transit for the wares of Marseilles, and greatly helped by Louis XI.'s institution of its commercial fairs in 1492, rose to vast importance in the sixteenth century, and was fitly styled, in Henry IV.'s days, the Golden Gate of France. The silk-trade found in it from the first a natural home, the produce of the town and its suburbs being augmented by the cocoons brought hither from more remote districts. In 1680 its silk-workers numbered nearly 12,000. Five years later they were reduced by the revocation of the Edict of Nantes to about a third, and there was no great increase till about 1750, when the old trade received fresh stimulus, and continued to grow till 1790, when it gave employment to 18,000 workpeople. The Revolution again reduced the number, which in 1800 hardly exceeded 3,000. Bonaparte's rule, however, began a revival, which has had no subsequent check. At the time of the peace of 1814 the town contained 12,000 silk-workers, and the number was nearly doubled in the two years ensuing. In 1837 there were 27,000 spinners and weavers. In 1863 there were about 10,000 master-workers and 60,000 journeymen ; and, as about as many labourers were employed in tool-making, growing, buying, selling, and other necessary occupations, the trade then gave work to more than a third of the entire population of 318,803, and to more persons than the whole town contained forty years before.

The proportion of master-workers to journeymen shows the nature of the silk-manufacture of Lyons. There are no great factories, as in England, with its cotton, wool, and linen trades. All the town is a vast factory, in which the master-workers, sometimes their own masters altogether, but oftener bound to silk-merchants, who lend them money for buying their material and paying their labourers, generally carry on their craft in meagre lodgings, one or two rooms serving for sleeping in, and another for spinning or weaving. The master works with his wife, two or three experienced labourers, and two or three apprentices, the hours of daily toil varying from twelve, in slack times, to twenty, when orders are most pressing. The Lyons weavers fare much better than the Spitalfields weavers, but their condition is, in most respects, far inferior to that of our own factory operatives. The spinners, who supply them with yarn, and who reside in the healthier suburbs, sometimes have happier times, but we must go to the romance-writers for a pleasant picture of their lot. " A particular charm," says M. Michelet, " surrounds the working of silk. It ennobles those who make it. In crossing our rudest countries, among the valleys of the Ardèche, where all is rock, where the mulberry and the chestnut seem to live without earth, on pebbles and air, where low houses in dry stone sadden the eye with their grey tints, everywhere I saw at the doors two or three bright-eyed girls, with brown skins and white teeth, who smiled at the passer-by, and spun gold."

One welcome phase in this factory-life of Lyons is the zeal shown in artistic instruction, by which the silks of France are rendered superior to nearly all those of other countries. The great school of St. Pierre gives free teaching to about two hundred students, whose special business it is to learn how best to devise beautiful patterns, and to apply them in weaving and dyeing. Here and elsewhere botanical gardens, halls of sculpture, and natural history museums do good work in the special and general education of the people, though most of them find a readier school for eye and hand in cultivating that love of flowers which is one of the most agreeable characteristics of the French temperament.

Moires, velvets, and the richest silken wares are made almost exclusively at Lyons. Ribbons are the staple produce of St. Étienne, the Coventry of France, where in 1864 there were 25,000 looms and 40,000 persons engaged in the trade, most of them, however, being peasant-farmers of the neighbourhood, whose children helped them in their light and dainty workmanship.

The use of little but hand-labour, and the continuance of the old-fashioned independence of work which characterises the silk-trade of France, are for the most part common also to its other textile manufactures. The result appears in the insignificance of its production of woollens, linen, and cotton fabrics, as compared with that of Great Britain. The making of cotton goods is more extensive than that of the other tissues ; but the difference and the cause of its sluggishness, as compared with the enterprise of our own country, can be understood by every one who, after visiting our busy centre of cotton industry, walks through the streets of Rouen, the Manchester of France. Here good work is done by the 50,000 or more men, women, and children employed in the trade—nearly half of the whole population—and the "rouen-neries," or printed cloths, for which they are especially famous, well deserve their fame ; but much of the labour still follows the old ways, and the best spinning and weaving in large establishments is done by Englishmen and other foreigners. Great factories seem out of place in France, and ill-fitted to the dispositions both of employer and of employed.

Mulhouse would be an exception to that inference, were not Mulhouse still more Swiss than French. A busy place of woollen manufacture from early times, calico-printing was begun in it in 1745, and it soon became a famous haunt of cotton spinners and weavers. Its annexation by France in 1795 did not greatly alter its character, while it facilitated the transit to it of cotton-fibre from Marseilles, Bordeaux, and Havre. Basle continued to supply most of the energy by which the manufacture was extended. Many large factories have been set up, and Mulhouse, lately making a special study of English arrangements, has taken the foremost place in the cotton manufacture of France. A large proportion of its 46,000 inhabitants find therein their chief employment.

If France shows us how a nation older than England has allowed us to get far ahead in manufacturing energy, and the national wealth that is acquired by it, we may see in the

United States what very rapid strides can be made in a new country, richly endowed with natural advantages, and peopled by a race well fitted to make use of them. The manufactures of the United States are still in their infancy, but the infantine robustness gives promise of unrivalled exploits in future years.

New York and Philadelphia, both of them great marts as well, are still the chief centres of manufacturing energy in America, New York having a slight pre-eminence as regards the value of its products, estimated in 1860 at about £32,000,000, and giving employment to 90,188 hands in 4,374 establishments. Most of those establishments, however, are devoted to minor trades, and Philadelphia surpasses it as a seat of great factories. Therein, in 1860, there were 6,467 establishments, giving employment to 107,931 persons, and producing goods worth more than £30,000,000 a year. Shoemaking, millinery, and fifty other trades help to swell those figures; but of staple manufactures in textile goods, ironwork, and the like Philadelphia now has a large share.

One of these, the Pascal Iron-works, may illustrate the progress of many. In 1821, when the city contained 120,000 inhabitants, a fifth of the number now resident in it, Stephen Morris opened a shop for making and selling stoves and grates. His success therein enabled him, in 1828, to take larger premises, in partnership with two others, and there set up a foundry for extensive iron-manufacture. In 1836 the making of wrought-iron tubes, for gas, steam, or water, became a special branch of work, and the firm now makes of them more than 5,000,000 feet a year. Other appliances for heating and lighting houses and buildings of all sorts were introduced by Morris and his successors, and the establishment in 1868 covered four acres of ground and gave employment to more than 1,100 workmen.

Philadelphia almost took the lead in American cotton-manufacture. In 1775 a society was formed for the advancement, in the town and its neighbourhood, of textile manufactures, and this was reshaped as the Pennsylvania Society of Manufactures and Useful Arts in 1787. By it great pains were taken to encourage native factories, but their growth was slow, both here and in other districts. The largest cotton-factory now in Philadelphia was started, in very recent times, by William Divine, an Irishman, born in 1801. First apprenticed to muslin-weaving in Belfast, he came in 1822 to Manchester, and was during five years engaged in silk-manufacture. In 1827 he resolved to emigrate, and a tedious voyage of twenty-one weeks conveyed him to New York, whence he at once passed on to Philadelphia. There he worked as a hand-loom weaver, earning a dollar a day, the usual wages, for the first month, after which his superior skill enabled him to obtain double the amount. After eleven years of such work, he had saved sufficient money to buy a set of wool-weaving machines, and to rent a room connected with a mill already established, and fed by its machinery. There he prospered, and in 1841 was rich enough to build a mill for himself. In that year he started the Kennebeck Factory, for woollen-manufacture. In 1846 he bought the Penn Factory, in which he had formerly worked as a weaver and foreman, and there began to spin cotton-yarn for himself, and to produce checks and printed goods. He subsequently opened another factory for woollen goods, and in these two he now gives employment to 200 looms, to 5,000 spindles, and to 350 operatives. Philadelphia in 1860 contained in all 132 cotton and woollen factories of that description, giving work to about 4,000 men and 5,000 women.

More strictly a manufacturing town than Philadelphia is Pittsburg, at the other end of Pennsylvania. Founded in 1765, it made but little progress till the close of the century, and in 1810 contained only 4,768 inhabitants. In 1860

its population, including its two great suburbs of Alleghany
and Birmingham, amounted to 160,000, more than 20,000
being employed in 1,191 manufacturing establishments,
large and small. It is reckoned that its trade has been
more than doubled during the past ten years, and its future
greatness can hardly be estimated. "Pittsburg," said an
American writer in 1866, "is the greatest and the richest
mining centre in America. Situated at the confluence of
Monongahela and the Alleghany, the banks of the former
ribbed with coal-veins and beds of iron-ore, from source
to mouth, and the banks of the latter, with its tributaries,
bordered by the richest oil-lands in the world; at the head
of navigation on the Ohio, by which she has commercial
intercourse with the whole great south and west, and the
cities across the ocean; at the junction of the two richest
rail thoroughfares in the country; yearly planning and
receiving new channels for her trade, east, west, north, and
south; forging the great guns and iron-clads that made the
old Union strong again, and making ploughshares, engines,
and implements of agriculture, for the 'piping times of
peace;' the centre of great steel, iron, and glass works; a
Newcastle, a Sheffield, a Birmingham, a Staffordshire; everything that any city could ever aspire to be, in commercial,
manufacturing, mining, and political position, is Pittsburg."

Pittsburg owes its sudden greatness mainly to its splendid
coal and iron fields. In 1868 it had thirty great iron-
factories, the annual produce of which was reckoned at
£1,200,000. It had also seven hardware establishments,
and as many steel-works, producing half of all the steel-
work in the United States, as well as fifty other factories for
the working up of iron in various ways. Its oldest staple
trade is glass manufacture, for which it has fifty-three
establishments, issuing £2,400,000 worth of glass every
year. Its youngest staple trade is oil-refining, which began
only about twelve years ago, and in 1868 gave employment

to more than 3,000 persons, and was worth more than £3,000,000. In 1859 Pittsburg produced 7,037 barrels of petroleum ; in 1865 the yield was about 1,200,000 barrels.

Other great centres of manufacturing energy are rising in the western districts of the United States, but the leading factories are still in the older settlements of the east, and they are most numerous in the New England States. Here began the manufacture of cotton, almost before it was practised in old England. Early in the eighteenth century, when the first colonists of Massachusetts and Connecticut were only a pastoral people, they began to spin and weave their own clothing, and it was to supply them with material that the first exportations of Barbadoes cotton-wool were made. That the trade should not have grown more rapidly than it did is hard to understand ; but it grew more rapidly in New England than anywhere else, and in the course of the present century has assumed considerable importance. It has given life, especially, to one notable trading-town.

Lowell, twenty-five miles north of Boston, was begun in 1821, by the purchase of four hundred acres of land, for £20,000, by the Merrimac Manufacturing Company, which set up its first cotton-mill in 1822. Other mills have been added, and in 1860 the company employed 2,400 operatives, who, by help of 2,380 looms and 85,720 spindles, turned 80,770 lbs. of cotton-fibre into 380,000 yards of cotton fabric every week. Other companies also followed in its lead, and the result has been the rapid growth of a handsome town, altogether devoted to manufactures. Its population was 6,477 in 1830, 20,981 in 1840, 33,385 in 1850, and about 40,000 in 1860. Nearly a third of the residents are actually employed in the cotton-factories, in the proportion of about two women to one man, their total weekly produce in 1860 being estimated at 2,463,000 yards ; while the other factories yielded in the same time about 44,000 yards of woollen cloth, about 25,000 yards of carpeting, and

50 rugs, besides an abundance of machinery and goods of all sorts requisite for carrying on the staple trade of the town. The special point of interest in Lowell, besides the fact that it is the largest cotton-manufacturing town in the United States, is the care taken by its New England founders, and maintained by their descendants, to promote the moral and physical well-being of the operatives. In connection with each factory are some twenty or thirty boarding-houses, in which, males and females being kept apart, cheap living is provided for all the workpeople. The girls earn from two to twenty shillings a week, besides their board, according to their age and efficiency, and the men receive on an average about two shillings a day. An hospital is provided for them, in case of sickness, and stringent rules prevail throughout the town for averting sickness, by careful ventilation, good paving, and the like. "The moral police," we are told, "which is established, appears to be of the greatest value, so far as it ensures a virtuous character and correct deportment. No persons are employed who are addicted to intemperance or guilty of immorality, and even association with persons of suspected character is deemed good ground for dismissal from the mills, and also for the rejection of all applications of this sort. Every person wishing to leave a mill can do so by giving a fortnight's notice, and the operative so discharged, having been employed during the year, is entitled to an honourable certificate. The names of all persons dismissed for bad conduct are entered in a book, which is sent to all the counting-houses in the city, and the individual is thus prevented from elsewhere obtaining occupation." There are evening-schools, lending-libraries, religious services, and public lectures in abundance; and the whole machinery is one of patriarchal government, mixed with Puritan socialism, which is unique among manufacturing arrangements.

"The population of Lowell," wrote John Greenleaf

Whittier, in 1843, "is constituted mainly of New Englanders; but there are representatives here of almost every
part of the civilised world. The good-humoured face of
the Milesian meets one at almost every turn; the shrewdly
solemn Scotchman, the Transatlantic Yankee, blending
the crafty thrift of Roger Snailsfoot with the stern religious
heroism of Cameron; the blue-eyed, fair-haired German,
from the towered hills which overlook the Rhine. Here,
too, are pedlars from Hamburg and Bavaria and Poland,
with their sharp Jewish faces and black, keen eyes. But
of all classes of foreigners the Irish are by far the most
numerous. Light-hearted, wrong-headed, impulsive, un-
calculating, with an Oriental love of hyperbole and, too
often, a common dislike of cold water and of that gem
which the fable tells us rests at the bottom of the well,
the Celtic elements of their character do not readily ac-
commodate themselves to those of the hard, cool, self-
relying Anglo-Saxon." That description is true still. Lowell
contains representatives of all the races that make up the
people of the United States, and shows how, by blending
all, the nation is working out its greatness.

Lowell suffered, like every other town concerned in the
manufacture of cotton goods, from the civil war that began
in 1861; and, even yet, it has hardly advanced upon the
position it had reached in 1860. In that year the whole
number of cotton-factories in the United States, more than
half being in New England, was 1,091. In these 46,766
men and 75,206 women were employed; and the produce
of their toil was nearly double that of 1850, being valued at
about £24,000,000. The woollen-factories of the United
States numbered 1,967 in 1860, and gave work to 25,926
men and 16,618 women; the value of the cloth produced,
nearly half as much again as in 1850, being about
£13,000,000.

CHAPTER X.

GREAT MARTS.

THE history of great factories is almost wholly modern;
the history of great marts is nearly as old as the history of
commerce itself. Babylon, Tyre, Alexandria, Venice, Antwerp, and the multitude of lesser marts that have arisen and
decayed in the course of centuries, show how, as soon as in
each age and nation trade became important, the importance was largely developed by the concentration of energy
in cities convenient for the resort of merchants, and for
bringing together and distributing the wares in which they
trafficked. A little has been already said concerning some
of the older marts. It will be sufficient here to notice some
of those which are still influential.

London, now the greatest mart in the world, and greater
than any of those which it has succeeded in pre-eminence,
has a commercial history covering more than twelve centuries. Bede says that, in 604, it had become, "by its
happy situation on the banks of the noble, navigable river
Thames, the emporium for many nations repairing to it by
land and sea;" and from that time, if not before, it began

to grow as a centre of trade. The growth at first was slow, but long before the Norman Conquest its convenient nearness to foreign ports had rendered it the chief trading-town of England, and, the same causes which produced its commercial supremacy leading to its selection as the centre of political government, its political importance greatly conduced to its commercial development. Special privileges, both of trade and of political self-management, were granted to it by William the Conqueror, and those privileges were confirmed and extended by later monarchs. "Amongst the noble and famous cities of the world," wrote William Fitz-Stephen, about the middle of the twelfth century, "London is one of the most renowned, on account of its wealth, its extensive trade and commerce, its grandeur and magnificence. To this city repair merchants of every nation in the world, bringing their commodities by sea:—

> " Arabia's gold, Sabæa's spice and incense,
> Scythia's keen weapons, and the oil of palms
> From Babylon's deep soil ; Nile's precious gems,
> China's bright shining silks, and Gallic wines,
> Norway's warm peltry, and the Russian sables."

In that description there was some exaggeration, as well as in Fitz-Stephen's statement that London in his time contained between 30,000 and 40,000 inhabitants. But that it was, even then, a large and rich trading-town is clear. "London," said another old chronicler, William of Malmesbury, "is a noble city, renowned for the opulence of its citizens, who, on account of the greatness of the city, are considered of the first quality, and rank as noblemen of the kingdom. It is filled with merchandise brought by the merchants of all countries, but chiefly those of Germany ; and, in case of scarcity in other parts of England, it is a granary, where corn may be more cheaply bought than anywhere else." The German merchants of the Steelyard, as we have seen, had for rivals traders from Lorraine and other parts, who came to deal with the local merchants already beginning to combine in guilds, and prepare for taking the place of the foreigners as chief merchants in the London market. The first native trading-ship of which we have record was the *Little Edward.* This ship, "belonging to the port of London, owned and commanded by John Brand, citizen and merchant of London, loaded with a cargo of wool, owned by three merchants of the hanse of Germany, who had lived in England in the enjoyment of the ancient privileges granted to them," was, in 1315, proceeding from London to Antwerp, when, off Margate, she was seized by the French, and taken to Calais. As compensation, £40 was claimed for the value of the vessel, and £1,200 for her cargo, by Edward II. That transaction aptly illustrates the method and the dangers of London commerce in the fourteenth century.

The London of the Plantagenets, all included within the old city walls, and with plenty of vacant space in it, was full of markets, and of other appliances for native and foreign trade, many of the localities of which are still marked by the names of streets and buildings. Westward from the Tower, along the water's side, from Billingsgate to Dowgate, were the rude quays and hythes at which the trading-vessels deposited their cargoes, and took in others of English produce; and north of it were great selds or warehouses, set up for this purpose, and extending to the Chepe, or market-street, portions of which are still known as Eastcheap and Cheapside, stretching from the Tower to St. Paul's Cathedral. In this street and its purlieus each trading class had its separate place of resort. In the open space near St. Mary Woolchurch was the Woolchurch Haw, the great meeting-place of wool and cloth merchants; Cornhill and Grasschurch-yard, to the east of it, being the haunts of dealers in corn and hay. Touching it on the western side, on the site now occupied by the Mansion House, was the Stocks Market, appropriated to butchers on flesh days, and to fishmongers on fish days, and hard by was the Poultry, for the use of poulterers. In that busy part room was afterwards found for Hebrew bankers, in Old Jewry, and, a little later, for Italian bankers, in Lombard Street. The western half of Chepᵉ was assigned to the grocers, the mercers, the goldsmiths, and other traders, whose shops extended to St. Paul's Churchyard, north of which was Smithfield, which gradually became a great market for dealers in live cattle, when it was not required for St. Bartholomew Fair. West of St. Paul's was the long thoroughfare which, after passing the river Fleet and the Temple Bar, was known as the dismal and unfrequented Strand, and led, through open fields, to the independent City of Westminster, which had its own nest of markets, the principal being at the gates of Old Westminster Hall.

A lively picture of the trading aspect of London in the fifteenth century appears in Lydgate's account of the experiences of London Lackpenny, a country bumpkin, who came up to try his luck in town. He went first to Westminster, but there, instead of getting any help, he was pushed about, and robbed of his hood and his purse :—

> "Within this hall neither rich nor yet poor
>   Would do for me aught, although I should die ;
> Which seeing, I got me out of the door,
>   When Flemings began on me for to cry :
> ' Master, what will you copen or buy ?
> Fine felt hats, or spectacles to read?
> Lay down your silver, and here you may speed.'

> " Then into London I did me hie—
>   Of all the land it beareth the prize.
> ' Hot peascods !' one began to cry,
>   ' Strawberries ripe, and cherries in the rise !
> One bade me come near, and buy some spice ;
> Pepper and saffron they gan me bede,
> But, for lack of money, I might not speed.

R

" Then to the Chepe I gan me drawen,
　　Where much people I saw for to stand.
One offered me velvet, silk, and lawn ;
　　Another he taketh me by the hand :
　　' Here is Paris thread, the finest in the land ! '
I never was used to such things indeed,
And, wanting money, I might not speed.

" Then went I forth by London Stone,
　　And throughout all Candlewick Street :
Drapers much cloth me offered anon ;
　　Then comes me one crying, ' Hot sheeps' feet ! '
　　One cried, ' Mackerel ! ' ' Ryster green ! ' another gan me
　　greet.
One bade me buy a hood to cover my head ;
But, for lack of money, I might not speed.

" Then into Cornhill anon I rode,
　　Where there was much stolen gear among.
I saw where hung mine owne hood
　　That I had lost among the throng.
　　To buy my own hood, I thought it wrong.
I knew it as well as I did my Creed,
But, for lack of money, I could not speed.

" Then hied I me down to Billinsgate ;
　　And one cried, ' Ho ! now go we hence ! '
I prayed a bargeman, for God's sake,
　　That he would spare me my expense.
　　' Thou goest not here,' quoth he, ' under two pence.
I wit not yet bestow any alms' deed.'
Thus, lacking money, I could not speed."

London Lackpenny fell in with only the retail dealers of
the metropolis. Before that time, however, native wholesale
merchants had become numerous and influential. Foreigners
still had much of the foreign trade, but Englishmen had
arisen as famous and enterprising as Walworth, Philpot, and
Whittington. By them, and such as them, trade was carried
on with near and distant parts of Europe ; and the trade
grew steadily in every later generation, till the foreign merchants, though not actually driven out of London, and, indeed, often treated more liberally than in the earlier times,

were forced into an insignificant position by the greater enterprise of London-born or London-bred Englishmen. The trading-guilds of the Middle Ages helped this progress ; the younger companies of merchants helped it still more. The wealth of industry that was developed throughout the kingdom under the Tudors, and the worthier position that England then acquired among the nations of Europe, encouraged and made easy the progress of all its trading-ports, but most of all of London.

Venice, in its palmiest days, had had a formidable northern rival in Bruges. Antwerp inherited the supremacy of both Bruges and Venice. But, in the sixteenth century, Antwerp began to be surpassed by London, and, in the seventeenth, the superiority was complete. " Shipped hence," said Lewis Roberts, in 1638, "the staple commodities of England, in former times, yielded by their returns from foreign parts all those necessities and wants we desired or stood in need of. But the late great traffic of this island hath been such that it hath not only proved a bountiful mother to the inhabitants, but also a courteous nurse to the adjoining neighbours ; for in what matter of traffic they have lost we have been found to have gained, and what they have wanted we have been noted to have supplied them with. Hath the proud and magnificent city of Venice lost her great traffic and commerce with India, Arabia, and Persia ? England hath got it, and now furnisheth her plenteously with the rich commodities thereof. Hath all Italy lost Venice, that fed it with those dainties? London now supplieth her place, and is found both to clothe and nourish it. Hath France almost lost the excellent commodities of Constantinople, Alexandria, Aleppo, and generally of all Turkey ? London can and doth furnish it. Nay, is Turkey itself deprived of the precious spices of India ? England can and doth plentifully afford them. Will you view Muscovy, survey Sweden, look upon Denmark, peruse the East Country,

and those other colder regions? There you shall find the
English to have been; the inhabitants, from the prince to
the peasant, wear English woollen linsey, feed in English
pewter, sauced with English spices, and send to their
enemies real English leaden messengers of death. Will you
behold the Netherlands, whose eyes and hearts envy England's traffic? Yet they must perforce confess that, for all their
great boasts, they are indebted to London for most of their
Syrian commodities, besides what other wares else they have
of English growth." Roberts, indeed, like many others in
his day, was nearly as much frightened as pleased at the wonderful progress that England had made in the commerce
that had London for its principal mart. " England," he said,
" being naturally seated in a northern corner of the world,
bending under the weight of too ponderous a burthen, cannot possibly always and for ever find a vent for all those
commodities that are seen to be daily exported and
brought within the compass of so narrow a circuit, unless
there can be, by the policy and government of the State,
a means found out to make this island the common emporium and staple of all Europe."

An emporium of more than all Europe England has
become, the whole island being enriched thereby, and
London more than any other part of it. The enterprise of
the East India Company, the Levant Company, and other
great trading corporations, brought to London a vast store
of the treasures of the East. The enterprise of other companies, by which the West Indies and the most favoured
parts of North America were colonised by Englishmen, provided a market for part of those treasures, and opened up
sources of even greater wealth. England made herself mistress of the seas by virtue of her naval prowess, shown in the
skill and heroism of her warriors; but she secured for herself
a much truer and more beneficial and more beneficent dominion, by the wise selfishness and indomitable energy dis-

played by her great merchants in trading with every part of the world, and in supplying every country with all the wares that it needed, in exchange for all the wares that it had to dispose of.

For nearly two centuries, London monopolised a very large proportion of this traffic, and of the wealth that was won by it. In 1732 the port had 1,487 vessels, Liverpool having only about 200, and Bristol not more than 300. At the commencement of the present century, London engrossed a third of the trade of the empire, and the annual value of its exports and imports exceeded £70,000,000. In 1860 it owned only a seventh of the 21,000 vessels belonging to all the British ports, but their aggregate tonnage was more than a fourth of the whole; and it had hardly less than a fourth of the entire trade of the kingdom, represented by more than £160,000,000 worth of exports, and about £210,000,000 worth of imports. Besides all that, its merchants are enriched by the profits upon a vast trade in articles produced in foreign countries, and sold by them to foreign countries, but which never enter the Thames at all; and further wealth comes to London from its gigantic share in all the great financial enterprises by which railways and other huge undertakings are rendered possible at home, and by which foreign loans, both national and private, are negotiated.

The great pivot of this purely financial trade is the Stock Exchange, in Capel Court, to which reference will be made hereafter. The great pivot of the general commerce of the City is the Royal Exchange, the first building for which was erected, at the instigation of Sir Thomas Gresham, in 1569, and destroyed by the Great Fire of 1666. Its substitute was also burnt to the ground in 1841, the present more commodious structure being completed in 1844. If all the bargains that have been struck, and all the achievements that have been begun by nods and whispers on that memorable site, during the past three centuries, could be recorded, a more

eventful story of trade, and not of trade alone, would be produced than any other mart in the world could, even in a small
degree, rival. "There is no place in town," wrote Addison,
in 1711, "which I so much love to frequent as the Royal
Exchange. It gives me a secret satisfaction, and in some
measure gratifies my vanity, as I am an Englishman, to see
so rich an assembly of countrymen and foreigners consulting
together upon the private business of mankind, and making
this metropolis a kind of emporium for the whole earth. I
must confess I look upon High Change to be a great council,
in which all considerable nations have their representatives.
Factors in the trading world are what ambassadors are in the
politic world. I am infinitely delighted in mixing with these
several ministers of commerce, as they are distinguished by
their different walks and different languages. Sometimes I
am jostled among a body of Armenians, sometimes I am
lost in a crowd of Jews, and sometimes make one in a
group of Dutchmen. I am a Dane, Swede, or Frenchman,
at different times; or rather fancy myself like the old philosopher, who, upon being asked what countryman he was,
announced that he was a citizen of the world. When I have
been upon the 'Change, I have often fancied one of the old
kings standing in person where he is represented in effigy,
and looking down upon the wealthy concourse of people
with which that place is every day filled. In this case, how
would he be surprised to hear all the languages of Europe
spoken in this little spot of his former dominions, and to see
so many private men who, in his time would have been the
vassals of some powerful baron, negotiating like princes for
greater sums of money than were formerly to be met with in
the royal treasury! Trade, without enlarging the British
territories, has given us a kind of additional empire. It has
multiplied the number of the rich, made our landed estates
infinitely more valuable than they were formerly, and added
to them an accession of other estates as valuable as the

lands themselves." The Royal Exchange has lost all the picturesqueness that it possessed in the days of Addison; but its national and international value has certainly not lessened in the century and a half that divide Queen Victoria's London from Queen Anne's.

The changes of the interval may be in some degree measured by the altered uses to which some notable buildings that sprang up in or near Addison's time have been put. Lloyd's Coffee-house, for example, started in Lombard Street, at the corner of Abchurch Lane, late in the seventeenth century, began only as a convenient place of gossip and refreshment for City people. It was a great meeting-place, "where the auctions are usually kept," when Addison wrote the *Spectator* only a lively club fit for Sir Roger de Coverley to be laughed at in; but gradually its social uses gave place to commercial. Transferred for a short time to Pope's Head Alley, the coffee-house was abandoned in 1774, and Lloyd's Rooms, then located in the upper part of the Royal Exchange, became strictly a business resort for ship-owners, ships' captains, and ship-insurers. More than a thousand insurance-brokers and underwriters there find a busy trade, in speculating upon losses by accidents at sea. Lloyd's agents are now established in every port of the world, and from each comes prompt information concerning the arrivals and departures, and the good fortunes, and the casualties of the many thousand vessels in which London merchants are interested.

Lloyd's, no longer a coffee-house, is cosmopolitan in its interests and information. Some other buildings, though still nominally coffee-houses, are hardly less active centres of business in special departments of the trade by which London has grown great. The North and South American Coffee-house, in Threadneedle Street, is the special haunt of traders with the vast continent that gives it its name, and especially with its greatest nation, the United States. All the Trans-

atlantic newspapers are here filed, for reference to the trade
details and political details, bearing upon trade, that they
furnish, and merchants are constantly looking in to consult
them, or to exchange other details of which they are possessed,
or to use those details in making bargains with one another
or jealously watching one another's operations. Of the Jerusalem Coffee-house, in Cowper's Court, Cornhill, similar use
is made by the thousands of merchants trading with the great
Eastern Hemisphere, from Bombay all the way round to
China and Japan, and across the Indian Ocean, down to the
great colonies of Australia and New Zealand. The Jamaica
Coffee-house, in St. Michael's Alley, on the other side of
Cornhill, has lost much of its importance with the compara-
tive decay of the West Indian trade, since the days when
Port Royal was a busier mart than Bombay, and there was a
larger trade with Barbadoes than with Victoria. The Baltic
Coffee-house, in Threadneedle Street, on the other hand, has
grown in value with the growth of English trade with Russia
and the other European countries that send us tallow, hemp,
and half-a-hundred other wares. Some old coffee-houses,
like Garraway's, in Change Alley, still retain a little of their
old character as refreshment-rooms ; but here the glass of
punch or the sandwich that is bought is wholly unimportant,
in comparison with the great contracts that are often proposed or concluded in the five minutes nominally set apart
for eating or drinking. The old-fashioned air that still per-
vades some of these old haunts contrasts strangely with the
ever new enterprise that is developed by the men who
frequent them.

   In trade with the United States London is surpassed by
Liverpool and Glasgow, but of the commerce carried on with
European countries, with India, China, and Australia, it has
still the largest share.

   London's chief rival in former times was Bristol. The
earliest record extant concerning this mart and its trade is

curious. " There is a seaport-town called Bristol," it was written, shortly after the Norman Conquest, " opposite to Ireland, to which its inhabitants make frequent voyages of trade. Wulfstan, Bishop of Worcester, cured the people of this town of a most odious custom, which they derived from their ancestors, of buying men and women in all parts of England, and exporting them to Ireland, for the sake of gain. You might have seen, with sorrow, long ranks of youths and maidens, of the greatest beauty, tied together with ropes, and daily exposed for sale ; nor were these men ashamed—oh, horrid wickedness !—to give up their nearest relations, even their own children, to slavery."

That trade, if the report of it was anything more than a Norman slander of the Anglo-Saxons, was soon exchanged for something better. During the Middle Ages, Bristol had an extensive trade with the Danes, who were then masters of a large part of Ireland. Not content with voyaging to Ireland, moreover, its merchants soon—while London still did little more than trade with the nations divided from it by only the British Channel and the German Ocean—went on more distant expeditions, to Denmark and Iceland, to the Mediterranean and the Levant. The extensive manufacture of woollen cloth that then sprang up on both sides of the Severn, in Wiltshire and in Devonshire, had Bristol, itself a busy cloth-making town, for its chief mart ; and enterprising merchants exchanged the native wares for foreign goods, by which the whole district was enriched. Most famous of all these merchants was William Canynge, who, during the eight years previous to 1460, had ten vessels, one of them with the unusually large burthen of 900 tons, and manned in all by 800 mariners, and who carried English trade farther than it had ever been carried before in native craft, before ending his days as a priest in the splendid church of St. Mary, Redcliff, which he spent much of his well-earned wealth in restoring. But other notable merchants were contemporary

with him ; among the number, Robert Sturney, who, having
gone with a hundred and sixty pilgrims on a pious visit to
Jerusalem, with which some trade was joined, continued to
carry on a brisk commerce with the Levant ; and John Jay,
who, not content with European trade, sent out a great ship,
in 1480, to seek for those fabled treasures of the West, which
soon afterwards Columbus reached, when, expecting to discover a new passage to India, he opened up America to
Europeans.

Bristol and the Cabots, Venetian traders who made it
their home, share with Spain and Columbus the honour of
discovering America ; and though the Bristol merchants,
landing on the barren shores of Labrador, gained nothing in
comparison with the advantages which Spain derived from
its acquisition of the West Indies and the neighbouring
mainland, their trading enterprise bore good fruit in the
sixteenth and following centuries. In the colonisation of
the British West Indies they had a large share, and, as long
as commerce with them had for its principal item traffic in
negro slaves, the supremacy of Bristol continued. Queen
Anne said that she never knew she was a queen until she
went to Bristol ; and its pomps and shows exceeded even
those of London in the eighteenth century. In 1761 the
town contained nearly 100,000 inhabitants. In 1861 its
population amounted to 154,093, and there had been in the
interval a steady growth in all the old ways of trade. In
the new ways of trade that have been opened up, however,
Bristol has been far surpassed by its younger rival, Liverpool, partly because of the greater energy of the traders of
Liverpool, but still more because of its convenient nearness
to the great manufacturing districts to which it has become
the chief mart.

Though a young rival, Liverpool is an old town. It
existed in Anglo-Saxon times, had a well-fortified castle
under William the Conqueror, and received from Henry II., in

1173, a charter directing that the whole estuary of the Mersey should be for ever free to "the men of Lyrpole," coming and returning with their ships and merchandise ; and, that charter being confirmed by King John in 1207, Liverpool was, by Henry III., in 1229, made a free borough, with a merchants' guild, and like liberties of tollage, passage, stallage, and customs to those enjoyed by the burgesses of London, Bristol, Hull, and other towns. For a long time, however, it was one of the smallest boroughs in the kingdom. In 1272 it contained only 168 houses, and in 1565 Stow reports that it had no more than 138 houses, scattered over seven streets, the market price of two of the principal houses being £10, while another was let for £4 a year. Yet long before that it had made a small beginning of that special trade which has mainly conduced to its greatness. In 1524 Leland said that there was "good merchandise at Lyrpole ; much Irish yarn that Manchester men do buy is there, and Irish merchants come much thither, as to a good haven ;" and Camden, writing in 1586, calls it "the most convenient and most frequented passage to Ireland." It had also, at that time, a little foreign trade. It was Humphrey Brooke who, in 1588, gave to Queen Elizabeth's ministers the first intimation of the coming of the Spanish Armada ; he having, he said, "departed out of St. Jean de Luce, in France, the day after the fleet set sail."

Its importance as a mart dates from the seventeenth century. Its merchants imported iron from Biscay, then the most famous iron district in Europe, and sent it to Birmingham, Sheffield, and other towns, to be converted into cutlery and hardware, much of which it received again for transmission to Ireland. It was also a great market for the woollen, linen, and cotton goods brought from Manchester, Blackburn, Wakefield, Halifax, and Bradford, which it fed with Irish flax, then its staple import. In carrying these wares to and fro, its traders found employment in

1618 for four-and-twenty ships. Its merchant navy was
more than ten times as great at the close of the century.
Being the chief mart of Manchester, it grew with the growth
of the famous manufacturing town.

Other causes conduced to its prosperity. Favoured by
Cromwell, as the best highway to Ireland, and made of
political importance by the great share taken by its leading
men in the Commonwealth strife, it had the great good
fortune of being directed by an excellent lord of the manor.
" It is of late," wrote one who visited the town in 1673,
" at the great charge and industry of the family of the
Moores, of Bank Hall, which family for some hundreds of
years have had a large property therein, and at present
combine chief lords and owners of the greatest share thereof,
having divers streets that bear their name, which hath so
enlarged the town that its church, though large and good,
is not enough to hold its inhabitants, which are many.
Amongst whom are divers eminent merchants and tradesmen, whose trade and traffic, especially into the West
Indies, makes it famous, its situation affording in great
plenty, and at reasonabler rates than in most parts of England, such exported commodities as are proper to the West
Indies, as likewise a quicker return for such imported commodities, by reason of the sugar-bakers and great manufacturers of cotton in the adjacent parts. Here is now erecting,
at the public charges, a famous town-house, placed on
pillars and arches of hewn stone, and underneath is the
public exchange for the merchants. It hath a very considerable market on Saturdays, for all sorts of provisions and
divers commodities, which are brought by the merchants,
and hence transported as aforesaid."

Having thus slowly made for itself a place among English trading-towns before the close of the seventeenth century,
Liverpool advanced mightily in the eighteenth, by means of
its energetic commerce in three special articles of traffic, of

which one was wholly wrong, and the other of doubtful value to the world. The first, in order of time, was the tobacco trade. Tobacco, in spite of the opposition of James I., and many who thought with him, in his days and after, had quickly come into favour with both Englishmen and foreigners, and, to supply their demands, had become the staple produce of Virginia. In the ten years from 1700 to 1709, the average annual importation of it to Great Britain amounted to 12,880 tons—7,857 tons for reshipment to other countries, and 5,023 tons, about two-thirds of the quantity now used by thrice as large a population, for home consumption. Bristol and Glasgow were enriched by the commerce, but neither of them had so great a share as Liverpool. Its chief merchants of a hundred and fifty years ago, Sir Thomas Johnson, Sir William Norris, and William Clayton, applied themselves to it with wonderful success, being led into a good deal of smuggling, by the exorbitant duties claimed for the revenue. Half the shipping and more than half the wealth of Liverpool was, during some years, devoted to this traffic. It was to meet its requirements that the Old Dock—the oldest dock in England—was begun in 1699, and completed about twenty years later, thereby enabling a far greater number of ships to load and unload at Liverpool than it could receive before, and tempting many shipowners to use its safe harbourage, instead of going to other ports. Thus a fresh impetus was given to the growth of the port. A tourist, writing in 1727, declared that, "in his first visit to Liverpool, in 1680, it was a large, handsome, and thriving town ; at his second visit, ten years later, it was become much bigger ; but, at his third visit, in 1726, it was more than double its bigness of the said second visit ;" and in 1760 it was said that " Liverpool, in point of a vastly-extended foreign commerce and mercantile shipping, is long since become undoubtedly the greatest and most opulent seaport in the kingdom, next after London and Bristol, probably employing about three hundred sail of her own, greater and lesser shipping, mostly in the Guinea and American trades.

That Guinea trade, joined with the American trade, provided the next and most reprehensible source of wealth to Liverpool. The Virginian and neighbouring colonists had learnt from the Spaniards the evil habit of employing negro slaves ; and Liverpool, sending its ships for tobacco, found it very profitable to send them first to the West Coast of Africa, and there take in human ballast. In 1709 it began its share in the slave trade with one vessel of thirty tons ; in 1760 the trade gave employment to seventy-four vessels, with an aggregate burthen of 8,178 tons, and enriched upwards of a hundred merchants, moɪe than half as many as were to be found in London and Bristol put together, those being the only two other towns largely concerned in this branch of commerce. It continued to grow during the next half century. In the ten years between 1795 and 1804, the busiest period of all, the Liverpool merchants shipped 323,770 slaves from Africa to America and the West Indies—the London share in the traffic including 46,405 slaves, and the Bristol people being responsible for the shipment of only 10,718. It was well, for the honour of England, that the trade was put a stop to in 1807.

But a hundred years ago no dishonour attached to it in the public estimation. Foster Cunliffe, the founder of a great trading family, and, according to his panegyrist, "a merchant whose honesty, diligence, and knowledge in mercantile affairs procured wealth and credit to himself and his country; a magistrate, who administered justice with discernment, candour, and impartiality ; a Christian, devout and exemplary in the exercise of every private duty ; a friend to merit, a patron to distress, an enemy only to vice and sloth," was one of the most energetic and prosperous of all the Liverpool slave-merchants. In 1753 he had four ships, fitted

to hold 1,120 slaves in all, which made two or three voyages
in the year between Guinea and the West Indies and North
America, and brought profit enough to stock a dozen vessels
with rum, sugar, and other articles, for sale in England.
Five of the twelve traded with Antigua, four with Maryland,
two with Montserrat, and one with Jamaica. As this instance
shows, the trade had been developed since its commencement. Instead of using the same vessels for slaves, tobacco,
and rum, and sending them the whole round, it was found
better to build ships specially adapted for human chattels,
and to let the others go to and fro with ordinary wares.
Thereby Liverpool was greatly enriched. During the seven
years ending with 1716, when the tobacco trade was the
chief staple, its annual shipping averaged 18,371 tons, being
one twenty-fourth that of all England. During the seven
years ending with 1792, when the slave trade had thrown
the tobacco trade into insignificance, the yearly average was
260,380 tons—more than a sixth of that of the whole kingdom ; that is, while the nation at large had in the interval
increased its shipping about three times, the maritime trade
of Liverpool had been multiplied by more than twelve.

The population of the town grew proportionately.
Between 1700 and 1752, the chief period of the tobacco
trade, the inhabitants had increased in number from 5.715
to 18,500. In the next half century, the chief period of
the slave trade, they had increased to 77,708. "This quon-
dam village," said Erskine, in 1791, "which is now fit to be
a proud capital for any empire in the world, has started up
like an enchanted palace, even in the memory of living men.
I had before often been at the principal seaports in this
island, and believing that, having seen Bristol and those
other towns that deservedly pass as great ones, I had seen
everything in this great nation of navigators on which a
subject should pride himself, I own that I was astonished
and astounded when, after passing a distant ferry and

ascending a hill, I was told by my guide, 'All you see spread out beneath you—that immense plain, which stands like another Venice upon the waters, which is intersected by those numerous docks, which glitters with those cheerful habitations of well-protected men, which is the busy seat of trade, and the gay scene of elegant amusements growing out of its prosperity, where there is the most cheerful face of industry, where there are riches overflowing, and everything that can delight a man who wishes to see the prosperity of a great community and a great empire—all this has been created by the industry and well-disciplined management of a handful of men since you were a boy.'"

That growth, however, was only an earnest of the progress yet to be made. In 1861 the population of Liverpool, six times as great as it was in 1801, was 437,740; and 4,682 vessels, with an aggregate of 2,658,732 tons, entered its harbour. The prime agent in this third stage of development, better than tobacco, and certainly better than slaves, has been cotton. Liverpool, as we have seen, began to rise from a village honoured with the name of a borough, by supplying Manchester with linen-yarn from Ireland. It was all along a chief mart for the sale of Manchester goods, woollen, linen, and, to the small extent of its trade therein, cotton. It now became a more important auxiliary to the manufacturing town and its hundred suburbs, by providing for it an ample store of the newer commodity. This trade, of course, grew naturally out of its old dealings with the West Indies and the United States, and it began more than a hundred years ago. In a Liverpool newspaper, dated the 3rd of November, 1758, appeared this novel advertisement: " To be sold by auction, at Forbes and Campbell's sale-room, near the Exchange, this day, at one o'clock, twenty-five bags of Jamaica cotton, in five lots." From that time cotton was regularly brought from the West Indies, and gradually Virginia, Maryland, and the other districts of the mainland

began to join in the trade. It only became important, however, about the commencement of the present century.
How it has grown and benefited other towns besides Liverpool we have already seen. By bringing cotton from America,
India, and other parts, Liverpool has vastly extended its
commerce, and if its staple trade is in importing the raw
fibre and exporting the manufactured cloth, that trade is
supplemented by commerce in a thousand other articles.
Liverpool is now a mart for everything, and for all the world.

The only British town that has kept pace with it is
Glasgow. But Glasgow, though as old as Liverpool, and,
in early times, much more famous on other grounds, is yet
younger as a busy place of trade. Early in the fifteenth
century, William Elphinstone, father of the Bishop Elphinstone who founded the University of Aberdeen, gained
celebrity by his shipments to France and other parts of
Europe of pickled salmon and dried herrings, in exchange
for which he received wine and brandy; and a hundred
years later we are told that Archibald Lyon, youngest son
of Lord Glamis, Earl of Strathmore, "undertook great
voyages and adventures, in trading to Poland, France, and
Holland," and that his son, and the husbands of his three
daughters, were all great merchants, and fathers of other
merchants; but most of the trade of Glasgow seems to
have been local and insignificant, until the union of England
and Scotland, in 1702, threw open to the northern kingdom
all the commercial facilities that the southern kingdom had
slowly acquired by centuries of enterprise and toil.

Very soon after that, Glasgow began to compete with
Liverpool in its lucrative tobacco trade. Six or eight adventurers chartered a ship, and sent it to Virginia with a
store of native produce, to be there sold, and the proceeds
spent in buying tobacco. The captain was appointed to act
as supercargo. "This person," says the old chronicler,
"although a shrewd man, knew nothing of accounts; and

S

when, on his return, he was asked by his employers for a statement of how the adventure had turned out, he told them he could give them none, but there were its proceeds, and threw down upon the table a large hoggar"—(that is, a stocking)—"stuffed to the top with coin. The adventure had been a profitable one ; and his employers conceived that, if an uneducated, untrained person had been so successful, their gains would have been still greater had a person versed in accounts been sent with it. Under this impression, they immediately dispatched a second adventure, with a supercargo highly recommended to them for his knowledge of accounts, who, on his return, produced a beautifully made out statement of his transactions, but no hoggar." Other enterprises succeeded in yielding both balance-sheets and money.

"I once asked the late Lord Provost Cochrane, of Glasgow, who was eminently wise, and who has been a merchant there for seventy years, "said Sir John Dalrymple in 1788, "to what causes he imputed the sudden rise of Glasgow. He said it was all owing to four young men of talent and spirit, who started at one time in business, and whose successes gave example to the rest. The four had not £10,000 amongst them when they began." These four enterprising youths were William Cunningham, Henry Ritchie, Alexander Spiers, and John Glassford. Glassford, during some years before his death in 1783, had twenty-five ships of his own, in which he each year imported £500,000 worth of tobacco ; and Spiers was still richer. They and others pursued their trade so successfully that Glasgow soon acquired more than half of the tobacco trade, then less prized than formerly by Liverpool, which found its chief profit in slave-dealing. In 1772 Glasgow imported 49,000 out of the 90,000 hogsheads brought into Great Britain, Spiers receiving an eighth of the Glasgow share, and Glassford an eleventh.

Very soon after that, mainly because of the American War of Independence, the tobacco trade began to decline; but the wealth and commercial energy that it had concentrated in Glasgow found exercise in other ways. Linen-manufacture had long before been established in the town and its neighbourhood, and the merchants had occupation in importing flax and exporting clothing. Cotton-manufacture had also, as we have seen, been introduced by David Dale and others, and iron-works of all sorts soon followed. Glasgow following closely the lead of Liverpool, and being, in fact, a Liverpool and a Manchester for Scotland, shared the prosperity of the southern towns. Many of its leading men, like the Monteiths, were both merchants and manufacturers: others were merchants alone. Trading at first chiefly with the West Indies and the United States, and therein having sugar and cotton for their staples, in succession to tobacco, its merchants have now learnt to trade with all the world, and Glasgow, from being 'an insignificant town, famous only for its pickled salmon and dried herrings, has become the third great British mart, inferior in size and trade only to London and Liverpool.

The same English trading enterprise that has led to the development of these marts at home, has effected yet greater wonders in the creation of other marts in the far East, in the far South, and in the far West alike. Brief reference to a few of the most notable of these will illustrate the growth of all.

Bombay, almost the oldest of them, built on a little island in one of the finest harbours in the world, was occupied by the Portuguese in 1532, and held by Spain till 1661, when it formed part of the Infanta Catherine's dowry, when she was married to Charles II. Even then it was not acquired without a struggle. Its Portuguese holders refused to admit the English, and it had to be besieged with heavy loss before the transfer was effected. The value of the port was better known to the Portuguese on the spot than to the

English at home. "It seems strange to me," said Pepys in 1663, "that such a thing as this, which was expected to be one of the best parts of the Queen's portion, should not be better understood; it being, if we had it, but a poor place, and not really so as was described to our King in the draught of it, but a poor little island; whereas they made the King and Lord Chancellor, and other learned men about the King, believe that that and other islands which are near to it were all one piece." It is to her possession of the "poor place," however, more than to any other single circumstance, that England owes her great Indian Empire.

At first Bombay, then containing about ten thousand natives, a few Portuguese, and fewer Englishmen, was used by its new owners merely as a military station, the old factory at Surat being retained as the chief trading-centre. Here the famous Sepoy army was begun, by the training of two or three companies of native soldiers, under English officers. These serving to keep order, the protection afforded by them was used as an inducement to native cotton-spinners, weavers, and traders of all sorts to immigrate from the mainland. Special privileges were also offered to Bombay manufacturers. By these means the native population was in a few years raised from ten to sixty thousand, and, unusual care being taken by the East India Company for the good government of the town, it rapidly acquired importance as a place of trade. Before the close of the seventeenth century it was, what it has ever since continued, the chief English mart in India.

Bombay was invaded by the great Aurungzebe in 1788. but the threatened danger was bought off, and soon the town became strong enough to send invading armies of its own across the mainland. Much of its later history is mixed up with the political history of the East India Company; and often political causes disturbed the progress of its commerce. But the commerce has grown steadily, being promoted not only by enterprising Englishmen, but also by the strange and enterprising race of Parsees, relics of the old fire-worshippers of Persia, who have made Bombay their special home.

The Parsees, aliens among the Hindoos and Mahometans with whom they live, have clung to English power and influence from its first appearance in India. As zealously devoted to commerce as the earliest Jews, to whose history theirs has some resemblance, their intimate acquaintance with India and its people, when both were strange to England, made them very valuable auxiliaries in early days, and their aid has been no less valuable in later times. To them Bombay owes half its prosperity. It is by their enterprise, mainly, that the splendid docks which the town possesses have been constructed, and in ship-building and use of the ships when built they show equal tact.

The growth of Bombay during the present century has been very rapid. In 1816 it had 161,338 inhabitants ; in 1864 the number was 816,562. About a hundredth part of these were Europeans, about a fifth Parsees, and the rest Hindoos and Moslems, of various creeds and castes. Bombay, aided by railway communication, is now the great centre for collection and distribution of all native produce, and of the wares brought from the other parts of the world. From Great Britain it receives each year about £8,000.000 worth of cotton and woollen goods, iron, hardware, and other articles, sending back £10,000,000 worth or more of raw cotton from the interior, and other native wares, and of silk, cotton, spices, and the like, brought by its merchant-ships from China and elsewhere. Its exports to China alone, in 1862, exceeded £6,000,000 in value ; its total exports in that year, conveyed in 3,052 vessels of 156,449 tons, being worth £18,622,462, while its imports, in 2,814 vessels, of 169,546 tons, were worth £9.468,965. It is a curious phase of Indian commerce from the earliest times, that it gives far more than it takes.

Calcutta, the second mart of India, differs greatly from Bombay. Its trade, chiefly internal—the old use of the Ganges being now supplemented by railways—is much more Oriental in its character. The English quarter of the town has handsome streets and noble buildings, justifying its claim to the title of "city of palaces." The native portion is a maze of narrow dirty streets, crowded with inhabitants, of whom many seem to combine in their characters all the European and all the Asiatic vices, whose only occupation is in a low sort of catering for the wants of both natives and foreigners. Founded in 1698, but of small account, Lord Clive, building Fort William in 1757, made it a chief seat of government. It had in 1866 a population of 377,924, besides some 177,000 daily visitors.

A younger and more promising mart than Calcutta, or even Bombay, which has grown out of English enterprise, is Melbourne. Sydney, founded in 1788, had become an important trading-place, and had colonised Van Diemen's Land, when, in 1802, the great Australian country now known as Victoria was discovered, and a feeble effort was made to plant a town on the present site of Melbourne; but that effort failed, and was forgotten for thirty years. In 1835, however, John Batman, a settler in Van Diemen's Land, crossed the channel with his family, and quietly took possession of the neglected district, and, before many months were over, his sole possession of it was disputed by another Van Diemen's Land colonist, John Pascoe Fawkner, who also crossed over, and built a hut for himself on the banks of the Yarra-Yarra. His petty quarrels with Batman helped to direct public attention to the district, and by the summer of 1836 Fawkner's hut was surrounded by 177 other adventurers, who built rude dwellings for themselves, and thus laid the foundations of the city of Melbourne. Its growth was rapid from the first. It had 11,738 inhabitants in 1841; 32,875 in 1846, and 77,345 in 1851. In the brief space of sixteen years it had become a great town, larger than Sydney; and even then it had handsome streets, great warehouses, and busy counting-houses, carrying on a thriving trade with the sheep-farmers of the interior, and the mother country, to which it sent vast supplies of native wool, in exchange for the home produce required for the use of the colonists.

Then, however, a wonderful discovery occurred, the results of which throw into the shade the achievements of the former half-generation. Gold was found in Bathurst, near Sydney, in February, 1851. In the following September, the Ballarat mines, within easy reach of Melbourne, were opened, and these proved only the firstfruits of a marvellous series of gold-findings, which eclipsed the old fables of El Dorado, and caused an unrivalled stream of immigration from all parts of the world to flow through the fortunate port of Melbourne. The strange and in many respects ugly story of the gold-seekings that ensued need not here be detailed. Their solid benefits appear in the extensive colonisation of Victoria, yielding better fruit than gold, and, most of all, in the growth of Melbourne. "A more striking contrast," says Mr. Therry, an old Australian judge, "could not well be furnished than the appearance Melbourne presented when I was there in 1845. and afterwards, when I visited it in 1856. In 1845 Bourke Street contained but a few scattered cottages, and sheep were grazed on the thick grass then growing in the street. It was only known to be a street in that year by a sign indicating 'This is Bourke Street.' In 1856 it was as crowded with fine buildings, and as thronged and alive with the hurrying to and fro of busy people as Cheapside at the present day. Two branches of Sydney banks supplied the district in 1845 with banking accommodation that only occupied them with business a few hours each day; in 1856 eight banks could scarcely meet the pecuniary exigencies of the community. In the principal street— Collins Street—there was, in 1845, but one jeweller, who

displayed a scanty supply of second-hand watches and pinchbeck brooches, in a shop similar to those in which pawnbrokers display their articles of used-up jewellery in the by-
streets off the Strand.   In 1856 might be seen in the same
street jewellers' shops as numerous and brilliant as those that
glitter in Regent Street.   The harbour of Hobson's Bay, on
the morning on which I left it for Sydney, in 1846, contained
two large ships, three brigs, and a few small colonial craft.
In 1856 the same harbour was filled with about two hundred
large London and Liverpool ships, and countless other
vessels from America, New Zealand, and other parts.   In
1845 there was little more than one clergyman of each
religious denomination.   In 1856 a numerous clergy of the
various denominations officiated ; the two principal, Church
of England and Roman Catholic, presided over by bishops
of their respective creeds.   In short, in size, in wealth, in
numbers, in varied social enjoyments, the humble town I had
quitted in 1845 had been transformed in 1856 into a splendid
city, and presented such a transition from poverty to splendour as no city of the ancient or modern world had heretofore exhibited in a corresponding period." In 1856, however, Melbourne had not 90,000 inhabitants ; now they are
above 160,000, and the town seems to have only begun its
career as a great Southern mart, capable of unlimited expan-
sion, to meet the growing requirements of the great Southern
continent that is being peopled with Englishmen, and that
may, ere long, become another Europe, or another America.

No American mart has grown so rapidly; but the nearest
counterpart to the development of Melbourne is to be found
in the progress of San Francisco, the youngest mart of that
American commerce in which New York led the way and
still has pre-eminence.

New York has had nearly eight times as long a period to
grow in as Melbourne, and is now ten times as large.   Its
site was discovered, in 1609, by Henry Hudson, in the course

of an expedition in search of the north-western passage to India, upon which he was employed by the Dutch, and the Dutch accordingly laid claim to the territory discovered, and in 1614 planted upon it their little town of New Amsterdam, calling the whole district New Netherlands. During sixty years their colony grew, in spite of English claims to possession of it, which issued in quarrels lasting till 1674, when the mastery of the English was formally acknowledged, and the name of the town was changed from New Amsterdam to New York. It had then about 2,500 inhabitants, and the population became about five times as numerous in the course of the ensuing century. Quarrels between the Dutch and English settlers, quarrels with the neighbouring colonies, quarrels with the native Indians, and quarrels with the French Canadians, however, retarded its progress, and until the War of Independence the town had an uneasy career.

Its first trade was with the Indians, for furs, while most of the colonists became farmers, and made good use of the fertile lands owned by them. "The bolting of flour and baking of bread," it was said in 1692, "hath been and is the chief support of the trade and traffic of this city, and maintenance of its inhabitants of all degrees." Therefrom arose more trade. As early as 1727 it was a ground of complaint that New York supplied Canada almost entirely with wheat and other articles of food, instead of leaving the traffic in the hands of the French. To Barbadoes and the other flourishing West Indian Islands, also, it sent its breadstuffs, receiving in exchange an abundance of rum and sugar, for the use of its own people and of the natives. The annals of the eighteenth century abound in curious controversies among English politicians concerning their trade complications, opposed, as they were, to the short-sighted views that then prevailed concerning the balance of trade, and other myths now happily obsolete. "There is yearly imported

into New York," it was said in 1732, "a very large quantity
of the woollen manufactures of this kingdom, for their clothing, which they would be rendered incapable to pay for, and
would be reduced to the necessity of making for themselves,
if they were prohibited from receiving from the foreign sugar-
colonies the money, rum, sugar, molasses, and cotton-wool
which they at present take, in return for provisions, horses,
and lumber, the produce of that province and of New
Jersey." New York not having much cloth-making of its
own, and therefore proving a good customer in the English
market, and also having no young iron manufactures to enter
into competition with the home trades, was less restrained
in its commerce with other colonies than some of the neighbouring ports ; but the obstacles thrown in its way by
narrow-minded statesmen at home were considerable, and it
had good reason for joining in the great war of free trade by
which the independence of the United States was brought
about. English folly necessitated that war, and New York,
at any rate, lost nothing by its issue.

Before the war began, New York, trading chiefly in
English-built and English-owned ships, shared with Philadelphia and Boston, which in the early times had surpassed
it as a trading-town, extensive traffic with the sugar islands
of the West Indies, sending to them flour, biscuits, fish,
timber, and other articles of native produce, and a smaller
traffic with British North America, just then vastly augmented
by the addition of Canada. Much American flour, also, was
brought to England, and some was sent to Portugal, Spain,
Italy, and even to the Levant. But England had sought to
check all trade that did not commend itself to the selfish
views of the moment, and her powers of checking it were
very great indeed. "She has cut off our trade with all the
world," was the just complaint of the " Declaration of Rights."
The English colonists, beginning to trade with all the world,
resolved that they would submit to no restraint. The

citizens of New York were among the first to take part in the rebellion, and, finding that by that step they had endangered all the commercial vitality they then possessed, and that all their trade was laid under embargo by the English, they entered heartily into the work until it was completed, and England, compelled to acknowledge the freedom of the United States, was forced to tolerate its commerce as that of an independent nation.

At the time of the Revolution, the trade of New York with England was surpassed by that of Philadelphia and Boston, and all these three northern ports together had less trade with the mother country than was possessed by Carolina, and only about half as much as that of Virginia and Maryland. New York had then much larger trade than many of its rivals with other parts, but it was only an inferior mart. A change, however, began before the close of the eighteenth century. In 1797, for the first time, it took precedence of all other ports, and since then its advance upon them has been rapid. The excellence of its harbour gave it an advantage over the New England and Pennsylvanian marts; the freedom of its institutions gave it a yet greater advantage over the marts of the slave states. With less local patriotism than any of them, it became a common centre for all the trade of the new empire. While the other ports sent abroad the special produce of their neighbourhoods, and brought back the special commodities that were most accessible in the districts visited by their ships, they all looked to New York to provide them with the other requirements of commerce. The leading mercantile houses in every town of the Union had their branches in New York, and very often these branches soon became the chief establishments, using their parents as mere agencies. Thus New York made progress, and earned its title of " the empire city."

The rapidity of its growth is shown by the statistics of its population. In 1697 it had 4,302 inhabitants. The number had risen in 1756 to 10,381, in 1790 to 31,131, and in 1820, when it was the largest city in the Union, to 123,706. In 1850 it amounted to 575,507, and in 1860 to 805,657, besides 266,661 in its great suburb of Brooklyn. The population of city and suburb cannot now be less than 1,500,000.

New York is now inferior to London alone as a great emporium of trade; and its very monotony of progress renders its history unromantic. Its sometime chief rival, New Orleans, has had a more chequered career.

New Orleans was founded on the Mississippi in 1718, by the French, as the capital of their colony of Louisiana. When Charlevoix visited it in 1722, it consisted, as he says, of "a hundred cabins, disposed with little regularity, a large wooden warehouse, two or three dwellings that would be no ornament to a French village, and the half of a sorry storehouse, which they were pleased to lend to the Lord, but of which He had scarcely taken possession when it was proposed to turn Him out to lodge under a tent." There was soon plenty of provision made for the teaching of religion, but not much heed was paid to commerce, or the wonderful facilities provided for it by the Mississippi, until New Orleans passed out of the hands of the French. Jesuits, priests, and Ursuline nuns were its most enterprising inhabitants. France, proposing to take possession of the whole American continent, failed in permanently holding any part of it. While Canada was being seized by England, Louisiana had to be ceded to Spain, and soon after its restoration the French were glad, in 1803, to sell the vast and sparsely-peopled territory to the United States.

New Orleans then contained about 8,000 inhabitants. That number was more than doubled by 1810. In 1830 it amounted to 46,310, in 1850 to 126,375, and in 1860 to 163,823.

For a time, New Orleans threatened to outstrip New York in the race for wealth. It soon surpassed Charleston, as a mart for the cotton and tobacco of the Southern States. The Central States and western territories were then beginning to be colonised, and the Mississippi and its tributaries offered twenty thousand miles of navigable watercourse, running in and out of a vast area of a million square miles, for çonveyance of their produce to New Orleans, and thence out into the Atlantic. New York, by help of canals, and, more recently, of railways, has absorbed much of this commerce. The merchants of New Orleans strove heartily to preserve it in its natural channel, and, with this end, made river navigation a scientific study. In 1810 the voyage from St. Louis to New Orleans, a distance of 1,500 miles, occupied a hundred and twenty days of tedious travelling in flat boats, pushed along by boatmen, who thrust their poles into the mud, and so, by walking aft, enabled the rickety craft to crawl and hobble down the river. In 1815 the first steamer plied on the Mississippi, and completed the voyage in twenty-five days. In 1860 it occupied only three days. The dangers of these flying steamers are famous, but American travellers and traders have been willing to run the risk, and New Orleans has received an immense accession of commerce, steamers giving speed, and an improvement on the old flat boats giving cheapness of transit.

The position of New Orleans is itself a wonder. Built on a swamp, from two to four feet below the level of the sea and river at high tide—causing it, till recent sanitary improvements were made, to be grievously plagued with yellow fever—it has to be protected by a high rampart, one part of which, known as the Levee, serves as a convenient landing-place. "The Levee of New Orleans," it was said, about thirty-five years ago, "is one continued quay, four miles in extent, and of an average breadth of

100 feet. It is fifteen feet above high water mark, and six feet above the level of the city, to which it is graduated by an easy descent, and, like the river it margins, it holds a serpentine course. It is constructed of deposit swept from the north by the Mississippi ; and the deposit is so great, and the consequent formation of land so rapid, immediately in front of that portion of the quay which is most used for the purposes of commerce, that it has, within a few years, become necessary to build piled wharves, jutting out from 50 to 100 feet into the river."

The progress of this Southern mart during fifty years was more rapid even than that of New York. In 1817 it collected for exportation 65,000 bales of cotton and 28,000 hogsheads of tobacco, besides other produce of all sorts. In 1848 its cotton exports amounted to 1,201,897 bales, and its tobacco to 60,364 hogsheads, and the increase of trade in many other important articles, especially bread-stuffs, had been very much greater. As early as 1822 its citizens began to anticipate the time when the town would be without a rival in the Old World or the New. "New Orleans alone," it was then said, "will be for ever, as it is now, the mighty mart of the merchandise and produce brought from more than a thousand rivers. With Boston, New York, Philadelphia, and Baltimore on the left, Mexico on the right, Havannah in front, and the immense valley of the Mississippi in the rear, no such position for the accumulation and perpetuity of wealth and power ever existed. Unless prevented by some great accident in human affairs, this rapidly-increasing city will, in no very distant time, leave the emporia of the Eastern World far behind."

The "great accident in human affairs" occurred in 1861. The great Southern Rebellion, partly instigated for the aggrandisement of New Orleans, led to its downfall. In 1860 the port cleared 1,293 vessels, with a total burthen of 894,353 tons. In 1861 it cleared 130 vessels, with a total burthen of 76,935 tons; and that sudden decimation has been followed by no sudden recovery. New Orleans may once more become a thriving port, but its hope of supremacy can never be realised. New York has now found, in railway communication, a better access to the West than even the Mississippi could furnish to New Orleans.

And in the West is growing up a mart which, though it can never stand alone, promises ere long to surpass even New York as a great American mart. In 1796 St. Louis had 891 inhabitants, and in 1830 no more than 5,852. In 1850 its population amounted to 77,860; it was 160,773 in 1860; and the last ten years have probably again more than doubled the number. A manufacturing town itself, St. Louis is in the centre of manufacturing districts, yet in their infancy, but possessed of wonderful resources for future development; yet more a mercantile town, it is the nucleus of a hundred markets, lately born or still to be started. Excellently placed on the Mississippi, and near to the Missouri and the Ohio, it has unrivalled facilities for inland water communication, and the Great Pacific Railway has now brought it within easy reach of both New York and San Francisco—the gates of the two great oceans, which, between them, wash the shores of all the civilised world.

San Francisco owes its progress, yet more than Melbourne, to gold discoveries. There is a romantic episode in its early history. Sir Francis Drake, seeking for Spanish booty in the course of his famous voyage round the world, visited its harbour in 1579, and there spent five weeks, repairing his ship and holding friendly intercourse with the natives. After two days of cautious exchanging of presents and other tokens of mutual kindliness, the English, who were in huts, with their ship on dry land, saw, with some fear, that the Indians were gathering in the distance in large numbers. "Presently," says the old chronicler of the voyage, "came down from the country a great multitude, and, among them, a man of goodly stature and comely personage, who was the king, accompanied by many tall and warlike men. Before his majesty advanced, two ambassadors presented themselves to the general, to announce his approach, and continued speaking for about an hour, at the end of which the king, making as princely a show as he possibly could, with all his train came forward, in the course of which they cried continually, after a singing manner, with a lusty courage. As they drew nearer and nearer unto us, so did they more and more strive to behave themselves with a certain comeliness and gravity in all their actions." The "comeliness and gravity" were of a curious sort. The men sang and danced as they approached; the women "tore themselves till the face, breasts, and other parts were bespattered with blood." As they bore no arms, save a few quaintly-ornamented clubs hanging from the necks of the chief persons, Drake made no opposition to their coming. "Then," proceeds the chronicler, "they made signs to our general to have him sit down; to whom both the king and divers others made several orations, or rather, indeed, if we understood them, supplications, that he would take the province and kingdom into his hand, and become their king and patron, making signs that they would resign unto him their right and title in the whole land, and become his vassals. That they might make us, indeed, believe that it was their true intent and meaning, the king himself, with great reverence, joyfully singing a song, set the crown upon his head, offering unto him many things, honoured him with the name of *hioh*—or 'king.' They added thereto, as it might seem, a song and dance of triumph, because they were not only visited of the gods, for so they still judged us to be, but that the great and chief god was now become their god, their king, and patron, and themselves were become the only happy and blessed people in the world, which thing our general thought not meet to reject, because he knew not what honour and profit it might be to our country. Wherefore, in the name and to the use of her Majesty, he took the sceptre, crown, and dignity of the said country in his hands."

To the district of which he was thus crowned king Drake gave the name of New Albion. He little thought that in its precincts, hidden only by a thin coating of earth, was Californian gold, but of his possessions no use was made by him or his countrymen during two centuries and a half.

San Francisco took its name from the mission of San Francisco de Assissi, founded in 1776 by two monks, who here established a missionary settlement, which flourished for about ninety years. In 1834 the religious supremacy gave way to the civil power, and from that time the town slowly grew. In 1847, however, it contained only a few rude cabins, and the entire population numbered only 459. Next year all was changed. In the spring gold was discovered in California, and San Francisco was altogether deserted for a few months. In the autumn its inhabitants returned, laden with treasure, and accompanied by thousands of other gold-finders and their satellites, who suddenly converted the little town into a busy mart. Gold being its first staple, it now deals extensively in everything that gold can buy. In 1860 it had 56,802 inhabitants. In the last ten years the population has doubled or trebled.

Very different from the sudden growth of new marts, like San Francisco, though greatly enriched by them and the new commerce they have created in recent times, is the slow growth of the old European marts. In illustration of the progress of these trading-towns, it will suffice, after what has been said concerning English ports, to refer briefly to the two of most importance in France—Marseilles and Bordeaux.

T

Marseilles is almost the oldest mart in Christendom. Founded by a Greek colony, six hundred years before the Christian era, it emerged from the obscurity into which it had fallen during the dark ages, and became a vigorous rival of Venice and Genoa in the times of their greatness. The exploits of Jacques Cœur in the fifteenth century have been already noticed. From his time till the present day it has continued to be the chief mart of France, and has grown with its growth. Its prosperity in the eighteenth century may be understood from the fact that 1,264 vessels entered its harbour in 1753. In 1821 it had 101,217 inhabitants. That number was doubled in the ensuing thirty years, and in 1866 the population amounted to 300,131. In 1864, 9,047 vessels, with an aggregate burthen of 1,667,419 tons, entered the port, and 8,893, with 1,657,831 tons in all, quitted it. Of this shipping one-sixteenth belonged to Marseilles itself, and nearly two-thirds to the rest of France. Of the remaining third, one-sixth was British, another sixth Spanish, a third Italian, and the rest chiefly Austrian. Raw silk is the staple import of Marseilles, but it also receives large supplies of cotton, coffee, sugar, and coals. There are numerous manufactories in the town and its neighbourhood, and the exports comprise, besides silk goods, every variety of French produce.

Bordeaux, with a population of 92,375 in 1820, and of about 190,000 in 1865, is a manufacturing town, as well as a mart for all sorts of articles ; but its staple trade has, from the earliest times, been in wine. It began to be famous as a port belonging, with the rest of Guienne and Aquitaine, to the English Crown, and to that circumstance was due the favour with which its merchants were regarded by mediæval England, and, in part, the importance of its later commerce with this country. The entire annual produce of the vineyards of France averages about 856,000,000 gallons, and of this some 25,000,000 gallons, or about half of the whole quantity exported from the country, passes out of Bordeaux. Its merchants collect, not only the produce of the neighbourhood, but large supplies from the Champagne and other districts, for shipment to England, the United States, and other countries.

CHAPTER XI.

MANIAS AND PANICS.

"The Madness of the Multitude" and its Variations—The Tulip Mania—
Manias of Discovery—The Darien Project—The Mississippi Scheme—
The Origin and Progress of English Stock-jobbing—The South Sea
Company and the South Sea Bubble—Contemporary Bubbles—Later
Developments of Stock-jobbing—Famous Stock-jobbers—Nathan
Meyer Rothschild and his Exploits—The Joint-stock Company Mania
and Panic of 1825-6—The Railway Mania and Panic of 1845-1847—
The Panics of 1857 and 1866.

WHEN the South Sea Bubble had been blown to its highest
and to its flimsiest hugeness, Sir Isaac Newton was asked what
would be the end of it. "I can calculate," he answered,
"the motions of erratic stars, but not the madness of the
multitude." The madness of the multitude has been stirred
up in strange ways, and has taken strange courses in each
age of the world, and in every line of thought and action;
and commercial follies are inferior only to religious follies in
the violence of their working, and in the mischiefs that they
have occasioned. Their issues, however, have not been
always mischievous. Just as the blind seekings of the old
alchemists after the philosopher's stone, and the power of
turning all meaner metals into gold, conduced greatly to the
development of modern science, so many famous manias,
the direct consequences of which have been only panics and
ruin to thousands, have, indirectly, been of great value, not
only as warnings to posterity, but in actually opening up
new and very helpful paths of trade.

One of the first great manias of modern times was one
of the most foolish. In the middle of the sixteenth century,
Counsellor Herwart, of Augsburg, a lover of rare plants, re-

ceived from Constantinople, where they had for a long time been cultivated, a present of tulips. Conrad Gesner saw them in bloom in 1539, and his praises, circulated throughout Europe, quickly rendered the flower very popular everywhere, but most of all in Holland. It does not seem to have been brought to England till 1600, and the fashion of tulip-growing never reached such a pitch in this country as on the Continent, though its virtues were sung by other poets as well as by Cowley in these lines :—

> "The tulip next appeared, all over gay,
> But wanton, full of pride, and full of play ;
> The world can't show a dye but here has place ;
> Nay, by new mixtures, she can change her face.
> Purple and gold are both beneath her care ;
> The richest needlework she loves to wear ;
> Her only study is to please the eye,
> And to outshine the rest in finery."

It was the unusual susceptibility of the tulip to variegations in colour, and delicacy of petals resulting from careful cultivation, that occasioned its great value in the eyes of curiosity-lovers in and out of Holland in the seventeenth century. For three-quarters of a century the love grew, and gardeners found it profitable to train and alter the plant until it was brought to a sickly beauty, all the more attractive to their customers because of the extreme care needed for keeping the exotic alive ; and in 1634 the artificial taste burst out into a mania. In that year the whole Dutch nation went mad about tulips. All ordinary trades were neglected, and rich and poor, young and old, alike devoted themselves to tulip-growing and tulip-selling. The price of bulbs rose every day, and those most in value were sold for enormous sums. In 1635 a good "Viceroy" was worth £300, an "Admiral Liefken" was worth more than £400, and a "Semper Augustus" could hardly be bought for £550. Of that last variety there were, early in 1636, only two good bulbs to be found in Holland. One, in Amsterdam, was sold for £450 a new carriage, two grey horses, and a set of harness. The other, owned by a lucky dealer in Haarlem, was exchanged for the fee-simple of twelve acres of building-ground. For one "Viceroy" bulb, at about the same time, were bartered two lasts of wheat, four lasts of rye, four fat oxen, eight fat swine, twelve fat sheep, two hogsheads of wine, four tuns of beer, two tons of butter, a thousand pounds of cheese, a bed, a suit of clothes, and a silver drinking-cup, the value of the whole being £240. We are told, among many like stories, of a Dutch merchant, to whom some good news was brought by a sailor, and who rewarded him with the present of a fine red-herring for his breakfast. On his way out of the counting-house, the sailor saw what he thought was an onion lying on a table, and, being fond of onions with his herrings, he quietly put it in his pocket. An hour or two afterwards he was finishing his meal, when the merchant and a whole bevy of clerks rush out to accuse and convict him of the theft, which they had just discovered. He had stolen and eaten, not an onion, but a valuable bulb, worth nearly £300, and the price of which, as the merchant said, "might have sumptuously feasted the Prince of Orange and the whole court of the Stadtholder;" and he had leisure for digesting it during several months' imprisonment with which his innocent felony was punished.

For more than a year the tulip-mania was at its height. Speculations in bulbs engrossed all the attention of moneyed men in the exchanges of Amsterdam, Rotterdam, Haarlem, Leyden, and every other town in Holland. In each the tulip-notary was, for the time, a more important man than the chief magistrate. The infection spread to other countries, and foreigners flocked to the Dutch marts to buy tulips for sale in their own lands; and the money brought by them and by buyers from country districts to Amsterdam and the large towns encouraged the idle belief that the tulip trade would be of more permanent profit to the country than traffic

with the East Indies, or any other branch of commerce in
which the Dutch had rendered themselves famous. But the
necessary signal soon came. Prices rose constantly till near
the end of 1636, when a fall began. Speculators, finding
that they were losing money by purchases they had already
made, refused to buy more, and thus still further reduced the
market value. A panic ensued, which brought thousands of
rich persons to beggary, and left a few fortunate adventurers
in the possession of vast wealth. Less injury was done by
this than by many other memorable manias; but years of
litigation among tulip buyers and sellers ensued, and there
was a long stagnation of the more legitimate trade of the
country.

England, at that time too busy with its political troubles,
and its preparations for civil war and the overthrow of
Charles I., took but little part in the tulip-mania, and lost
nothing by the tulip-panic. The high value set upon tulips
in consequence of this whim, however, has been enduring in
this country. In 1800 their average price was fifteen guineas
apiece, and in 1835 a "Miss Fanny Kemble" bulb was sold
in London by public auction for £75. In Holland the
mania for tulip-growing is not dead yet.

Very different from the tulip folly was a series of manias
that excited Europe, and spread far beyond European limits,
in the fifteenth and following centuries. The earliest of
these was, in some measure, connected with the projects of
the old alchemists. While mistaken men of science sought
in their closets to find out the philosopher's stone, and the
secret of transmuting useless ores to gold, men of action
were panting to discover the islands of perpetual youth and
the lands of inexhaustible wealth, that were supposed to
exist somewhere in undiscovered quarters of the world. The
exaggerated stories of Marco Polo and other travellers concerning the countries they had visited passed from mouth to
ear with ever fresh exaggerations, until, shortly before the

time of Columbus, the belief was prevalent that in the far East, near the unknown site of the Garden of Paradise, was a region of boundless wealth and boundless happiness. A score of different fables, based on traditions handed down from ancient times, and, to some extent, justified by the treasures obtained by the Venetian merchants from Oriental traders, found credence in and before the fifteenth century, and proved of notable benefit to the world, by furnishing supporters to more sober adventurers, like Prince Henry of Portugal and Christopher Columbus. They helped to make possible the discovery of America, and, as soon as America was discovered, they took bolder shape, and proved of further benefit by encouraging its exploration and colonisation. It was the quest of the fountain of life that led to the conquest of Florida. It was the quest of El Dorado, the Golden City of Manoa, the Golden Lake of Parina, and kindred golden myths, that led to the conquest of Peru, Guiana, and all the intermediate northern parts of South America.

These and others like them were manias which would have been altogether beneficial, had the men who devoted their lives to them been honest and generous enough to make good use of their successes, seeing that, when the fables that produced them were exploded, facts better than any fables were brought to light. Some kindred manias, however, were less fortunate in their issues.

One of the first and most notable of these was the Darien project, by which Scotland was nearly ruined in the closing years of the seventeenth century. Its author was William Paterson, the founder of the Bank of England, who urged upon both James II. and William III. the expediency of colonising the Isthmus of Darien, and using it as "the key of the Indies and door of the world." Paterson, ignorant of the inhospitable nature of this tract of land, but attracted by its wonderful fitness, had other things been propitious, for a

great emporium of trade between Europe and Asia, advocated the project again and again, before it was taken up, in
1695, by the Scots. " Being an isthmus, and seated between
the two vast oceans of the universe," he said, " it is furnished
on each side with excellent harbours, between the principal
of which lie the more easy and convenient passes between
the one and the other sea. These ports and passes, being
possessed and fortified, may be easily secured and defended
against any force, not only there, but that can possibly be
found in those places, which are not only the most convenient
doors and inlets into, but likewise the readiest and nearest
means of gaining, and afterwards for ever keeping the command of, the spacious South Sea, which, as it is the greatest,
so it is by far the richest, side of the world. These ports so
settled, with passes open, through them will flow at least two-
thirds of what both Indies yield to Christendom. The time
and expense of the voyage to China, Japan, and the richest
part of the East Indies, will be lessened more than half, and
the consumption of European commodities soon be more
than doubled, and afterwards yearly increased."

No commercial speculation ever entered upon was
worthier in design or more honestly propounded, and, as far
as lay in his power, worked through by its author, than this
Darien project, but its history was painfully disastrous.

Paterson erred in thinking that the Isthmus of Darien
was, "in healthfulness and fruitfulness," a fit place for an
army of raw colonists to suddenly take possession of and
make their home without careful preparation and pioneering.
He erred, also, in trusting the large enterprise which he
projected to a nation so poor as Scotland was two centuries
ago. That, indeed, he did not at all intend. His first and
constant idea was to employ upon it an abundant store of
English capital, and when, in 1695, his Scottish friends
proposed to make Edinburgh the headquarters of the project,
he expected that more than half the funds to be collected

would come from wealthy English speculators. English
jealousy of Scotland, however, as well as the special jealousy
with which the East India Company, the Levant Company,
and other trading associations, regarded the establishment
of a powerful rival, caused his anticipations to fail. As soon
as the Scottish African and Indian Company, as it was
styled, took shape in Edinburgh, a hue-and-cry was raised
against it in London. King William III. and some of his
shrewdest advisers, men like Lord Halifax and John Locke,
approved of it; but it was fiercely denounced in Parliament,
as a project wildly fanatical in itself, and certain to bring
about war with Spain, by its tampering with the Spanish
monopoly of trade with Central America. The impeachment of Paterson and his chief fellow-workers was even
proposed in the House of Commons, and though this was
soon abandoned, every sort of influence was used to bring
the men and their arguments into discredit. These so well
succeeded that whereas more than £300,000 had, in the
course of a few days, been promised by wealthy Londoners,
these promises were speedily recalled, and, after long effort,
hardly a tenth of that sum was actually raised in England.
The whole burthen of the project fell upon Scotland, and
then more than eighteen months had to be spent in preach-
ing up the scheme among Scotchmen, before a capital of
£400,000 could be collected. Paterson himself subscribed
£3,000, and a crowd of noblemen and merchants made
large contributions; but most of the shares were taken by
humbler adventurers, who found it hard to scrape together
a few pounds, and to whom loss of their money would be
ruin. The mania ran through Scotland, however, and by
the middle of 1697 much of the available wealth of the
country was in the hands of the African and Indian
Company.

Then difficulties arose about building ships and collecting stores, for which Leith, at that time a very poor port,

though the best in Scotland, offered few facilities. Paterson went to Amsterdam and Hamburg to buy articles that could not be obtained in Edinburgh, and to pay for them he entrusted a London merchant with £25,000. The London merchant proved dishonest, and defrauded the Company of about £8,000 before his peculations were discovered. That loss was more than the Company could bear; but, through Paterson's excess of honesty, it led to the ruin of the whole project. The fraudulent agent having been appointed by him, he rashly took upon himself the responsibility of the whole misfortune, and declared himself indebted to the Company for all the £8,000 that had been stolen. In part payment thereof, he gave up his £3,000 share, and being unable to pay the rest, he offered the directors "either to dismiss him out of the Company's service, allowing him time to recover some fortune or employment, and then, as he became able, he would pay by degrees; or to retain him in their service, and allow him, out of the Company's free profits, some reasonable consideration for his pains, charges, and losses in promoting the same, out of which allowance he doubted not, in a few years, to discharge the balance." The latter alternative was chosen; but the directors of the Company meanly and unwisely degraded him from his natural position as leader of the project, and retained him in a subordinate capacity.

Thereby the Darien scheme was ruined. After long delays, a party of twelve hundred adventurers quitted Leith in July, 1698, and another party followed in August, 1699. Paterson went with the first company, not as its general, but as an adviser, whose advice was not to be taken. With notable folly, the direction of the voyage, the planting of the colony, and the business to be done afterwards were intrusted to seven incompetent councillors, with equal powers. Paterson complained of this arrangement at starting, and complained of the bad provisions with which the party were

supplied, but he was overruled, both then and all through
the tragic history of the expedition. Painful, by reason of its
monotony of sadness is his record of the enterprise, in which
nothing was done as he wished and had purposed. " During
the voyage," he says, " our marine chancellors did not only
take all upon them, but likewise browbeat and discouraged
everybody else. Yet we had patience, hoping things would
mend when we came ashore. But we found ourselves mistaken ; for though our masters at sea had sufficiently taught
us that we fresh-water men knew nothing of their salt-water
business, yet, when at land, they were so far from letting us
turn the chase, that they took upon them to know everything
better than we. I must confess, it troubled me exceedingly
to see our affairs thus turmoiled and disordered by tempers
and dispositions as boisterous and turbulent as the elements
they are used to struggle with, which are at least as mischievous masters as ever they can be useful servants." The
ignorant leaders of the expedition insisted upon landing on
what Paterson called "a mere morass, neither fit to be fortified nor planted, nor, indeed, for the men to lie upon ;" the
absurd reason given for this being that thereby labour would
be saved in supplying the colonists with water. After two
months had been wasted, and many men had been weakened,
if not killed, by their unhealthy situation, the colony was
transferred to another part of the isthmus. Already, however, most of the provisions brought from Scotland had been
eaten or lost. The colonists were in no condition to sow
and reap for themselves. All their time was spent in building houses and laying out grounds, negotiating with the
native Indians, and protecting themselves from the jealous
treatment of the Spanish settlers in the neighbourhood.
Many died of starvation, many others fell victims to the
fevers of the tropics. At length all the survivors, a bare
eighth of the twelve hundred that had gone out, expecting to
found a more successful trading-colony than had yet been

established, painfully toiled home again, in the autumn of 1699. They had hardly gone when the second party arrived ; but the new-comers, seeing the ill-success of their predecessors, wisely abstained from making much effort at continuing the exploit. Attacked by Spanish war-ships, they speedily capitulated, and made their way back to Scotland. Thus ended Paterson's great Darien scheme

At home the troubles were long felt. Scottish trading energy seemed to have spent itself upon this luckless project, and the rich found themselves poor, and the poor yet poorer, by reason of the loss of all the capital they had embarked, and the restraining of all fresh enterprise during the next few years. The union between England and Scotland, which Paterson greatly helped to bring about, and in which he made ample atonement for the mischiefs which he had innocently occasioned, soon remedied the evil, and the northern country, now one in commercial as well as in political interests with the southern country, quickly recovered its equilibrium, and entered on a new career of prosperity.

More lasting depression followed upon a yet greater mania, akin to the Darien project in its ostensible purposes, though in nothing else, which soon afterwards arose in France. Its author, a countryman, and, perhaps, at one time an acquaintance, of Paterson's, was the celebrated John Law.

Law, born in 1671, was the son of a wealthy goldsmith in Edinburgh, who died in 1688. The young man came to London, took high rank among its fops and gallants, spent all his fortune, and in 1697 killed an antagonist in a duel. Being imprisoned for that offence, he contrived to escape, and the next twenty years were passed by him as a gambling adventurer in Scotland, Flanders, Holland, Germany, Hungary, and France. As early as 1705 we find him advancing the false monetary system for which he was afterwards notorious. In that year he addressed to the people of Edinburgh "two overtures for supplying the present scarcity of coin and improving trade, and for clearing the debts due by the Government to the army and civil list, by issuing paper-money." But the cautious Scots were in no mood to listen to him, and they were altogether deterred by two able pamphlets, in which Paterson showed the mischief of that and all other "imaginary projects," and maintained that there could be no national credit without solid cash, and no national progress without persevering industry. Law was as unsuccessful in the like arguments which he offered to Louis XIV. and other foreign princes, until the death of Louis, and the appointment of the foolish Duke of Orleans as Regent of France, in 1715, paved the way to his better fortune.

France was then on the verge of bankruptcy. Misgovernment had ruined the credit of the State, and the frauds of men in office, and their allies in the trading community, had crippled all the resources of the country, and brought its commerce almost to a standstill. By depreciating the coinage, and by violent raids upon some great delinquents, who gladly paid high bribes in order that they might escape punishment, the Regent attempted to tide over the difficulty; but after a few months affairs were in a worse state than ever. Then Law appeared at Court, and, with a mixture of truth and folly, urged that a metallic currency was by itself quite inadequate to the commercial needs of France, and proposed that a national bank should be set up, which should collect and distribute the royal revenues, and issue paper-money on their security, and on that of the public lands. His proposals were readily listened to, and, though they were not altogether adopted, he was allowed, in May, 1716, to establish a bank with a capital of 6,000,000 livres, one-fourth in specie, the rest in State-paper, and to issue notes, payable on demand, which were to be accepted in payment of taxes, and to have full currency throughout the kingdom. Law's bank succeeded so well that in the course of a year his notes were worth fifteen per cent. more than gold and silver money, which was liable to depreciation at the whim of the Crown. The favour which he won thereby with statesmen, courtiers, and common folk made easy the adoption of a new project, the Mississippi scheme, which he now devised.

While the English colonists were making sure their position on the eastern coast-line of North America, above and below New York, the French, having conquered Canada, gradually extended their power in the interior, pushed southwards along the Mississippi till they reached its mouth, and then founded New Orleans. From the vast territory thus acquired, and vaguely described as Louisiana, they expected great benefits; and their national vanity was quickened by the hope that, in due time, they would be able, from their inland vantage-ground, to drive the English and all other aliens into the sea, and thus to gain possession of the whole North American continent. But, in spite of the efforts of Colbert and other bold statesmen at home, and of skilful and indefatigable generals in Canada and Louisiana, their Transatlantic possessions proved only a source of weakness to France. No firm footing was gained even on the St. Lawrence, and on the Mississippi nothing but barren victories resulted from the martial energy that there had ample play. France was beginning to grow tired of its American colonies, when Law and his friends revived the old notion, really a true one, that under the prolific soil of Louisiana there was boundless mineral wealth—not gold, as they represented, but coal and iron, which are better than gold. Law proposed that a new company should be founded to utilise the wealth of this great district, that miners and traders should be sent out to it, and that, with the proceeds, the French exchequer and the whole French nation should be mightily enriched. The proposal was agreed to. The company was incorporated in August, 1717, with a nominal capital or 100,000,000 livres, and with it was associated Law's bank, with enlarged functions and privileges, and finally converted into the Royal Bank of France. The processes by which the company and the bank played into each other's hands, and quickly flooded the country with paper-money, need not be detailed. The Parliament of France boldly and honestly opposed their mischievous follies, and Law was more than once impeached and denounced as an enemy to the country. But the Regent supported him, and soon encouraged him in more extravagant measures than he would have dared by himself to adopt; and the people of France, from peer to peasant, rushed madly into the tempting maze of speculation prepared for them.

Early in 1719, when the mania was at its height, the Mississippi Company was re-organised and endowed with exclusive trading privileges to the East Indies, China, and the South Seas, under the new name of the Company of the Indies. Fifty thousand fresh shares were created, with a nominal value of 25,000,000 livres, and upon them Law promised an annual profit of 120 per cent. So great was the demand for these shares that their number was increased to three hundred thousand, and all were taken up in a few weeks. Country folks crowded up to Paris, and nearly every resident therein joined in the insane rush. Law's house in the Rue de Quincampoix was besieged from morning to night by a rabble of dukes, duchesses, merchants, milkmaids, and all other representatives of *noblesse* and *bourgeoisie.* So many were there crushed to death or maimed for life that Law had to remove to the Place Vendôme, and at length to take the great Hôtel de Soissons, the garden of which, covering several acres, was large enough to hold a few of the most eager speculators. Law's antechambers were crowded with persons of all ranks, who waited all day long, and day after day, for their turn to obtain the coveted shares; and the shares, as soon as they were bought, were taken into the great market in the garden, there to be traded with among the thousands who were ready to pay any price that was asked for them, and who generally sold them again at yet higher rates. The turmoil of speculation, which lasted for a year, has no parallel in the history of financial follies.

Curious stories by the dozen are told concerning this turmoil and its consequences. A cobbler, whose stall was near to the headquarters of the speculation, gained 200 livres a day by providing standing-room and pens and paper for the adventurers. A hunchback, whose deformity was his only stock-in-trade, made a fortune by turning himself into a movable writing-desk. A lady, who had long in vain sought access to Law's counting-house, devised an original plan for meeting him. Ordering her coachman to run up against a post as soon as he could meet the great financier in the streets, she drove about incessantly for three days before Law came in sight. At last she was lucky enough to see him approaching her. "Upset us now, for God's sake, upset us now!" she shouted. The coachman obeyed, and she was thrown upon the pavement. Law ran to assist her, escorted her into his house, and there heard that the lady suffered from nothing but want of Mississippi shares, and so was induced to place her name on the list of applicants.

All ordinary occupations were neglected during this time of frenzy, save those by which the wisest persons grew rich in catering for the extravagant ways of living that it begot or quickened. Costly viands abounded. Pictures, jewellery, and the like were brought to Paris in greater quantities than ever, and sold for fabulous sums. Thousands of paupers were enriched, and as many wealthy men were impoverished. A few speculators were notably fortunate, among the rest Louis XIV.'s illegitimate son, the Duc de Bourbon, who rebuilt the palace at Chantilly, and bought vast estates with his profits on Mississippi paper. Many foreigners, too, went

U

to Paris to speculate shrewdly in paper money, and then took their proceeds in solid coin out of the country, and native adventures followed the same wise course. We are told, for instance, of one Vermalet, who covered a cart-load of gold and silver, worth nearly 1,000,000 livres, with hay and stubble, and, disguising himself in a peasant's blouse, quietly smuggled it into Belgium, and thence to Amsterdam.

It was by such draining out of the real money of France that the inevitable sequel of the Mississippi mania was hastened. In the first week of 1820, Law began to find that he had not enough coin in his bank to meet the requirements of his customers. Depreciation of the already depreciated gold and silver money was resorted to, but in vain. In vain, also, an edict was obtained restricting specie payments to each person to one hundred livres in gold, and five livres in silver. These measures only informed the public of the coming danger, and increased the demand for coin which could not be supplied. So desperate were affairs at the end of February, that the Regent forbade any one, under heavy penalties, to have more than 500 livres of coin—about £20 —or any jewels or other commodities that could be easily transported, in his possession ; and, in order that crimes of this artificial sort might be detected, informers were to be entitled to half the worth of the illicit valuables which they brought to light. Thereby all social relations were wantonly disturbed, and public confidence in the paper currency was utterly destroyed. "Never," says a contemporary historian, "was seen a more capricious Government; never was a more frantic tyranny exercised by hands less firm. It is inconceivable to those who were witnesses of the horrors of those times, and who look back upon them now as on a dream, that a sudden revolution did not break out, that Law and the Regent did not perish by a tragical death. They were both held in horror, but the people confined themselves to complaints. A sombre and timid despair, a stupid consternation, seized upon all, and men's minds were too vile even to be capable of a courageous crime."

It was well that the "courageous crime" was not perpetrated. France suffered enough without it; and perhaps the hundreds of thousands who were ruined by Law's folly—we have no reason to say that he was guilty of more than most cruel folly—had sufficient wisdom to see that the folly was also their own. But the national and individual distress that ensued was altogether grievous. Law, who, after being exiled from France, resumed his old gambling habits, and died a pauper, in Venice, in 1729, had issued notes to the nominal value of 2,700,000,000 livres, which soon shrivelled into worthless paper, and left France with a national debt of 3,100,000,000 livres, and so unhinged the trade and capital of the country that the mischief could never be adequately repaired. French commercial prosperity is almost a novelty of our own days.

The age of the Mississippi mania in France was also the age of the South Sea mania in England; but here fortunate circumstances rendered the national folly much less disastrous. The South Sea mania was only the most memorable episode in two centuries of stock-jobbing, which, as it fills an important place in our commercial history, and is the chain on which all our great manias and all our great panics have been suspended, needs to be briefly traced to its commencement.

The word stock, in its present commercial sense, was first applied to the shares of the East India Company, and of the other great associations established during the seventeenth century, for foreign and colonial trade. At first the stock was not marketable. A separate subscription was made for each enterprise, and the subscriber was held responsible for his shares until the transaction was completed, and his portion of profits, if there were any, was assigned to him. But soon the shares became permanent, and their holders were enabled, if they chose, to dispose of them like any other property, for whatever they were worth. Then the National Debt was begun, starting from Charles II.'s illegal seizure, in 1679, of the money lodged for safety in the Mint; and it was soon found to be a convenient means for investment of the savings of persons who had no commercial facilities for applying them in enterprises of their own. There was plenty of this surplus cash floating about, or, rather, until space was found for it to float in, hoarded up by its owners. Pope's father, when he retired from business, carried £20,000 down to his country-house, to be locked up in a strong box, and taken out, a little at the time, as he had need of it. Thousands of rich men did the like, while others, afraid of keeping so much money in their own hands, entrusted it to the goldsmiths and others, who, in those days, took the place of regular bankers, paying them, however, for the trouble of taking care of it, instead of receiving from them interest for its use. To all such people it was a great boon to have opportunities of profitably investing their money, instead of merely stowing it away. During the troublous times of Stuart misrule, they did it with fear and trembling; but no sooner had William III. taken possession of the English throne, than the public stocks, for which Government was held responsible, and the private stock of the East India, and other trading-companies, came to be eagerly sought after, and bandied about from one hand to another, as they rose or fell in value.

Addison, in the *Spectator* has a pleasant allegory, "or what else the reader shall please to call it," as he says, of a beautiful virgin, seated on a throne of gold, in the old meeting-place of the Bank of England, whose name was Public Credit. "The walls, instead of being adorned with pictures and maps, were hung with many Acts of Parliament, written in gold letters. At the upper end of the hall was the Magna Charta, with the 'Act of Uniformity' on the right

hand, and the 'Act of Toleration' on the left; at the lower end
of the hall was the 'Act of Settlement,' which was placed full
in the eye of the virgin that sat upon the throne. Both the
sides of the hall were covered with such Acts of Parliament
as had been made for the establishment of the public funds.
The lady seemed to set an unspeakable value upon these
several pieces of furniture, insomuch that she often refreshed
her eye with them, and often smiled with a secret pleasure as
she looked upon them, but, at the same time, showed a very
particular uneasiness, if she saw anything approaching that
might hurt them. She appeared, indeed, infinitely timorous
in all her behaviour, and she changed colour and started
at everything she heard. She was, likewise, as I afterwards
found, a greater valetudinarian than any I had ever met with,
even in her own sex, and subject to such momentary con-
sumptions, that, in the twinkling of an eye, she would fall
away from the most florid complexion and the most healthful
state of body, and wither into a skeleton. Her recoveries
were often as sudden as her decays, insomuch, that she would
revive in a moment out of a wasting distemper into a habit
of the highest health and vigour. I had very soon an oppor-
tunity of observing these quick turns and changes in her
constitution. There sat at her feet a couple of secretaries,
who received, every hour, letters from all parts of the world,
which the one or other of them was always reading to her,
and according to the news she heard she changed colour,
and discovered many symptoms of health or sickness. Behind the throne was a prodigious heap of bags of money,
which were piled upon one another so high that they touched
the ceiling. The floor, on her right-hand side and on her
left, was covered with vast sums of gold, that rose in pyra-
mids on either side of her; but this I did not so much
wonder at, when I heard that she had the same virtue in her
touch which the poets tell us a Lydian king was formerly
possessed of, and that she could convert whatever she pleased

into that precious metal." Addison goes on to tell how, at
the threat of danger to the commonwealth, nine-tenths of the
bags of money collapsed, and the heaps of gold were turned
into heaps of paper, and Public Credit nearly expired ; and
how, on the return of safety, the lady revived, and her sur-
roundings were restored to their former grandeur—showing
that national wealth varies greatly and constantly, with the
various prospects of national liberty and mutual trust.   And
William Paterson, writing in 1716, five years after Addison,
expresses the same truth in other words.   "The present
public credit," he says, "hath at least a hundred feet, some
greater, some smaller, some weaker, some stronger ; and,
possibly, this may be the reason why the public credit is so
apt to reel and totter, that stocks and other public securities
often fall or rise four or five, and sometimes fifteen or sixteen per cent., on very slight occasions."

Out of this rise and fall of public stocks arose the trade
of stock-jobbing.   As a trade, it seems to have been publicly
recognised in 1688.   With that year, the year of William III.'s
coming to England, began a swarm of financial projects,
fraudulent and honest, wise and foolish, all offering facilities
to capitalists for the investment of their money, and all intended by the men who started them and kept them afloat
to be sources of profit to themselves.   These men, the men
who made it their business to deal in the shares of the real
and bubble companies newly-established, as well as in the
public funds and the stock of older corporations, were
thenceforward known as stock-jobbers, and they soon
became famous, and had a locality of their own in the City
of London.   "The centre of jobbing," said one of the
pamphleteers who assailed them in 1692, "is in the kingdom
of 'Change Alley and its adjacencies.   The limits are easily
surrounded in about a minute and a half.   Slipping out of
Jonathan's into the Alley, you turn your face full south ;
moving on a few paces, and then turning due east, you

advance to Garraway's ; from thence, going out at the other
door, you go on still east into Birchin's Lane ; and then,
halting a little at the Sword-Blade Bank, you immediately
face to the north, enter Cornhill, visit two or three petty
provinces there on your way to the west, and then, having
boxed your compass, and sailed round your stock-jobbing
globe, you turn into Jonathan's again." In this same year,
1692, Shadwell, only living long enough to do it, wrote his
comedy of "The Stock-jobbers," wherein the merits of the
Mouse-trap Company and the Flea-killing Company are
seriously discussed, and a party of Puritans consider whether
it is lawful for the godly to have shares in a company about
to be established for importing rope-dancers from China,
yielding at last to the arguments of one who says that those
whose consciences forbid it need never go and look at the
rope-dancing, if, indeed, they ever have the chance. "The
thing is like to take," he adds. "The shares will sell ; and
then we shall not care whether the dancers come over or no."

The trade, growing up like a mushroom, took root like
an oak. The successful establishment of the Bank of England, at Paterson's suggestion, in 1695, gave it great encouragement, and encouragement as great came from the
turmoil o. continental war, in which England was then and
for some time afterwards engaged. Sir Henry Furness, the
Bank Director, found it profitable to have a complete courier
system of his own, and, thereby receiving news of good or
bad occurrences long before even the Government advices
arrived, to use his early information in successful bartering
of stock. It was said by his detractors that he never
scrupled to invent reports of victories or defeats, and that
most of his great wealth was amassed by means of these
false reports, and the immense advantage which they gave
him. Another story is to the effect that Medina, the
Jewish banker and jobber, attained a like end by contracting
with the Duke of Marlborough for early expresses, in return

for a secret payment of £6,000 a year. Such statements as these may not have been true ; but it is clear that stock-jobbing, from its very commencement, offered great temptation for dishonesty, and that there were many who yielded to them. " It is a complete system of knavery," it was said in 1701, "founded in fraud, born of deceit, and nourished by trick, cheat, wheedle, forgeries, falsehoods, and all sorts of delusions, coining false news, whispering imaginary terrors, and preying upon those they have elevated or depressed." "The stock-jobbers," said another pamphleteer of the same year, "can ruin men silently, undermine and impoverish them, by the strange and unheard-of engines of interest, discount, transfers, tallies, debentures, shares, profits, and the devil and all of figures and hard names."

These were engines, however, that steadily gained favour, both with the many who were damaged by them, and with the few who used them for their own advancement. All the stock-jobbers, of course, were not dishonest. Thomas Guy, the benevolent founder of Guy's Hospital and of various useful charities in his native town of Tamworth, was one of the most prosperous of them, and he seems to have worked honestly from first to last. And there were many like him. Perhaps, indeed, these honest men, in giving their countenance to the movements of the dishonest, did most harm of all. At any rate, incalculable harm was done. The stock-jobbers ran riot for forty years. Then came the South Sea Bubble, and the hundreds of other bubbles that were blown round about it, until, all rushing together, they suddenly collapsed, and brought grievous distress upon the people of England.

The Bubble expanded slowly during eight years. In 1711, six years before Law's Mississippi Company was formed, Robert Harley, Earl of Oxford and Lord Treasurer, procured an Act of Parliament, appointing that, "to the intent that the trade to the South Sea be carried on for the

honour, and increase of the wealth and riches of this realm,"
a company should be formed with the exclusive privilege of
trading, colonising, and fighting in the southern seas, and
along the whole western side of South America. The members of this South Sea Company were to be the holders of
the Government bonds for the National Debt, then amounting to nearly £10,000,000, the interest of which, if not
the principal, it was thought could easily be paid out of the
profits of commerce with the gold and silver districts of
Peru and Chili. After the company was formed, it trans-
pired that the King of Spain claimed more than a fourth of
their profits for permitting English merchants to deal with
his colonists, and then only sanctioned their sending one
shipload of negroes every year; but even with this limitation great benefits were anticipated, especially as the English reckoned that, if they were only allowed to trade at all,
they could make the trade as extensive as they liked. The
preparations were tardy, and the first vessel did not leave
England till 1717; then the war with Spain, which broke out
in the following year, made orderly commerce with Chili and
Peru impossible.

But before this the South Sea stock-holders discovered
that South Sea traffic was an unimportant part of their enterprise. From the first, the new company was in favour
with the public, and a busy trade was carried on in its shares.
The Mississippi Company, started in Paris in 1717, showed
how this trade might be augmented. The South Sea Company offered to increase its capital, and so be able to lend
£2,000,000 to the State, and the Bank of England, stirred
up to rivalry, made a similar offer. A fierce war was carried
on between the Bank and the Company during more than
two years, and, in their efforts to outbid one another with
the Government and the country, a turmoil of stock-jobbing
was engendered, which received no check from the wretched
failure of the Mississippi scheme in 1719. By the com-

mencement of 1720 the South Sea stock had risen nearly
two hundred per cent. in value, and all that its holders
desired was, by promises that could not possibly be realised,
to raise the value yet more, and so to sell their shares at
great profit. In this they succeeded for a time. The Company triumphed over the Bank. In February, 1720, a bill
was brought into Parliament, authorising it to take upon
itself the whole National Debt, growing rapidly, and then
exceeding £30,000,000, and the bill became law in April.

In vain Sir Robert Walpole warned the country that
"the great principle of the project was an evil of first-rate
magnitude. It was to raise artificially the value of stock, by
exciting and keeping up a general infatuation; and, by promising dividends out of funds which could never be adequate
to the purpose, it would hold out a dangerous lure to decoy
the unwary to their ruin, by making them part with the
earnings of their labour for a prospect of imaginary wealth."
The warning was unheeded. The madness of speculation
that had just ruined France had seized England, with nearly
equal violence. Pope's satire was sober history when, pro-
phesying after the fact, he said :—

> " At length corruption, like a general flood,
> So long by watchful ministers withstood,
> Shall deluge all ; and avarice, creeping on,
> Spread like a low-born mist, and blot the sun.
> Statesman and patriot ply alike the stocks ;
> Peeress and butler share alike the box ;
> And judges job, and bishops bite the town,
> And mighty dukes pack cards for half-a-crown ;
> See Britain sunk in lucre's sordid charms,
> And France revenged on Anne's and Edward's arms."

The South Sea mania, rampant in February, 1720, increased
till August, when each £100 share was worth £1,000.
'Change Alley, swarming with professional and amateur
stock-jobbers of every rank and of both sexes, was aptly
compared by Swift to a gulf in the South Sea.

" Subscribers here by thousands float,
    And jostle one another down,
Each paddling in his leaky boat,
    And here they fish for gold, and drown.

" Now buried in the depths below,
    Now mounted up to heaven again,
They reel and stagger to and fro,
    At their wits' end, like drunken men.

" Meantime, secure on Garraway Cliffs,
    A savage race, by shipwrecks fed,
Lie waiting for the foundering skiffs,
    And strip the bodies of the dead."

Humbler poets described the mania in street ballads and coffee-house epigrams without number. One said—

" Then stars and garters did appear
    Among the meaner rabble,
To buy and sell, to see and hear
    The Jews and Gentiles squabble.

" The greatest ladies thither came,
    And plied in chariots daily,
Or pawned their jewels for a sum
    To venture in the Alley."

The South Sea Bubble was only the greatest among a crowd of great bubbles. The older companies shared in the brief show of imaginary prosperity. East India Stock, worth £100, rose to be worth £445; and African Stock, advanced in value from £23 to £200. There is extant a list of nearly two hundred principal bubble companies started in this year of bubbles, their nominal capital varying from £1,000,000 to £10,000,000 apiece, and the total of the whole exceeding £300,000,000. " Any impudent impostor," says the contemporary historian, " whilst the delusion was at its height, needed only to hire a room at some coffee-house or other house near Exchange Alley for a few hours, and open a subscription-book for somewhat relative to commerce, manufacture, plantation, or some supposed

invention, either hatched out of his own brain or else stolen
from some of the many abortive projects of former times,
having first advertised it in the newspapers of the preceding
day, and he might in a few hours find subscribers for one
or two millions, in some cases more, of imaginary stock.
Many of these very subscribers were far'from believing
those projects feasible. It was enough for their purpose
that there would soon be a premium on the receipts for
those subscriptions, when they generally got rid of them in
the crowded alleys to others more credulous than themselves." One company, with a capital of £3,000,000, was
"for insuring to all masters and mistresses the losses
they may sustain by servants;" another was "for furnishing merchants and others with watches;" a third,
with a capital of £1,000,000, was "for a wheel for perpetual motion;" a fourth was for making salt water
fresh; a fifth was "for planting mulberry-trees and
breeding silkworms in Chelsea Park;" and a sixth was
designed " to import a number of large jackasses from Spain,
in order to propagate a larger kind of mule in England"—as
if there were not already jackasses enough in London. So
preposterous were many of the genuine projects, that it is
hard to say whether it was in jest or in earnest that an advertisement was issued announcing that " at a certain place, on
Tuesday next, books will be opened for a subscription of
£2,000,000 for the invention of melting sawdust and chips,
and casting them into clean deal boards, without cracks or
knots." Another advertisement invited speculators to pay
£2 as a deposit on each of five thousand £100 shares in
" a company for carrying on an undertaking of great advantage, but nobody to know what it is," the remaining £98
for each share being due in a month's time, when the details
of the scheme were to be published. The name of the promoter of this secret company was never known, but his
advertisement drew so many adventurers on the appointed

day that in less than six hours he had received a thousand deposits of £2 each. With that success he was satisfied. Instead of waiting for another day, in which his transparent fraud might be exposed, he pocketed the £2,000, and decamped the same night.

The South Sea mania lasted a shorter time and had fewer victims in England than the Mississippi mania in France; but it was great enough to prove a source of ruin to hundreds of thousands, and of serious national discredit. During eight months every coffee-house was a stock exchange, subject to no laws of honesty, and swayed by rampant folly; and the milliners' shops were put to like uses by those ladies who could not stand the crush of the men's meeting-places. Wealth changed hands with unheard-of rapidity, and was steadily concentrated by the hundreds of knaves to whom thousands of fools were willing dupes. According to the old epigram—

> " This evil Solomon espied
>   Among the rabble rout,
> That beggars did on horseback ride
>   Whilst princes walk on foot.
>
> " South Sea has verified the same ;
>   For mighty men of late
> Are brought to poverty and shame,
>   Whilst scoundrels ride in state."

But their skilful horsemanship was brief. Quarrels among the South Sea directors opened the eyes of the public, and the great bubble and all the lesser bubbles suddenly collapsed. Early in August, 1720, the South Sea shares were bought eagerly for £1,000 apiece ; late in September they could not be sold for £150. George I., then in Hanover, hurried back to England. Parliament made a searching inquiry into the state of affairs. Many ringleaders of the fraud were severely punished ; and efforts were made to lessen the misfortunes of those whom they had beguiled. In February, 1721, the chief culprit, Aislabie, the Chancellor

of the Exchequer, who had used his official position to inflate
the bubble, was committed to the Tower of London, and a
huge bonfire on Tower Hill showed him, on the first night
of his captivity, what sort of vengeance the London mob
would have been glad to execute on him and his accomplices.
Great injury was done to multitudes, and the commerce of
the country was crippled during many years. But England
was rich enough and English enterprise was diverse enough
for the disaster to be much less keenly felt by the whole
nation than was that greater one which Law and his patrons
had provoked in France.

It would have been almost well had the retribution been
more violent, and an end been thus put to the vicious
ways of trade which rendered the social history of 1720, as
Smollett said, "a detail of transactions which only serves to
exhibit an inanimate picture of tasteless vice and mean
degeneracy." Stock-jobbing was hindered, but not crushed,
by the bursting of the South Sea Bubble, and a few years
served to render it at any rate as vigorous as it had been
before 1720. Statesmen and satirists sought in vain to do
away with it, and no good came of an Act of Parliament " to
prevent the infamous practice of stock-jobbing," passed in
1734, and of which Sir John Barnard, a great London merchant, and an intelligent champion of free trade and of
various enlightened views of commerce in the House of
Commons, was the most eloquent and energetic supporter.
"The many bad consequences of stock-jobbing are well-
known," he said, in one of his speeches on the subject,
"and it is high time to put an end to that infamous practice.
It is a lottery, or, rather, a gaming-house, publicly set up in
the middle of the City of London, by which the heads of our
merchants and tradesmen are turned from getting a liveli-
hood by the honest means of industry and frugality, and are
enticed to become gamesters by the hope of getting an
estate at once. It is not only a lottery, but one of the worst

sort, because it is always in the power of the principal managers to bestow the benefit tickets as they have a mind. The broker comes to a merchant and talks to him of the many fatigues and dangers, the great trouble and small profits, that are in his way of trade ; and, after having done all he can to put him out of conceit with his business, which is often too easily effected, he proposes to dig for him in the rich mine of 'Change Alley, and to get more for him in a day than he could get by his trade in a twelvemonth. Thus the merchant is persuaded. He engages, he goes on for some time, but never knows what he is a-doing till he is quite undone."

By the law which Sir John Barnard was instrumental in passing, it was provided that "all contracts and agreements whatsoever which shall be made or entered into to put upon or to deliver, receive, accept, or refuse any public or joint-stock, or other public securities, or any part or share therein, shall be null and void, to all intents and purposes whatsoever." This law, the only law of importance concerning stock-jobbing to be found in the English statute-book, still remains in force ; but its force only helps to keep rogues from punishment. It makes stock-jobbing debts illegal, just as betting debts are illegal, and thus, while speculators are not at all, or very slightly, restrained by it, it gives immunity, as far as the law is concerned, to the dishonest. The only tribunal by which they can be punished is the Stock Exchange Committee, which summarily expels from the great meeting-place of the stock-jobbers every one who fails to fulfil his engagements.

For about a hundred years the London jobbers had Jonathan's Coffee-house, in Sweeting's Rents, for their chief resort, the whole of Sweeting's Alley and the neighbouring parts being also frequented by them in busy times. In 1804 the growth of business made necessary the establishment of a more convenient haunt, and accordingly the

Stock Exchange, precursor of the building that now occupies
the same ground, was erected in Capel Court, on the site
of the old mansion of Sir Thomas Capel, who was Lord
Mayor in 1504. At first this building was used only for
traffic in English funds, dealers in foreign stock being left
to carry on their trade where they chose, generally in the
Royal Exchange. But soon the Stock Exchange was thrown
open to stock-jobbing of all sorts ; dealings in English
funds being conducted in one part of the house, foreign
stocks being bought and sold in another department, and the
railway and other share market having also a province of
its own. The establishment now contains about a thousand
members, each being elected by ballot, and passing through
a period of probation before he is admitted to the full
privileges of the society and has a voice in the election of
the committee by which, in the ordinary way, the Stock
Exchange is absolutely governed, the government to some
extent applying to the many other establishments that, in
imitation of the London Stock Exchange, have been set up
in all the chief centres of provincial trade. The members
are of two sorts, jobbers and brokers, neither of whom are
allowed to carry on any other business, although they may
be, and are, for the most part, chiefly agents of the thousands upon thousands of outsiders, who make a trade or
an amusement of speculation in stocks and shares. These
outsiders are stock-jobbers too, although, their names not
generally appearing in the transactions in which they take
part, the nominal responsibility rests with the jobbers and
brokers who have access to the Stock Exchange. The
jobber is, or is supposed to be, a wealthy man, possessed
of all sorts of stocks and shares, which he is ready to sell,
and of means with which to buy any others that are offered
to him on satisfactory terms. The broker is avowedly the
agent of other people, commissioned to buy and sell such
shares as they require or have for disposal.

This trade, within proper limits, is, of course, a necessary branch of English commerce; and for many generations it has been honestly pursued by honest men without number. But its opportunities for dishonesty are great, and by use of these opportunities the turmoil of speculation has been promoted, and manias and panics, more or less momentous, have followed one another in quick succession ever since the beginning of the trade. The old offence of the dishonest stock-dealers and their patrons and their followers, practised long ago, and practised still, has been " the getting up of companies," the reckless encouragement of new ways of speculation in which the public may be induced to invest their money, in order that brokers may secure their certain and jobbers their uncertain profits. Another offence which, though of long standing, has lately been committed with unexampled impudence, is of a different sort. It consists of two complementary processes, known in Stock Exchange phraseology as " bulling " and " bearing." The Stock Exchange and the stock-brokers' offices are open every day and all day long, but stocks and shares can only be actually transferred at stated periods, intervals of four weeks being fixed for English Consols, and a fortnight for most other kinds of shares and foreign stocks. Hence the buying and selling of scrip throughout the intermediate time is all in anticipation of the delivery-days, and the time between one delivery-day and another is available for any shameless gambling in which the jobber chooses to engage. In it he is free to "buy" and "sell" a thousand shares, though he may have in his possession neither a single one, nor the means of purchasing it. If he buys, it is of course in expectation that, before delivery-day comes round, the shares will have risen in value, and he will thus be able to sell them again, and pocket the difference between the two prices. If he sells, he expects, on the other hand, that prices will fall, and that, in consequence, he will be able to buy shares enough to meet his obligations, and thus also make money by the transaction. In the first instance he is a "bull," speculating for a rise; in the other he is a "bear," speculating for a fall. If he is prudent and honest, he can generally, like his peers in the betting-ring, make a safe book by hedging one speculation against another. If he is reckless and dishonest, he can often help himself by means of the "tricks, cheats, forgeries, falsehoods, and all sorts of delusions, coining false news, and whispering imaginary terrors" that were complained of in 1701.

We have seen how stock-jobbing began in England. It is not necessary to describe the details of all its later stages. In spite of the Act of 1734, its field of operations has, ever since that year, been steadily enlarged, both through the rapid increase of the National Debt, and through the yet more rapid development of all kinds of mercantile and manufacturing energy. For great factories and trading concerns, and yet more for docks, canals, and other public works undertaken in furtherance of the interests of commerce, large sums of money had to be borrowed; and all the bonds and pledges issued in acknowledgment of these various debts being taken into the market, just like Government stock and the shares in public companies, passed from hand to hand at varying prices, according to the varying prospects of success and the chances of prompt return of the capital embarked in them. By all such means the stock-brokers and stock-jobbers were supplied with business during the eighteenth century.

The trade, however, has assumed very much more gigantic proportions during the last sixty or seventy years, most of its chief promoters not being themselves members of the Stock Exchange—only stock-jobbers, as it were, on the sly. Pre-eminent among these men were Abraham and Benjamin Goldsmid, one of whom died in 1808, the other in 1810; Sir Francis Baring, who also died in 1810, and Nathan

Meyer Rothschild, who fairly entered on his wonderful career of prosperity in the latter year, and held his place without a rival—unless Alexander Baring might be called one—till his death in 1836. The Goldsmids and the elder Baring made their fortunes, and helped to enrich half the members of the Stock Exchange, by their successful negotiations of the English loans made necessary by Pitt's persistent carrying on of his great war with France, agreeable to antique theories of fame and glory, but productive of incalculable misery to the nation at large. Rothschild was also a contractor for the English Government ; but his prosperity resulted chiefly from his introduction of continental loans into the English market. The vast trade in foreign Consols, which now gives occupation to hundreds of merchants, bankers, and stock-dealers, and finds favour with thousands of speculators, owes its origin entirely to him.

Rothschild was the very type and perfection of a stock-jobber. His first great undertaking, after settling in London, was the buying up, in 1810, of a number of Wellington's drafts for expenses incurred by the army in Spain, floating about or sinking in the market. Having paid for these much less than their nominal value, he straightway claimed their redemption at par, and, Government not being able to do this, he furnished the necessary funds from his own well-filled coffers ; thus, by one clever trick, making a large profit as a jobber and another large profit as a money-lender. " It was the best business I ever did," he said, twenty years after. But he did plenty of other business of a like sort, Wellington being again an unconscious sharer in the most notable of all. Rothschild was at Hougoumont on the memorable day of the battle of Waterloo, watching its incidents almost as eagerly as either Napoleon or his great antagonist could do. Immediately the issue of the battle was clear, he hurried off, and, with help of carriages and horses, carefully appointed along his route, reached England a day before any other messenger arrived. During that day his secret agents, on the strength of a report, said to have originated with him, that the English forces were defeated, bought at panic-prices, a cartload of shares, bonds, stock, and scrip of every sort, all of which, as soon as the true news arrived, and confidence was thereby restored, he was able to sell again for their real value; thereby, it was rumoured, he cleared £1,000,000.

Nathan Rothschild was an honest and a good man in his way. He conferred many benefits on English commerce; but, in showing how sharp practice in money-making may be brought to perfection, he did more harm than can ever be atoned for.

He rarely failed in his speculations. Therein he differed from the crowd of men, most of them more dupes than knaves, who brought about the chief financial disasters of the present century.

The first of these, the greatest English mania since the South Sea Bubble, and, notwithstanding the changes wrought by a century of commercial progress, curiously like it in some respects, began in 1824. In that year the South American colonies of Spain achieved their independence, and thus was opened up to England that same trade with the eastern shores of the Pacific from which the South Sea Company had expected to derive boundless wealth. The old expectations were revived, and British sympathy for the young republics of Chili and Peru came in aid of commercial speculation. When the Peruvian loan was brought into the London market, so great was the demand for its stock that it was sold by public auction, in the Royal Exchange, and until its financial worthlessness was discovered, a constant trade was eagerly carried on in it. Much more extensive were the private and joint-stock enterprises promoted by persons who honestly thought that another El Dorado was before them, and by others who were ready to make profit out of the delusions of their neighbours. A vast quantity of English capital was sunk in projects for trade of all sorts with Mexico and South America. Other projects floated merrily in the stream of speculation that was thus started, and the Joint-Stock Company Mania of 1825 was the result.

"In all these speculations," says a chronicler of the day, "only a small instalment, seldom exceeding five per cent., was paid at first, so that a very moderate rise in the price of the shares produced a large profit on the sum actually invested. If, for instance, shares of £100, on which £5 had been paid, rose to a premium of £40, this yielded on every share a profit equal to eight times the amount of the money which had been paid. This possibility of enormous profit, by risking so small a sum, was a bait too tempting to be resisted. All the gambling propensities of human nature were brought into action, and crowds of individuals of every description—the credulous and the suspicious, the crafty and the bold, the raw and the experienced, the intelligent and the ignorant, princes, nobles, politicians, placemen, patriots, lawyers, physicians, divines, philosophers, poets—intermingled with women of all ranks and degrees, spinsters, wives, and widows, hastening to venture some portion of their property in schemes of which scarcely anything was known except the name." The Anglo-Mexican mining shares, on which only £10 were paid, sold for £43 on the 10th of December, 1824, and for £150 on the 11th of January, 1825. The Real del Monte shares, with £70 paid up, rose in value during the same short period from £550 to £1,350. About three hundred joint-stock companies were brought out during 1824 and 1825, and their nominal capital amounted to £180,000,000, though the amount paid up was hardly £18,000,000. Most of them, of course, had nothing to do with the Spanish-American projects, save that they were off-shoots of the speculative spirit thereby aroused, and often

started only to enable adventurers to recover their losses
upon the earlier schemes. Banking companies, canal com-
panies, gas companies, insurance companies, sugar com-
panies, fishing companies, and early-milk-delivery companies
were among the number.

The mania was at its height during the first four months
of 1825. During the next seven months there was a struggle
between mania and panic, desperate expedients being resorted to in order to maintain public confidence, and devise
new projects to prop up those that were falling. In
December the crash came. To avert it heavy drains were
made upon the bullion reserve of the Bank of England,
heavy drains having previously been made in furtherance of
the speculations. At the end of November, 1824, the Bank
reserve was £11,323,760. At the end of November, 1825,
it was only £3,012,150, and that scanty store was nearly
exhausted during the ensuing weeks. It was said, indeed,
that the Bank was only saved by the accidental finding of
two million one-pound notes, which had been packed away
and lost sight of some time before.

Other banks were not so lucky. A great Plymouth
bank, Sir William Elford's, failed on the 29th of November.
One as great in Yorkshire, that of Wentworth and Company,
immediately followed; and the news of these disasters told
grievously in London. On the 3rd of December the Bank
of Poole, Thornton, and Company, one of the largest in
London, was in such difficulties that the directors of the
Bank of England had to meet on Sunday and agree to
advance it £300,000 before banking-hours on Monday.
Thereby Poole's house was saved for a week, but it fell on
the following Monday, the 12th of December; and Williams,
Burgess, and Company had to close their doors on Tuesday.
Other London banks failed, and at least eighty country
banks were ruined by their fall. "On Monday morning the
storm began," said the Deputy-Governor of the Bank of Eng-

land, "and till Saturday night it raged with an intensity that it is impossible for me to describe. On Saturday night it had somewhat abated. The Bank had taken a firm and deliberate resolution to make common cause with the country, and on Saturday night it was my happiness, when I went up to the Cabinet, reeling with fatigue, to be able to call out to my Lord Liverpool, and to the members of his Majesty's Government then present, that all was well."

All was not well; but the crisis had been checked by the arbitrary but wise policy of the Bank of England in issuing, between Wednesday and Saturday, more than £5,000,000 of notes in excess of their bullion reserve, which could be measured by handfuls, and their Government securities. Old Londoners still remember with a shudder the horrors of that week ; how hundreds of men, supposed to be rolling in wealth, wandered distractedly up and down the streets, fearing that in an hour or two they might be bankrupts ; and how thousands watched their movements with ghastly interest, knowing that the bankruptcy of those in whom they trusted meant starvation to themselves.

Many did starve. When public confidence was restored, and the troubled sea of commerce was smooth again, the waters rippled over wretched dupes without number, undone for ever by their own folly and the temptings of those who had led them into speculations beyond their means. Old men lay down to die under the load of disgrace that they had brought on themselves. Young men rushed into mad acts, with the blind hope of retrieving their fortunes ; and the silent wretchedness of widows and orphans, robbed of their all, furnished a strange contrast to the gratulations of those who had prompted the mania and made money out of the panic.

The tide of speculation proceeded without very much abatement. Many of the joint-stock companies formed in 1824 and 1825 were built on firm bases, honestly supplied

real needs of commerce, and, having proved their stability
during the panic, flourished after it more than ever.   Other
laudable enterprises followed their example and shared their
success ; while there were plenty of other schemes, wrongly
devised, or wrongly conducted, which during their long or
brief careers, proved pitfalls to the unwary, and, in painful
ways, continued to teach the trite and little-heeded lesson
that " honesty is the best policy."

During the forty years following upon 1825, English
trade throve wonderfully ; but there has been a monotony of
variety in its progress, tempting fanciful observers to pro-
pound a law of financial tides and storms.   After a crisis
there is a lull of a year or two, in which speculators are
cautious and " money is tight."   Then speculating energy
revives and steadily gains force during seven or eight years,
until it develops into a mania, lasting for about a year, and
ending in another panic.   The sequel of our last panic does
not conform to that hypothesis, but it was nearly true
between 1825 and 1865.

The joint-stock mania of 1825 was followed by the less
disastrous mania of 1835 and 1836, and that by the great
railway mania of 1845.   Railway construction, begun with
Stephenson's famous exploit on the Manchester and Liverpool line, had given healthy occupation to English capitalists,
and proved of inestimable advantage to Englishmen of all
grades during fifteen previous years ; but its progress was
only too slow until the close of 1844.   Then there was a
sudden outburst of well-guided and misguided zeal.   In
January, 1845, sixteen new railway companies were registered.
In April fifty-two were started.   From that time till the
autumn eight, ten, or more new schemes were brought out
every day.   In September, the most prolific month of all,
the number was four hundred and fifty-seven, making for the
year then ended a total of a thousand and thirty-five, to
which three hundred and sixty-three were added in October.

Nearly every village in the kingdom was to have a line or a branch of its own; and all our colonies, as well as foreign countries, were to be similarly blessed by English enterprise. The island-rock of St. Kitt's, for instance, four miles wide and fifteen long, was to have a railway, for the benefit of its negro inhabitants. The capital required for British schemes alone was more than £100,000,000, and nearly as much was asked for foreign projects.

But none paused to consider where this wealth was to come from. Stock-jobbers and their myrmidons, known as "alley-men," puffed, and believed their own puffs. Merchants and retail traders, seeing the real value to them of improved communication between one place and another, rushed madly into the speculation, and manufacturers followed as eagerly. Persons of all grades and classes shared the infatuation. For three-quarters of a year London was giddy with a tumult far greater than that which arose in 1825, and worthy to be compared with the tumult of the South Sea Bubble year; and the excitement of London spread to every other town in the country, with a force for which previous manias furnished no parallel. Earlier manias were concentrated in the metropolis; but the railway infatuation ran through every district in England, Scotland, and Ireland, through which the railways were to run. Some of the projects, as the last quarter of a century has proved, were, of course, sound in conception and wisely conducted; but most of them, whether born and bred of folly or of fraud, were utterly preposterous, and, in many cases, no lawless art was spared in working upon the greed of the public, and fostering the delusion by which it was being ensnared. "Rigging the market" was the most successful art. Immediately after the announcement of a new project, it was given out that all the shares were taken up. The few that had been really issued were bought and sold at high premiums by secret partners in the scheme, and thus a demand

was created for the unissued shares, and they were then
sold with enormous profit. The promoters of hundreds of
companies knew from the commencement that their projected lines would never be established; but they could
make money by projecting them, and thus their sole object
was achieved. It was with them as with Shadwell's Flea-
killing Company, so long as shares were taken and deposits were paid up, there was no need for seeing whether
the fleas could really be killed.

One cause of the mania was the abundance of capital
and the low rate of interest which speculators in the funds
and other safe channels of investment could obtain for their
money at the close of 1844. The Bank rate of discount
was then only 2½ per cent., and so it continued for a
year, and Government securities yielded a correspondingly
low profit. The temptation to invest in enterprises promising to yield four, six, or eight times as much interest
was too great for incautious capitalists, and even the cautious
were disarmed by the great favour with which the Government approved and Parliament sanctioned a vast number of
railway projects. Both Government and Parliament began
to assume a different attitude in the autumn of 1845, and
thereby a slight check was given to railway speculation.
Many projects collapsed, and others lost favour. But the
mania continued, as far as most of the schemes already propounded were concerned, throughout 1846 and half of 1847.
The rage for excessive speculation once aroused, moreover,
found vent in other ways as well as in railroads. The high
price of corn, especially, caused merchants to import great
quantities of grain from abroad, and this brought about the
crash. Railway shareholders, including corn-merchants, as
well as every other class in the country, were called upon
for fresh instalments of the amount promised by them to
lines in process of construction, just at a time when an un-
expectedly favourable harvest brought down the price of

wheat, and rendered all speculations therein unprofitable. The result was the failure of one great house after another, and a panic which spread all over the country.

The panic began, after more than two years of mania, on the 9th of August, 1847, when Leslie, Alexander, and Company declared themselves unable to meet their liabilities, amounting to £500,000. Other failures, to the extent of £700,000, followed within a week, and in succeeding weeks the heap of ruins accumulated with terrible rapidity, till the money involved amounted to £15,000,000. The fall of mercantile houses necessitated the fall of banks that had lent them money, and the fall of banks brought speculators of every class to bankruptcy. There is a terrible similarity in panics, and the miseries that ensued in 1847 differed only from those of 1826 in that they were more wide-spread, and, by reason of the continuous demands for instalments of the capital pledged for railways that were being laid down, more far-reaching.

There was another panic in 1857, here especially noteworthy because one of its causes, if not the principal, only indirectly a commercial one, was the war-mania which caused England to join with France in strife with Russia, and to achieve a victory that brought all the consequences of a defeat. Another cause was the spirit of over-trading that had found such strange development in 1844, and the ensuing years, and had received no adequate check even from the troubles of 1847.

It was as a curb upon this tendency to over-trading, and as a protection to speculators who, for every two or three pounds that they contributed to the old joint-stock companies, might in the course of years be compelled to pay fifty or a hundred, that the "Limited Liability Act" was passed in 1862. If productive of some good, however, it also produced much fresh evil. Its limitations provoked a false confidence in the minds of investors, and yet left them subject to liabilities which might cause their ruin. And, while ostensibly protecting honest men who are not supposed to understand all the ramifications of commercial adventure, it was pernicious in that it also, but much more efficiently, lessened the responsibilities of the dishonest men who start new undertakings, and modify old ones, with the sole or chief purpose of encouraging speculation. It begot a limited liability mania, which, in 1865, caused the formation of two hundred and eighty-seven companies, with an aggregate authorised capital of more that £100,000,000, but with only £12,000,000 of paid-up deposits. The failures of 1866 and a panic not yet allayed were the results.

There have been plenty of other manias, and consequent panics, besides those here enumerated, many in England, many in the United States and elsewhere. There have also been panics without number, great and small, hardly to be attributed to commercial manias. Diverse in origin, in progress, and in effect, caused sometimes by fraud, sometimes by folly, sometimes by nothing but misguided wisdom, they all teach one transparent lesson of prudence and honesty; but when that lesson is duly learnt and truly practised, the romance of trade will have reached a climax indeed romantic.

CHAPTER XII.

OLD-WORLD commerce was great, but even the names of the men who promoted it, and whom it enriched, are, for the most part, unknown to us. The biographical interest of trading history hardly covers five centuries, and commences with those famous merchant-princes of Italy who, more than any others of the Middle Ages, aided the revival of commerce in modern times, and, in so doing, by accident or design, gave notable help to the progress of political and scientific, and even of literary and religious enlightenment.

One family of these merchant-princes is especially remarkable. There were Medici at Florence in the commencement of the fourteenth century, if not during all the previous centuries in which the chief inland city of Italy had been making itself famous among the foremost cities of the world. Venice, first of all the northern commonwealths, had risen from obscurity by reason of her merchant-enterprise, and become the world's great mart—

> " A ruler of the waters and their powers ;
> And such she was ; her daughters had their dowers
> From spoils of nations, and the exhaustless East
> Poured in her lap all gems in sparkling showers :
> In purple was she robed, and of her feast
> Monarchs partook, and deemed their dignity increased."

Genoa, on the other side of the Peninsula, had learnt to vie with Venice in commercial greatness. Florence, no less commercial, but debarred by her position from maritime exploits, had taken the lead in manufacture of the woollen and silken wares for which the material was collected by her friendly rivals, and had found a yet greater source of influence by early development of the banker's calling. It was by her banking especially that Florence won her greatness. With agencies in all the other busy towns, her citizens drew from all abundant wealth, which, before it bore fruit in luxurious degradation, enabled them to wage a noble and successful war against Suabian tyranny, and, when that was over, to fight somewhat less nobly against aristocratic tyrants at home. A worthier liberty was achieved by Florence than by any of the other Italian cities, or by any of the young commonwealths then rising in Europe. The struggle between conservatism and radicalism was carried on with varying benefit, but more beneficially than elsewhere in the Florence of the fourteenth and fifteenth centuries; and, though nowhere else were Guelph and Ghibelline divisions greater, the contest was controlled by the hard-working spirit of its citizens and the common sense of dignity, with generally true views as to the method of its attainment and preservation. As we often see in later periods, but in a way for which contemporary history furnishes no parallel, we find men constantly rising from the ranks and taking high place in civic councils, gradually losing the plebeian sympathies with which they began, but not quickly sinking into useless aristocrats under the load of their own aggrandisement. These sources of prosperity were not very permanent, but they lasted through several generations; and the Medici played a famous part in the city's healthy growth before they took the lead in its unhealthy sequels.

While they were quietly working their way to influence, earlier Florentine traders achieved greater wealth and fame.

In the thirteenth century the Mozzi and the Spini acted as Papal bankers and farmers of the Papal revenues. In the fourteenth century the Peruzzi, the Bardi, and the Alberti had agencies in Venice, Naples, Rome, Perugia, Sienna, Avignon, Paris, Brussels, Bruges, and even in London, York, and Hull. It was to a great extent by means of money lent to him by the Peruzzi that Edward III. was able to carry on his war with France; and the English monarch's failure, in 1346, to pay 1,365,000 golden crowns which he owed to the Florentine bankers caused a panic which was felt throughout Europe.

The Medici began to be notable late in the fourteenth century. Salvestro de' Medici was gonfaloniere in 1370; and he was elected for another period of two months' signory in May, 1378. Florence was then seething with opposition of the plebeian community to the capitani and the aristocratic oligarchs. Salvestro was called upon to violate his duty for the gratification of his superiors. He refused, and, on the 18th of June, when he was chairman of the signory, he summoned a meeting of the whole body of citizens, designing to submit to them a law for the repression of the capitani. But his law was not approved by his colleagues, and, on their rejection, he rushed angrily from the council-board to the public meeting, and addressed it in words never forgotten. "Citizens!" he exclaimed, "I have striven to-day to purge this city of the pestilent tyranny of the great and overbearing. But I have not been permitted to do so; my colleagues will not allow it. It would have been for the welfare of the citizens and of the entire city, but I have not been listened to or received the attention due to your gonfaloniere. Since I am powerless, therefore, to do good, I will no longer hold office, either as prior or gonfaloniere. I shall retire to my own house, and you may make whom you will gonfaloniere." He was not suffered to retire. A shout of approval greeted him; a flame of democratic zeal

spread through the meeting and through the city, and the
flame took real shape in the burning of palaces and houses
in the aristocratic quarter. The mob ruled in Florence for
a month, and though order was then restored, and the
tumult was soon followed by rejoicings and submission to
the capitani, and Salvestro de' Medici narrowly escaped vengeance for his contumacious action, a beginning was then
made of that popular supremacy which the later Medici
were to turn altogether to their own advantage.

Salvestro de' Medici returned to his banking, and his
name is afterwards only vaguely met with in Florentine
history as a champion of the people, other champions being
his kinsmen and partners, Averardo and Vieri. One episode
in Vieri de' Medici's banking history aptly illustrates the
condition of affairs in Florence. In 1389 the Duke of
Milan was scheming for the city's overthrow. That did not
hinder his keeping a banking account with the Medici; but
one day an agent of the duke entered the bank, and asked
in his name for a thousand crowns in a sealed bag. Vieri
paid the money, but, suspecting treachery, tracked the messenger until he discovered that the bag was handed as a
bribe to one of the gonfalonieri then in office. The func-
tionary was brought to justice, and branded as a traitor, and
Vieri became more popular than ever. Averardo, the other
cousin, made but little stir in Florence; but he was the
father of Giovanni de' Medici, and Giovanni was the father
of Cosmo and head of all the famous Medici of the Middle
Ages and of later days.

Giovanni de' Medici, then about sixty, and representative
of the wealthiest and most influential family in Florence,
was chosen gonfaloniere in 1421. His election was opposed
on the ground of his great riches and his great talents.
Niccolo da Uzzano, his chief opponent, showed from the
history of the commonwealth, says the old historian, "how
great was the danger of drawing up a man who enjoyed so

great and universal a reputation, and how easy a thing it was to prevent an evil in its beginning, and how exceedingly difficult to remedy mischief when it had grown strong; there were many capabilities and qualities in Giovanni de' Medici which very much surpassed those of Salvestro, and it therefore behoved the citizens to be very careful what they were putting their hands to." That argument, that Giovanni de' Medici was too able a man for office, shows the defect of Florentine institutions at that time. They could only be propped up by weak and unambitious men.

Giovanni was accordingly kept down till Florence could not do without him. He was then placed in power, and the fears of his enemies were realised. · His election to the signory, though only for two months, began the supremacy of a family that could never afterwards be suppressed. Giovanni, however, worked quietly and unostentatiously. He toiled on at his ledgers, handed money across the counter, and sent it to distant parts of the world, was courteous to every one, and straightforward in all his dealings. The result, whether he cunningly planned it or not, was the acquisition of all that power for which he seemed to care little. During the brief remainder of his life he was the most popular man in the commonwealth, trusted by all classes, consulted on all public business, employed in every sort of work. He unobtrusively effected a great reform in the method of taxation, which brought much ease to the community, while it increased its revenues; and he as unobtrusively effected other changes. His son Cosmo blamed him for want of ambition; but his mode of life did more than anything else could do to help Cosmo's own ambition. "He was a merciful and charitable man," said Macchiavelli, "and not only gave assistance to those who asked it of him, but often, unasked, succoured the poor in their need. He felt kindly towards all men, and was not chary of praise to the good or of compassion to the bad. He was a partisan of peace,

W

and always sought to avoid war.   He asked for none of the
honours of the State, and enjoyed them all.   As a magistrate, he was gracious and affable ; not endowed with much
eloquence, but abundantly gifted with sagacity and prudence.
His outward appearance was of a melancholy cast, but
in conversation he was agreeable and facetious.   He died
enormously rich in treasure, but richer still in good repute
and in the goodwill of his fellow-citizens.   And this inheritance was not only maintained, but was increased by his son
Cosmo.

Giovanni de' Medici died in 1429, leaving 178,000
golden florins ; and that vast wealth was vastly increased by
his descendants.   At one time they had sixteen branch banks
in the various capitals of Europe.   Their network of finance
covered the whole civilised world of the West, and contributed mightily to their growing riches and to their growing
influence.   It is noteworthy that these Medici, like other
mediæval merchants, but unlike most modern traders, stuck
to business long after they had made politics their foremost
employment ; but from the time of Giovanni's death their
commercial history becomes insignificant, in comparison with
their political influence.   The story of that influence need
not be given here.   To tell it in detail would be to recount
all the later and the most familiar portion of Florentine
history.   From 1433, when Cosmo de' Medici was banished
from Florence for ten years, to be recalled in less than a
year, this is especially the case.   Every one knows how he
returned to be "the father of his country" during thirty years.
And the power of his wealth, and of other valuable properties
besides wealth, spread far beyond Florence.   "He not only,"
says Macchiavelli, "overcame the domestic opposition and
civic rivalries of his enemies, but also conquered that of
many foreign powers, and that with such rare felicity and
prudence that whoever opposed him lost his money and his
time, if not his territory ; as the Venetians can well testify,

who, as long as they were allied with him, were constantly
victorious over the Duke Filippo Visconti, but disunited
from him, were as constantly beaten, first by Filippo and
then by the new duke, Francesco Sforza. And when they
were leagued with Alfonso against the Republic of Florence,
Cosmo, by means of his credit, so emptied Venice and
Naples of money, that they were constrained to make
peace on such terms as were granted to them. Cosmo had
a higher renown and wider reputation than any citizen,
not a man of arms, that Florence or, indeed, any other
city had ever possessed. He surpassed every other man
of his times, not only in authority and wealth, but also
in liberality and prudence, for the chief among all the
qualities that made him the first man in his country were
his generosity and munificence. After his death it was
found that there was not a single citizen of any position
to whom Cosmo had not lent large sums of money. His
magnificence was shown also by the abundance of buildings undertaken by him. He rebuilt from their foundations
the convents and churches of San Marco and San Lorenzo,
and the monastery of Santa Verdiana, in Florence, and San
Girolamo and the Badia, on the hill of Fiesole, and a church
of the Franciscans in the Mugello. Besides all this, he
erected altars and chapels of exceeding splendour in the
church of Santa Croce, in that of the Servites, in that of the
Holy Angels, and at San Miniato, and furnished them richly
with all things needed for the celebration of holy worship.
To these sacred edifices must be added his own private
residences, one of which, in the city, is a mansion befitting
such a citizen, and four others in the country are all palaces
of royal magnificence, rather than what might be expected to
belong to a private person. And, as if it did not suffice him
to be known throughout Europe for the splendour of his
buildings, he erected an hospital for poor and infirm pilgrims
at Jerusalem."

Cosmo de' Medici, born in 1389, and dying in 1464, was the most notable of all the merchant-princes on record. His descendants, though many of them merchants, were chiefly memorable as princes. From him sprang Lorenzo the Magnificent, Pope Leo X., and Pope Clement VII., Catherine, the queen-mother of France, who instigated the Massacre of St. Bartholomew, and Alexander, the first Duke of Florence, who culminated the change from the popular influence in their own city of the early Medici to the tyranny of the later. From his brother Lorenzo, the younger son of old Giovanni, issued the long line of Medicean Grand Dukes of Tuscany, who reigned from 1537 to 1737.

A merchant family of a very different sort to the Italian Medici, but hardly inferior to it in commercial importance, was that of the Bavarian Fuggers, whose name, during the Middle Ages, was often Italianised into Folcari. John Fugger was a weaver in a village out of Augsburg, in the middle of the fourteenth century. His son, the second John Fugger, transferred his weaving business to Augsburg, in which he acquired rights of citizenship in 1370, through marriage with a citizen's daughter. Augsburg was then the chief seat of linen manufacture in Europe and, advantageously placed on the highway between Venice and Bruges, a great emporium of trade in all native and foreign wares for which there was a market in the surrounding countries. John Fugger throve here. Starting as a humble weaver in 1370, he died in 1409, one of the richest and most enterprising of the merchants of Augsburg. His sons, Andrew and James, followed in his steps, and greatly augmented the family wealth and influence. The offspring of the elder withdrew from commerce, and entered the ranks of the nobility, as founders of the house of Fugger the Roe ; but trade was followed successfully by nearly all the eleven children of the younger son. Three of these especially—Ulric, George, and James—were renowned for their industry, integrity, and shrewdness. All three married ladies of rank, and were themselves ennobled. They did not abandon linen manufacture, but prospered most as merchants, and became rivals of the Medici and all the other Italian financiers in banking enterprise. They were the Emperor Maximilian's chief bankers, and found for him the money with which he was able to wage his European wars. James Fugger was also a great miner, and opened up the mineral treasures of the Tyrol, where he built the famous Fuggerau Castle. He died without issue. Ulric also was childless. But George, the second of the three brothers, had two famous sons, Raymond and Anthony, and by them, and especially the younger, the family was raised to its highest pitch of greatness.

They owned the gold-mines of the valley of the Inn and the silver-mines of Falkenstein and Schwartz. They had banking and commercial agencies in Venice, Genoa, Antwerp, and a dozen other marts. Their ships went into every sea, and brought wealth from every port. Once nearly twenty of their vessels were captured in the Baltic, by a fleet of the Hanseatic League, whose monopoly they were assailing by traffic with the northern ports of Europe. They joined in Portuguese expeditions to the East Indies and in Spanish expeditions to the West. Maximilian employed them in diplomacy, as well as in financial agencies, and his son, Charles V., found them yet more useful. When the Emperor was at Paris, and the Crown jewels of France were shown to him, he exclaimed, with more pride than good taste, " I know a weaver in Augsburg who could buy all that." Anthony Fugger was the weaver. Charles was sumptuously entertained by him for a year and a day, during his attendance at the famous Diet of Augsburg in 1530, and to the conclusion of that or of some later visit is referred a mythical story which has its counterpart in the traditional biography of many another great merchant. " I feel myself," Anthony Fugger is reported to have said, " so amply repaid by the

honour of this visit that this bond is now useless," and
thereupon producing the Emperor's bond for 800,000 florins,
he threw it into a fire of cinnamon-wood that was burning
in the hall.　An odd bargain, showing more business-like
qualities. is on record between Anthony Fugger and our
own Edward VI.　In 1551 the Augsburg merchant lent
£60,000 to the English King, part to be repaid in May and
part in August.　But in April Edward found himself unable
to meet his liabilities, and was forced to make a compromise
thus quaintly worded in the King's own journal : " First,
that the Fulcare should put it off for 10 per cent.; secondly,
that I should buy 12,000 marks, at six shillings the ounce ;
thirdly, that I should pay 100,000 crowns for a very fair
jewel, four rubies, marvellous big, one orient and great
diamond, and one great pearl."　That transaction shows
very plainly how the Fuggers and their peers and rivals made
money in old days.

Anthony Fugger died worth 6,000,000 solid golden
crowns, besides jewels and treasures of immense value, great
houses and estates in various parts of Germany, and trading-
factories all over Europe and in both the Indies.　He was
known as Anthony the Rich, and concerning him a ghost-
story is extant, which they who like may believe.　" It was
told me at Naples," said George Sandys, the gossiping old
traveller, in 1610, " by a countryman of ours, and an old
pensioner of the Pope's, who was a youth in the days of
King Henry, that it was then generally bruited throughout
England that Mr. Gresham, a merchant, setting sail from
Palermo, being crossed by contrary winds, was constrained
to anchor under the lee of the island of Stromboli, which
place is commonly affirmed by the Roman Catholics to be
the jaws of hell.　Now about midday, when for certain
hours it accustomedly forbeareth to flame, he ascended the
mountain with eight of the sailors ; and, approaching the vent
as near as they durst, amongst other noises they heard a voice

cry aloud, ' Dispatch ! dispatch ! the rich Anthony is coming !'
Terrified herewith, they descended, and anon the mountain
again evaporated fire. But from so dismal a place they
made all the haste they could ; when, the wind still thwart-
ing their course, and desiring much to know more of this
matter, they returned to Palermo ; and forthwith inquiring of
Anthony, it was told them that he was dead, and, com-
puting the time, they did find it to agree with the very
instant that the voice was heard by them. Gresham reported
this at his return to the King, and the mariners, being called
before him, confirmed by oath the naration. In Gresham
himself it wrought so deep an impression that he gave over
all traffic, distributing his goods, a part to his kinsfolk and
the rest to good uses, retaining only a competency to himself, and so spent the rest of his life in solitary devotion."
Dates and circumstances contradict this record ; but it is as
trustworthy as most other ghost-stories.

Anthony Fugger hardly deserved to be cast into ever-
lasting torment, through the jaws of Stromboli. He vied,
in a humble way, with the Medici in his patronage of art
and literature, and, like some of his ancestors and many of
his descendants, he was as charitable and good-hearted as
he was honest and enterprising. Schools, hospitals, alms-
houses, and endowments of all sorts, in and out of Augsburg, still attest his benevolence, and that of his father,
uncles, and sons. These sons and other descendants of the
family, retaining their interest in the trade still carried on in
their name, gradually settled down as landed proprietors.
In 1619 there were five branches of the family of Fugger,
including forty-seven counts and countesses, and three hundred and sixty-five members of all grades. Of the descendants of Raymond and Anthony Fugger alone there are now
four great branches, owning large portions of Bavaria, and
retaining the name of feudal lordship over 50,000 or more
dependants.

Hardly inferior to the Fuggers, in commercial dignity, under Charles V., were the Welsers, also Augsburg merchants, who, among a crowd of other famous exploits, farmed the South American province of Venezuela, and fitted out several expeditions in search of El Dorado, whereby they gained less gold than that which came from more commonplace trade in districts nearer home.   Another, and rather earlier merchant-prince, Jacques Cœur, the Frenchman, has been already described ; and of earlier and later English merchants something has also been said.

The growth of British commerce in the Middle Ages is illustrated by the familiar history of men like the De la Poles of Hull, Walworth, Philpot, and Whittington of London, and the Canynges of Bristol ; and the greater achievements of the Greshams—with the exception of that uncle of Sir Thomas Gresham whom Anthony Fugger's ghost, as we have seen, is recorded to have driven from trade into the priesthood—inaugurate the greater age of commerce that began with the Tudors.

Sir Thomas Gresham was the greatest English merchant of the old stamp, and no mean rival of Anthony Fugger. Living long in Antwerp, and having agencies all over Europe, his commercial and financial operations on his own account were hardly more important than the political services which he rendered to Edward VI. and Queen Elizabeth.   He had many notable contemporaries and immediate successors, who were more strictly and exclusively merchants.   One of the chief of these was Sir Edward Osborne, who began life as an apprentice to Master William Hewit.   Hewit's warehouse and counting-house were on Old London Bridge, and his little daughter Anne, tumbling out of the window and falling into the Thames one day, was only saved from drowning by the bravery of young Osborne, who jumped in after her.   Her grateful father gave her to him for a wife when she was old enough to marry, and in the end bequeathed to him his wealth and business. Osborne made good use of his inheritance, and was one of the first of those enterprising merchants who, not content with the old-fashioned European trade to which Gresham devoted himself, sent their ships into far-off seas, and were the pioneers of trade and colonisation in distant lands. He traded with the West Indies when the West Indies were hardly known to Englishmen. He was the chief founder of the Levant Company; and almost the first Englishmen who went to India in search of new ways of trade were sent by him.

A yet more enterprising merchant of the same sort was Sir Thomas Smythe, one of the founders of the East India Company, and its first governor, holding the office over and over again, as often as he would allow himself to be elected, till the end of his life, and, whether holding it or not, its real master. To him, more than to any other single man, our present vast empire in India and the imperial trade carried on with it, owe their origin. But with that work and the profit that it brought him Smythe was not satisfied. For twelve years he was governor of the Virginia Company. Under his skilful rule, the colony, which had failed under Raleigh's planting, prospered greatly. From the board-room in London he ruled it with despotic power, and thus the same merchant, who was the chief promoter of British intercourse with India, was also the chief promoter of that famous group of colonies out of which the United States of America has grown. Sir Thomas Smythe, dying in the same year as his sovereign, was the greatest English merchant in the days of James I.

He had many famous contemporaries, many good and many bad. One of the worthiest was renowned Sir Hugh Myddelton, who turned aside from commerce with India and America, to construct the New River which gave wholesome water to thirsty Londoners, and a fresh impetus to

engineering skill.   One of the worst, if not the worst, was
Sir Giles Mompesson, who turned aside from foreign trade to
traffic in monopolies, which brought upon him and Charles I.
the just wrath of the House of Commons, and to engage in
yet worse traffic, which caused Massinger to paint his portrait,
hardly exaggerated, as *Sir Giles Overreach*, in " A New Way
to Pay Old Debts."   When *Lord Lovell*, whom he wishes
to marry his daughter, asks him—

> " Are you not frighted with the imprecations
> And curses of whole families, made wretched
> By your sinister practices?"

Sir Giles Overreach answers—

>   " Yes, as rocks are
> When foamy billows split themselves against
> Their flinty ribs ; or as the moon is moved
> When wolves, with hunger pined, howl at her brightness.
> I am of a solid temper, and, like these,
> Steer on, a constant course.   With mine own sword,
> If called into the field, I can make that right
> Which fearful enemies murmured at as wrong.
> When in bitterness they call me
> Extortioner, tyrant, cormorant, or intruder
> On my poor neighbours' rights, or grand encloser
> Of what was common, to my private use,—
> Nay, when my ears are pierced with widows' cries,
> And undone orphans wash with tears my threshold,
> I only think what 'tis to have my daughter
> Right honourable ; and 'tis a powerful charm
> Makes me insensible of remorse, or pity,
> Or the least sting of conscience.   I am marble.
> Nay more, if you will have my character
> In little, I enjoy more true delight
> In my arrival to my wealth by dark
> And crooked ways, than you shall e'er take pleasure
> In spending what my industry hath compassed."

Of dishonest merchants, as in every other walk in life,
there have been many to throw an ugly shade over the history of commerce, and by the contrast to render brighter
the careers of traders who, though they may not have seen,

or cared to see, that their enterprise was, at every turn, rich in beneficent results of every sort, chose honourable ways for their own advancement, and understood that, in helping others, they were most surely augmenting their own wealth.

There is, for the most part, less of striking personal incident in the lives of modern English merchants than in those of their predecessors. A few familiar stories of beggar-boys who have risen to be millionaires, by steady perseverance and quick perception of the ways in which to make best use of the chances open to them, illustrate the careers of thousands of great merchants. There is plenty of romance still in ledgers and office-stools, cheque-books and cash-boxes; but there is more variety and charm in the history of the heroes of such lately-born commerce as we find in England's great American offshoot than generally occurs in the recent trading annals of our own country.

The first great American merchant was Sir William Pepperell, the son of a Cornish fisherman who, thriving in his humble trade at home, emigrated to New England in Charles II.'s time, and in 1679 settled at Kittery Point, in Maine, where he married the daughter of a ship-builder. The building of small ships and filling them with fish for coasting and West Indian trade were then the chief occupations of all New Englanders who were not farmers, and the elder Pepperell grew rich thereby. He was a soldier, having repeatedly to withstand the efforts of the native Indians to recover their fatherland, as well as a merchant. His son, born in 1696, was trained in both pursuits. He was a shop-lad, busy with trade in lumber, fish, provisions, and other ships' stores, before he was sixteen, when, several of his friends having been murdered in the streets of Kittery, he had to go out and take vengeance on the aggressors. Business alternated with fighting, however, and when his father died in 1734, young Pepperell succeeded to the management of a thriving trade, and the ownership of more ships,

warehouses, mills, and farms than any other merchant in
New England possessed at that time ; he was also colonel of
the militia of Maine.   During the next five-and-twenty years
he prospered in both ways.

The most famous exploit in his career occurred in 1744.
In that year, England and France being at war, Governor
Shirley, of Massachusetts, conceived the bold design of
capturing Louisbourg, "the Dunkirk of America," a strong
town built on Cape Breton, with a stone rampart twelve
yards high, and a ditch twenty-seven yards wide, which had
been twenty-five years in building, and had cost 30,000,000
livres.   Eighty-six heavy guns, mounted in three batteries,
were supposed to render it impregnable, and made a safe
harbour for French trading-ships, and a nest for the French
privateers, that dashed out to sea and darted along the
coast to do serious damage to the English vessels going to
and from the American colonies.   Failing in obtaining the
assistance which he sought from home for what was considered a Quixotic enterprise, Shirley consulted Pepperell,
who, being the most popular as well as the richest man in
those parts, quickly collected about four thousand sturdy
volunteers for land-fighting, and rendered further help by
contributing to the organisation of a volunteer fleet of a
hundred armed vessels.   He was appointed commander-in-
chief of the land forces dispatched to Cape Breton, and
was a chief adviser in the naval operations by which his
siege of Louisbourg was aided.   The siege lasted seven
weeks.   In the end Louisbourg surrendered, and this victory,
when reported to England, was acknowledged, amid bonfires
and fireworks, to be the most valiant and beneficial in the
whole war.   Mr. William Pepperell, merchant, was made Sir
William Pepperell, Bart.; and when, five years afterwards,
he visited London, he was feasted by its citizens and welcomed at Court with all the honour due to a hero.   When,
shortly afterwards, a great French armament was fitted out

to recover Louisbourg, and take vengeance on Massachusetts, Pepperell was at the head of the movement for its resistance; but shipwreck and pestilence anticipated the work of soldiers and sailors, and from that time the English possession of Louisbourg was undisputed.

Sir William Pepperell did other service to the mother country, and helped to enrich himself, by his ship-building. One vessel especially, the *America*, carrying forty-four guns, which he constructed for the British Government, was for a long time one of the best in our navy, and proved useful in the war which too soon broke out between England and her colonists.

In that war Pepperell did not live long enough to take part. In 1748 he retired from active business. In February, 1759, Pitt made him a lieutenant-general, the first native American to receive that honour; but he only enjoyed it for a few weeks. He died in the following July.

Massachusetts had several other famous merchants in that and the following generation; the most famous of all, by reason of his achievements apart from commerce, being John Hancock. Hancock, the son of a clergyman who died young, was born at Quincy, near Boston, in 1737, and after more careful education than was then common in the American colonies, entered the counting-house of his uncle, a merchant of Boston. That was in 1754. In 1764 his uncle died, and he succeeded to the business. Though showing himself a skilful merchant, he found time for further studies, and became a leader in intellectual society and a favourite with all classes. In 1766 he was chosen representative of Boston in that memorable General Assembly, in which armed resistance of England was threatened unless its tyrannical measures of taxation and interference with local affairs were rescinded. Hancock and Samuel Adams were the great promoters of the opposition. Hancock's sympathies with English refinements, and his prominent

position in American society, caused Lord North to make
special efforts to withdraw him from the revolutionary party
which he was helping to form, and to bribe him to fidelity
to the mother country.   But those efforts were indignantly
rebuffed, and their only effect was to make Hancock a more
zealous secessionist than ever.   He was then, and with good
reason, denounced as " the arch-rebel."   He and Adams,
outlawed for their patriotism, had, during some years, to lead
the life of fugitives, and in all their wanderings became fire-
brands of revolution.   They were concealed in Lexington
on the memorable 19th of April, 1775, when the first blood
was shed, and the brief victory of General Gage was the
signal for general insurrection, quickly issuing in a lasting
triumph.   It was in vain that, in June, a pardon was offered
to all rebels except Adams and Hancock, whose offences
were too great to be forgiven.   All Americans shared the
spirit of Adams and Hancock, and they had Washington for
their general.   The battle of Bunker's Hill, on the 17th of
June, 1775, was followed by the congress of delegates from
all the insurgent colonies which met in Philadelphia, and
Hancock, representing Massachusetts, though almost the
youngest man amongst them, was chosen its president.
Modest and true-hearted as he was, he is said to have been
so astonished at this great mark of confidence, that he
urged the selection of some older man, and refused to take
his seat until one brawny colleague took him up in his arms
and forced him into it.   Once installed in the office, however, he held it worthily.   To the Declaration of Independence, issued in 1776, his signature, as president, was first
affixed.   Ill-health caused him to retire for some time from
public life in 1777, when the independence of the United
States was completed ; and he took no very prominent part
in the later work, but he was Governor of Massachusetts
from 1780 till 1793, with an interval of two years   He died,
at the age of fifty-six, in 1793.

John Hancock stands pre-eminent among the merchant-patriots of the United States. But trade was soon resigned by him for better work, while others of his day and of his temper continued to apply themselves to commercial as well as to political affairs. One of his most notable contemporaries was Elias Hackett Derby, of Salem.

Salem, near Boston, began even before it to be a busy haunt of trade, and one of its first merchants was Roger Derby, who emigrated from Devonshire in 1671, and who, dying in 1698, left a great house, a warehouse, a wharf, and a keen commercial spirit to his son Richard, who, in turn, bequeathed all these, and more, to a son of the same name. Richard Derby the younger, born in 1712, traded with New York and other towns on the coast, and often sent his ships on more adventurous voyages to the West Indies and to Europe. Many fights between his captains and the buccaneers of Jamaica and the Spanish Main are recorded. During the French war, between 1756 and 1763, he was especially famous for his trading enterprise. He owned several great ships, armed with eight or twelve guns apiece, which went to and fro, adding privateering to regular commerce, and greatly enriching himself and his family. He had six giant sons, the shortest of whom was six feet six inches tall, all trained to seamanship, to commerce, and to war; and of these Elias, the second, born in 1739, was the most remarkable.

At the commencement of the War of Independence, when Boston declared against the English, great efforts were made to secure the fidelity of Salem. The British Government offered to make it, instead of Boston, the chief town of Massachusetts, and the promise of extensive ship-building and the armed protection of its commerce rendered the bribe a great one. The Derbys, and the other merchants of Salem, however, bluntly refused, and though their patriotism brought heavy loss at first, the ultimate gain was vast. Elias

Derby had seven ships of his own trading to the West Indies, some of which were seized, while the rest proved useless for their old purposes. The young merchant turned them into privateers, and employed all his own property, and all his influence with his merchant-brothers and his brother-merchants, in increasing the number. Before the war was over he was concerned, more or less, in the fitting out and vigorous use of as many as a hundred and fifty-eight privateers, mounting in all more than two thousand guns, and the exploits of these vessels fill an important place in the history of the war. One of them, the *Revenge*, a ten-gun sloop, captured four Jamaica-men, laden with rum, on its first expedition in 1777, and that success was followed by many other like achievements, by which England suffered and New England gained. The names given to some of these vessels aptly show the temper of the men who owned them. One was the *Tyrannicide*, and proved a fit associate for the *Revenge;* but Captain Hunsdon, who at first commanded it, made himself especially obnoxious to the British after his transfer to another, the *Pickering*, a tough little schooner carrying fourteen guns. In 1780 she had just taken a ship of her own size in the Bay of Biscay, and was towing her into port, when the *Achilles*, a forty-two-gun frigate, came up. Hunsdon bravely prepared to meet this foe of thrice his own strength, fought desperately within sight of some hundred thousand Spaniards who crowded down to the shore to watch the result, and was cheered by their shouts of sympathy when he forced the *Achilles* to withdraw and leave him in quiet possession of his prize. It was by prowess of that sort that American independence was achieved.

In the Salem privateering Elias Derby is supposed to have had at least a fourth share ; of many vessels he was sole owner, of nearly all the rest he was a part proprietor. He made ship-building his great study during war-time. He established great building-yards, and constructed a multitude of better ships than other merchants then generally possessed ; and these ships, planned for fighting, he easily converted, as soon as peace was restored, into trading-vessels, which went into every sea. Between 1785 and 1799, thirty-seven of his merchantmen made a hundred and twenty-five voyages, of which forty-five were to the East Indies and China. Of the American trade with the East Indies he was the father ; and while that branch of commerce, as far as England was concerned, was a monopoly of the East India Company, he set the fashion, which others quickly followed, of carrying free trade into the distant East, and of taking home tea, silk, and a hundred other wares, which could be sold in America at a very much lower price than those obtained through England. The value of that trade to the United States in their infancy can hardly be over-estimated: its value to Derby himself was very great. In the ten years ending with 1799 he increased his wealth five-fold ; and when he died, in that year, he was the richest merchant in America. Four sons and a dozen other kinsmen succeeded to his enterprise, and maintained the fame of his name in Salem and all over the United States.

Pepperell, Hancock, and Derby were all native New Englanders. Hardly less memorable was Stephen Girard, a Frenchman, who became a citizen of Philadelphia, and the greatest of its early merchants. His career was a strange one. The son of a sea-captain, he was born at Bordeaux in 1750. When he was about ten, and could barely read and write, he went as cabin-boy in a vessel bound for the West Indies. There, or on the voyage thither, he lost one eye, and this misfortune and the ridicule it brought upon him roused his temper, and rendered it more difficult for him, without money and without friends, to fight his way in the world. Fight he did, however, and with notable success. From a cabin-boy he rose, before he was twenty, to be the captain and part-owner of a small ship trading between the

x

West Indies and New Orleans, then a French port. In 1769 he quitted the sea, went to Philadelphia, and there opened a little shop for retail trade, partly stocking it with goods brought from San Domingo. In that business also he prospered, until it was destroyed by the war, and he had to begin life again as a bottler of claret and cider, at Mount Holly, until he had saved money enough to return, in 1780, to his former trade between New Orleans and the West Indies. Peace and its opportunities brought him back, two or three years later, to Philadelphia, and that town then became his home for nearly half a century. He brought with him some strangely-gotten wealth. Two of his ships were lying in the harbour of San Domingo when insurrection broke out. A crowd of planters hurried down with as much of their treasures as they could carry, and left them on board while they returned for more. Most of them were murdered before they could get back to the harbour, and, in consequence, Girard's vessels went home to New Orleans laden with valuables for which no claimants could be found, and which he was thus left to take as his own.

If there was questionable honesty in that proceeding, Stephen Girard proved himself an honest man during his long residence in Philadelphia. The selfishness and moroseness which had been shown by him in his early struggles for life also peeled off, and he became a patriot and a philanthropist.

In 1793 a terrible plague of yellow fever broke out in Philadelphia. Most of the inhabitants fled for their lives, and the dying were left to die untended. "While the pestilence was raging at its utmost height," we are told, "an individual of low and square stature was perceived alighting from a coach which drew up before an hospital where the most loathsome victims of the disease had been collected. The man entered this living sepulchre, and soon returned bearing in his arms a form that appeared to be suffering in the last stages of the fever. The man who performed this act was Stephen Girard, and it is a well-attested fact that, during the prevalence of the disease, he continued a constant attendant in the hospital, performing all those offices which would seem revolting to the humblest menial." Another hospital was full of patients, but all its attendants save three had died or run away, and there were no funds for nourishing the sufferers. Girard gave both money and attendance. He took upon himself the entire management of the house. "The deplorable situation to which fright and sickness have reduced the inhabitants of our city," he wrote, in a quiet matter-of-fact way, which precisely illustrates his character, "demands succour from those who do not fear death, or who, at least, do not see any risk in the epidemic which now prevails here. This will occupy me some time, and if I have the misfortune to succumb, I will have at least the satisfaction to have performed a duty which all owe to each other." He did not succumb. During sixty days the rough sailor-boy, who had become a hard merchant, was in constant attendance, nursing the sick with all a woman's care and tenderness. His example encouraged others to work with him; but only when the violence of the plague was removed, and he had made arrangements for providing for those who had recovered, and for the orphans left by the dead, did he go back to his counting-house, there to furnish another instance of the double blessing that springs from "the quality of mercy."

In 1797 and 1798 the fever broke out again, and he again, by personal services and liberal contributions, helped the sufferers. "During all this frightful time," he wrote to a doctor of his acquaintance, "I have constantly remained in the city, and, without neglecting my public duties, have played a part which will make you smile. Will you believe, my friend, that I have visited so many as fifteen sick people in a day? And—what will surprise you still more—I have lost only one patient, an Irishman, who would drink a little. I do not flatter myself that I have cured one single person ; but you will think with me that, in my quality of Philadelphian physician, I have been very moderate, and that not one of my *confrères* has killed fewer than myself."

It seemed as if the very name of " brotherly love," which William Penn had given to his city of Philadelphia, had effected a revolution in Girard's character. Contemning Christianity, and scorned by his enemies and all Pharisees as an atheist, he showed a true Christian spirit in all his relations with the poor and needy who were around him. He was profuse in his charities during life, and 2,000,000 out of the 9,000,000 dollars which he left behind him were applied in founding the Girard College for Orphans in Philadelphia. Nearly all the rest of his wealth was divided among hospitals, schools, and the like, or left to be spent in street improvements and similar beneficial works, in Philadelphia, New Orleans, and other parts.

Stephen Girard's philanthropy did not hinder his money-making, and therein he helped his adopted country as well as himself. He had been rich enough, on his second settlement in Philadelphia, to start at once as an enterprising merchant. His commerce throve, and in the end he became the greatest banker in the country. In 1812 he purchased the old Bank of the United States, to which a renewal of its charter had been refused, and commenced banking operations with a capital of 1,200,000 dollars. Vast business came into his hands, and none the less because he steadily refused to countenance the speculative disposition then abroad in America. He never discounted an accommodation bill, and never renewed a promissory note ; thus setting an example which was of great benefit to the nation, and securing for himself unlimited confidence. The Girard Bank came to be regarded as the safest establishment in the

United States. " The establishment of this bank," says a native writer, "exhibited to the country the novel spectacle of a private American banker conducting his institution upon a large scale, and conferring upon the community advantages nearly as great as those which had been received from State or national auspices   And this bank rendered important services to Government. The fiscal affairs of the nation had been thrown into confusion by the dissolution of the former bank, and the suspension of specie payments added to the general confusion ; yet, while the public credit was shaken to its very centre, and the country was involved in difficulties springing from its exhausted finances and the expenses of war, the bank of Mr. Girard, not only received large subscriptions for loans, but made extensive advances to the Government, which enabled the country to carry on its belligerent enterprises—loans, too, which were the spontaneous act of patriotism, as well as of prudence.   This aid appears to have been rendered from time to time down to 1817, when the second national bank superseded his assistance.   In spite of the suspension of specie payments by the State banks, resulting from the ' Non-Intercourse Act,' not a single note of his own was suffered to be depreciated, and he was thus enabled, in 1817, to contribute effectually to the restoration of specie payments."

Girard's long and useful life, lasting till 1831, overlapped that of many younger men, and made him a contemporary of merchants still active in the service of their country.   In Philadelphia he has had many noteworthy successors ; but the modern development of New York as the chief trading capital of America has drawn to it a yet greater number of enterprising merchants.

One of these was Thomas Eddy, whose Quaker parents emigrated from Ireland about the middle of the eighteenth century, and settled in Philadelphia.   There he was born, in 1758. In 1779 he went to New York, with ninety-six dollars

in his possession, a very scanty education, and no knowledge
of business. He made money, however, out of the turmoil
then caused by the English occupation of New York, trading
thence to England and Ireland, where he had a brother and
a friend for partners. In 1782 he returned to Philadelphia,
hoping to increase his business; but there, two years afterwards, taking part in tobacco speculation, he was ruined
through the failure of some of his fellow-speculators. He
worked on quietly till he had paid his debts, and then came
to England for a few years. In 1792 he started again in
New York, this time to succeed beyond his expectations.
The funding of the public debt in that year gave new life to
the trade of stock-jobbing, and Thomas Eddy, following it
honestly, was quickly enriched by it. He made good use
of his riches, and of the leisure that they brought him. His
zeal in the reformation of prisons, and of the penal code of
New York, which still sanctioned whipping-posts, pillories,
and other mediæval tortures called punishments, procured
for him the title of the Howard of America. He did other
useful public work, reconstruction of the New York Hospital
and the introduction of savings-banks into the State being
among the number. His greatest commercial enterprise,
also, was undesignedly philanthropical. Of the Erie Canal
he was the chief projector in 1810, and he worked on at
its extension till his death in 1827.

Another representative merchant of New York was
Gideon Lee, born of poor parents, at Amherst, in Massachusetts, in 1778. "I remember," he wrote in his old age,
"when I was a lad living with my uncle, it was my business
to feed and milk the cows; and many a time, long before
light in the morning, I was started off in the cold and snow,
without shoes, to my work, and used to think it a luxury to
warm my frozen feet on the spot just before occupied by
the animal that I roused. It taught me to reflect and to
consider possibilities; and I remember asking myself, 'Is

it not possible to better my condition?'" He settled that
it was possible, and, having gone without shoes hitherto,
resolved to make shoes for other people as well as for himself. He apprenticed himself to a shoemaker and tanner;
and, as soon as his apprenticeship was, over, he set up for
himself. The first hundred dollars that he earned he spent in
improving his education at Westfield Academy. Then he
went to his trade again, and he throve so well in it that he
eventually removed to New York, and there became a great
leather-merchant and a dealer in everything, dying rich and
famous for his honesty and worth in 1841. One anecdote
illustrates his character. A trader, richer than he was, was
once in his shop, boasting that he had overreached this person, that person, and others; "and now," he added, "I
have gained an advantage over you." "That may be,"
answered Gideon Lee, "but if you will promise never to
enter my office again, I will give you that bundle of goat-
skins." The man promised, took up the bundle, and walked
away. Fifteen years afterwards he again came into the
office. "You have broken your word," exclaimed Lee, who
had never seen him in the interval. "Pay me for the goat-
skins!" "Oh, I am quite poor," replied the man, "and
have been very unfortunate since I saw you." "Yes,"
answered Gideon Lee, "and you always will be poor;
that miserable desire of overreaching others must ever keep
you so."

Let one other New York merchant be mentioned. Jacob
Little was born, in 1797, at Newburyport, Massachusetts,
where his father was a well-to-do merchant, until the war with
England ruined him in 1812. In 1817 young Little went
to New York, and was for five years a clerk to Jacob Barber,
one of the chief traders then in the city. In 1822 he started
business for himself as a specie-broker, having a humble
office in Wall Street. He toiled up during twelve years,
often giving eighteen hours a day to business. His evenings

he spent in going round to the shops and buying up worn-out coin, which he disposed of in the mornings. Thus he gradually worked his way into larger trade. In 1834, and for thirty years afterwards, he was the leading financier and banker in New York, sometimes making 200,000 dollars in a year. He was the "Railway King" of America, known as "the Napoleon of the Board." His success in railway speculations made him many enemies, and in 1834 there was a plot laid for his ruin. It was known that he had contracted to sell a large quantity of Erie stock; but no one would sell him the scrip which he needed to complete his bargain. Crowds assembled on delivery-day to see his expected ruin at two o'clock; but at one o'clock he quietly walked into the Erie Railway Company's office, produced bonds for money lent by him to the Company, asked for shares which, according to the stipulation made therein, he was entitled to receive on demand, and thus baffled his rivals. Thrice he nearly failed, and had to suspend payment, but each time he quickly retrieved his position; and it was a common saying that "Jacob Little's suspended paper was better than the cheques of most merchants." In railway shares he traded successfully to the last, and in 1847 he was invited to join in starting the first telegraph projected in America, between Boston and New York. That proposal he declined, and thereby he was prevented from being the richest man in America. He was nearly the richest man, however, until the Southern rebellion swept away most of his fortune. He died in 1865.

New York, during the last hundred years, has produced or drawn into it a multitude of famous merchants, of whom these three may serve as specimens. Boston, also, has had many, but none more remarkable than the Lawrences. Samuel Lawrence, descended from John Lawrence, a native of Suffolk, who emigrated in 1630, was a respectable farmer in Massachusetts a century ago. When the war broke out in 1775 he ran seven miles in forty minutes, to tell all his neighbours and dependants that the English were marching into Boston, and to summon many of them to follow him as volunteers for the defence of their homesteads ; and during the next three years he was a soldier. Once he had a holiday for his wedding, but while he and his bride were standing up in church the alarm-bell rang. He had to beg the parson to hurry over the service, ran off the moment it was done, and only saw his wife now and then, for a few hours at a time, until the war was ended.

His hardly-used wife bore him, besides other children, four famous sons, William, Amos, Abbot, and Samuel. William, born in 1783, was intended to be a farmer. Amos, three years younger, began life as shop-boy in a general store at Groton, where everything was sold, from pins to rum. So much rum was also drunk on the premises that Amos Lawrence, in disgust, resolved, when he was fifteen, never again to drink spirits, or anything with spirit in it ; and it was partly to his carrying out of that resolution that he attributed his success in life. In 1808, his apprenticeship being over, he left Groton for Boston, there to set up business for himself, with help of 1,000 dollars which his father mortgaged his farm to lend to him. " I told him he did wrong," Amos wrote afterwards, " to place himself in a situation to be made unhappy if I lost the money. He told me he guessed I wouldn't lose it." Nor was it lost. Amos lived frugally, worked hard, and prospered. The debt on the farm was soon paid off, and his shop was quickly turned into a merchant's counting-house. In 1808 Abbot Lawrence, his younger brother, was apprenticed to him, and in 1809 the eldest son, William, also came to him as a clerk. William started a separate business, however, in 1810, afterwards taking the other brother, Samuel, as his partner. This firm was less notable than that of Amos and Abbot Lawrence. It took that name in 1814, when the younger brother had

completed his apprenticeship, and the elder was able to put
50,000 dollars into the concern, the savings of seven years.
Both brothers were mightily enriched by their enterprise,
and found wise use for their riches.

Amos Lawrence was a simple, honest merchant, and a
good man. When ill-health caused his retirement from
business, he used to spend much of his leisure in buying nick-
nacks and valuables of all sorts, and putting them up in neat
parcels to be sent round, with kind messages, to his poor
neighbours; a parcel of books or a case of instruments for
this hard-working student, a neat bundle of clothes for that
well-behaved damsel, a box of crockery and other household
utensils for yonder newly-married couple, a pair of spectacles and a large-type Bible for these old people—and inside
each parcel there was generally a five or a fifty dollar note,
according to the needs of the neighbour to whom it was
sent. For public charity, moreover, Amos Lawrence was
justly famous. He died on the last day of 1852, and then
it was found that since 1828 he had given away to benevolent institutions of various kinds at least 639,000 dollars.

Abbot Lawrence was hardly less charitable, but he was
able to do good work in other ways. First coming to England, soon after the year 1814, in furtherance of his own and
his brother's business, he came again in 1849 as representative of the United States at the Court of Queen Victoria,
and during four years he stoutly maintained the honour of
his country. He was a great promoter of railways, and
all through life a zealous friend to native manufacturing
energy. Of Lowell he was one of the founders; and in 1847
he started a scientific school in Harvard University, with
the main object of encouraging American industry. He
died in 1855.

A richer merchant, and to that extent, if not otherwise,
a more philanthropic man than any of the Lawrences, or any
other American merchant, was George Peabody. Peabody's

uneventful life of successful trade in both hemispneres, and
his large-hearted charities, both in the land of his birth and
in the land of his adoption, are too well known to be repeated here. There is a quiet romance, most pleasant and
instructive, in the career of that true-hearted grocer's boy of
Danvers, who became a great merchant in Baltimore, and a
greater merchant in London, who, without knowing it, was
the greatest hero of commerce in our day, and whose body
was conveyed with fitting pomp by men-of-war of both
nations from his death-place in England to his burial-place
in America. He had done much, as other great merchants
have done, but not yet with complete success, to turn swords
into ploughshares and spears into reaping-hooks; and when
all was over, the implements of war were turned into marks
of peace, and the roar of cannon, instead of betokening unholy slaughter, was muffled into an impressive utterance of
holy grief at the death of a good man and a great merchant.

Another good man and great merchant, worthy to be
named in the same breath with George Peabody, was
Jamsetjee Jejeebhoy. This eminent Parsee, the son of
poor parents in Bombay, was born in 1783. He became a
clerk in the office of Framjee Messerwanjee, an earlier Parsee
merchant of Bombay, who, valuing his great business abili-
ties, made him his son-in-law and partner in 1800, when he
was only seventeen years old. Before settling down in
Bombay, he made several trading-voyages to the distant East
and the distant West; he went five times to China, and he
came once, at any rate, to England. In the course of one of
the Chinese expeditions, being on board a vessel in the fleet
commanded by Sir Nathaniel Dance, he narrowly escaped
capture by the French. On another occasion, when off the
Cape of Good Hope, he was actually captured by them.
He lost all his property, and, after long waiting at Cape
Town, had to make the best of his way in a Danish ship to
Calcutta, and so back again to Bombay. All that was before

the peace of 1815. The happier times that followed were so helpful to the great Indian mart that its imports rose from £870,000 in 1814 to £3,052,000 in 1819, and they have never ceased growing during the subsequent half-century. It was Jamsetjee Jejeebhoy's good fortune to be resident in Bombay from the commencement of that rapid improvement, and to have wisdom to use it for his own and his fellow-men's advantage. In 1820 he was acknowledged to be the greatest merchant in Bombay, and his supremacy became more and more marked during the next eight-and-thirty years. His commerce spread over all the world. His philanthropies were chiefly local. In 1822 he released all the poor debtors in Bombay by paying their debts. Between that year and 1858 he spent more than £250,000 in benevolent and beneficent work of all sorts. He gave £44,000 to the Parsee Benevolent Institution, £15,000 to the Dhurumsulla, or Poor Asylum of Bombay; he endowed the Jamsetjee Hospital with £16,000, and the Jamsetjee School of Industrial Art with £10,000. He constructed the Poona Waterworks, at a cost of £18,000; and he contributed £15,000 to the causeway and arched stone bridge, undertaken by the Indian Government, mainly at his instigation, from Mahim to Bandora, thus connecting the island of Salsette with the island of Bombay. In acknowledgment of his great services, he was knighted in 1842; and English appreciation of his large contributions to the Patriotic Fund was shown by the baronetcy conferred upon him in 1857. "By industry and liberality" was the motto which he set upon his coat-of-arms. He died in 1859, and all Bombay mourned over his grave.

The names of Sir Jamsetjee Jejeebhoy and of George Peabody, both English and yet not English, fitly close our little series of notable merchants illustrating the romance of trade.

INDEX.

CASSELL, PETTER, AND GALPIN, BELLE SAUVAGE WORKS, LONDON, E.C.

STANDARD WORKS.

Cassell's Illustrated History of England, from the Earliest Period to the Present Time. With about 2,000 Illustrations. NEW TONED PAPER EDITION. Complete in 9 Vols., cloth, each, 9s.

Cassell's Illustrated History of the War between France and Germany. With 500 Engravings and Plans of the Battle-fields. Complete in Two Volumes. Extra crown 4to, cloth, 9s. each ; or bound in half-calf, 30s.

British Battles on Land and Sea. By JAMES GRANT, Author of "The Romance of War," &c. With about 600 Illustrations. *Complete in 3 Vols.,* extra crown 4to, cloth gilt, 9s. each.

Old and New London. Vols. I., II., and III. now ready, with about 200 Illustrations in each ; extra crown 4to, cloth gilt, 9s. each.

The History of Protestantism. By the Rev. J. A. WYLIE, LL.D. Vol. I., with upwards of 200 Original Illustrations. Extra crown 4to, 620 pages, cloth, 9s. (*To be completed in 3 Vols.*)

Cassell's History of the United States. Vol. I., with 200 Illustrations and Maps. Extra crown 4to, 620 pages, cloth, 9s. (*To be completed in 3 Vols.*)

The Bible Educator. Edited by the Rev. E. H. PLUMPTRE, D.D., Professor of Exegesis of the New Testament, King's College, London. With 400 Engravings and Maps. Complete in 4 Vols., cloth, 6s. each ; or in Two Double Vols., 21s.

Cassell's New Popular Educator. Revised to the Present Date, with numerous Additions. Complete in Six Vols., 412 pp. each, cloth, 6s. each ; or Three Vols., half-calf, £2 10s.

Cassell's Popular Recreator. A Guide and Key to In-door and Out-door Amusement. Complete in Two Vols., with about 1,000 Illustrations, cloth, 6s. each ; or One Vol., 10s. 6d.

Cassell's Technical Educator. With Coloured Designs and numerous Illustrations. Complete in Four Vols., extra crown 4to, cloth, 6s. each ; or Two Vols., half-calf, 31s. 6d.

The Book of the Horse. By SAMUEL SIDNEY. With Twenty-five Fac-simile Coloured Plates from Original Paintings, and upwards of 100 Woodcuts. 600 pages, demy 4to, cloth bevelled, gilt edges, 31s. 6d. ; half-morocco, £2 2s.

The Illustrated Book of Poultry. By L. WRIGHT. With Fifty Coloured Portraits of Prize Birds, and numerous Engravings. Demy 4to, 600 pages, cloth bevelled, gilt edges, 31s. 6d. ; half-morocco, gilt edges, £2 2s.

Cassell's Household Guide. With *Coloured Cookery Plates,* and Illustrations on nearly every page. Complete in Four Vols., 6s. each ; or Two Vols., half-calf, £1 11s. 6d.

Cassell's Guinea Illustrated Bible. With 900 Illustrations. Royal 4to, 1,476 pages. Cloth gilt, 21s. ; leather, 25s.

Cassell's Bible Dictionary. With 600 Illustrations. Imperial 8vo, 1,159 pages, cloth, 21s. ; morocco, 40s.

The Child's Bible. With 220 Illustrations. Demy 4to, cloth gilt, £1 1s. ; leather, 30s.; morocco elegant, 42s.

MISCELLANEOUS WORKS.

Book of Good Devices, The. Edited by GODFREY GOLDING. With 1,900 Precepts for Practice. Cloth, bevelled, gilt edges, 3s. 6d.

Chapters on Trees. A Popular Account of their Nature and Uses. By M. and E. KIRBY. Profusely Illustrated. 320 pages, extra crown 8vo, cloth gilt, 5s.

Civil Service, Guide to Employment in the. *New Edition.* With an Introduction by J. D. MORELL, LL.D. Cloth, 2s. 6d.

Civil Service, Guide to the Indian. By A. C. EWALD, F.S.A. *New and Cheaper Edition.* Cloth, 2s. 6d.

Dictionary of Phrase and Fable. By the Rev. Dr. BREWER. *New and Cheaper Edition.* Demy 8vo, 1,000 pp., cloth, 7s. 6d.

Facts and Hints for Every-day Life. A Comprehensive Book on Every Subject connected with the Comforts of Home and the Health and Prosperity of its Inmates. *Second Edition.* 2s. 6d.

Half-Hours with Early Explorers. By T. FROST. Profusely Illustrated. *Second Edition.* Cloth, 5s.

Hymns and Poems for Little Folks. Uniform with "The Children's Album." With 150 full-page Pictures. Super-royal 16mo, 320 pages, cloth, 3s. 6d.

Manners of Modern Society. A Comprehensive Work on the Etiquette of the Present Day. *Fourth Edition.* Cloth gilt, 2s. 6d.

North-West Passage by Land. By Viscount MILTON and Dr. CHEADLE. *Original Edition,* demy 8vo, cloth, with 22 Plates, 21s. *New and Cheaper Edition,* crown 8vo, with Map and Illustrations, 2s. 6d.

Notable Shipwrecks. By UNCLE HARDY. 320 pages, crown 8vo, with Frontispiece. *Second Edition.* Cloth gilt, 5s.

Our Children, and How to Rear and Train Them. A Manual for Parents, in the Physical, Educational, Religious, and Moral Training of their Children. Crown 8vo, cloth, 3s. 6d.

Pictures of School Life and Boyhood. Selected from the Best Authors, and Edited by PERCY FITZGERALD, M.A. 256 pages, crown 8vo, cloth gilt, with Frontispiece, 3s. 6d.

Practical Poultry-Keeper, The. *Eighth Edition.* By L. WRIGHT. Illustrated with numerous Wood-cuts, 3s. 6d. ; or with Eight new Chromo Plates, 5s.

Soldier and Patriot. The Story of GEORGE WASHINGTON. By F. M. OWEN. 256 pages, cloth, bevelled boards, 3s. 6d.

The Three Homes. A Tale for Fathers and Sons. By F. T. L. HOPE. 400 pages, crown 8vo, cloth, gilt edges, 5s.

Truth will Out. By JEANIE HERING, Author of "Golden Days," "Little Pickles," &c. 240 pages, crown 8vo. With Frontispiece. 3s. 6d.

Young Man in the Battle of Life, The. By the Rev. Dr. LANDELS. Fcap. 8vo, 292 pages. *Third Edition.* Cloth gilt, 3s. 6d.

CASSELL'S EDITION OF THE POETS.

In fcap. 8vo, bound in cloth extra, with Illuminated Title. Illustrated with numerous full-page Engravings on Wood, from Designs by Eminent Artists. In cloth gilt, 3s. 6d.

Longfellow.	Cowper.	The Book of Humorous Poetry.
Scott.	Milton.	Ballads, Scottish and English.
Byron.	Pope.	
Moore.	Burns.	Lives of the British Poets.
Wordsworth.	The Casquet of Gems.	

CASSELL'S LIBRARY EDITION OF THE POETS,

In BOLD, READABLE TYPE, with Memoir of each Poet, Notes, and Critical Dissertation, bound in cloth, as under :—

Scott's Poetical Works. Three Vols., cloth, 2s. each.

Burns' Poetical Works. Two Vols., 2s. each.

Thomson's Poetical Works. One Vol., cloth, 2s.

Young's Poetical Works. One Vol., cloth, 2s.

Dryden's Poetical Works. Two Vols., cloth, 2s. each.

Milton's Poetical Works. Two Vols., cloth, 2s. each.

Goldsmith, Wharton, and Collins' Poetical Works. One Vol., 2s.

☞ *The following CATALOGUES of Messrs.* CASSELL PETTER & GALPIN'S PUBLICATIONS *can be had from all Booksellers, or post free on application to the Publishers :—*

CASSELL'S COMPLETE CATALOGUE, containing a complete List of Works, including Bibles and Religious Literature, Children's Books, Dictionaries, Educational Works, Fine Art Volumes, Handbooks and Guides, History, Miscellaneous, Natural History, Poetry, Travels, Serials.

CASSELL'S EDUCATIONAL CATALOGUE, containing a description of their numerous Educational Works, &c., with Specimen Pages and Illustrations, including their Elementary and Technical Series, together with a List of their Mathematical Instruments, Water-Colours, &c.

Cassell Petter & Galpin : London, Paris & New York.